ADMINISTRATION

The Word and the Science

ADMINISTRATION
The Word and the Science

A. Dunsire
SENIOR LECTURER, DEPARTMENT OF POLITICS
UNIVERSITY OF YORK

A HALSTED PRESS BOOK

John Wiley & Sons
New York

This edition was first published in 1973 by Martin Robertson & Company Ltd., 17 Quick Street, London N1 8HL.

Published in the U.S.A. by the Halsted Press, a Division of John Wiley & Sons, Inc., New York.

ISBN: 0 470–22752–4
Library of Congress Catalog Card No: 73–7176

Printed in Great Britain

Contents

Preface

Consider the following:

1 Method of administration: place pill in large end of tube provided, insert in horse's mouth, and blow sharply through small end. (*Old joke.*)

2 The government of persons is replaced by the administration of things and the direction of the processes of production. (*Engels, 1878, 309.*)*

3 The Treasury itself is rather an office of superintendence and appeal than an office of administration. It requires, therefore, a smaller staff than might be expected... (*Sir Reginald Welby, Permanent Secretary, 1879.*)

4 It is customary, in debates of the House, to allow priority to members of the administration who wish to speak... (*Alpheus Todd, (1869), 1889, 400.*)

5 Administration.–Five per cent of the annual income of fund shall be transferred to the general funds of the party to pay for administrative expenses of the fund. (*Labour Party Constitution, The Parliamentary Fund, 1906.*)

6 When two men co-operate to roll a stone that neither could have rolled alone, the rudiments of administration have appeared. (*Simon, Smithburg, Thompson, 1950, 3.*)

I dare say each of these quotations is perfectly intelligible to you, even out of context. But now, having replaced 'administration' in one of them by some word or phrase which retains the sense of the quotation, try substituting that word or phrase in another quotation. It will not always make sense.

There are, of course, a large number of words like that in English, and before indulging in the hair-splitting exercise of trying

---

* This is the only footnote in the book. I prefer to put all I have to say in the text; and references will be given in brackets in the text, as here.

'*Engels, 1878, 309*' means that the quotation or point referred to will be found on page 309 of the book by Engels that was published in 1878, the full details being given under 'Engels' in the booklist at the end of the book.

'*Todd, (1869) 1889, 400*' means page 400 of a book by Todd that was first published in 1869, although the edition actually being used is that of 1889–the details again appearing in the booklist under 'Todd'.

to sort out all these shades of meaning, one should certainly ask, Does it matter? If it is clear enough in context, is that not all that is required? To a practising administrator, of all men, cerebration about 'administration' in the abstract goes decidedly against the grain; and if he should argue for getting on with the job, never mind what it is called, I would have a great deal of sympathy with his point of view.

But it is simply the case that positions of battle, of a sort, are today taken up over what is and is not 'administration'; peace and harmony, and even salary level, may hang on a verbal usage. The Maud Committee on Management in Local Government wrestling with a distinction between the work proper to elected members and the work proper to officers; the Fulton Committee on the Civil Service considering the relationship between generalists and specialists; the Parliamentary Commissioner for Administration and the Select Committee arriving at the limits of his competence—each is an example of a live debate in recent British history where arguments have been led which, to carry the weight they were designed to carry, needed the kind of consensus on the meaning of the key word 'administration' that was and is clearly lacking. A fascinating sidelight on the Vietnam war revealed that peace talks were endangered by the translation of *chanh-quyen* as 'administrative' (rather than 'governmental') which the Nixon Administration, or Government, wrongly thought meant a major concession.

One justification for investigating the evolution of the term, demonstrating its diversification into so many usages, would therefore be the intent that men would stop arguing from a statement of what 'administration' means. No one usage that *is* a current usage is any more 'correct' than another, as any good dictionary makes clear. Diversification, however, may have a pattern; and even the showing of the pattern may help in understanding the evolution of the thing the term denotes. If that can be identified, and the class of thing it is be described, it will matter less that men dispute its label; as there is no difficulty to a botanist in identifying a common flower that has different names in various parts of the country, if he has either a specimen or a technical description of its salient parts. Yet in the field in which we are interested, it is not so much that we use different terms for the same thing that creates difficulty, as that we use the same term for different things. Koestler says of the Eskimos that they

... have several words for various kinds of snow where we have only one; but Malinowski's savages had only one word, *manna wala*, for all insects and birds—except those that can be eaten. (*Koestler, 1964, 612.*)

If *manna wala* serves to make the only distinction the savages are interested in, what a remote and academic activity it is to carefully separate out the millions of different sorts of *manna wala*! For every thousand English gardeners who can name each species of flower in the garden, there is perhaps one, who can do the same for his weeds—or who would see any point in doing so. The simple ideas 'sky' and 'stars' which serve most of us quite adequately to describe what we see, even during a flight, will not suffice to communicate the notions we shall all develop as space travel increases.

Distinctions are hair-splitting only so long as we do not need them for purposes of our own; if we do come to need them, yet do not quite realise it, we may go on using one term in several senses, and fail to communicate.

This is just what I think has been happening with 'administration'. It is surely a commonplace that *all* the kinds of activity we may wish to denote by this term have been increasing absolutely in their occurrence, in the modern Western world at least, over the last few generations—some of them, a thousandfold, and exponentially, or so we may fear. Problems associated with this have become large enough to need separate diagnosis, and a name. The literature now abounds with distinctions between administration and something else where not long ago it did not: between administration and ideology, politics, policy, government, judicial process, law, management, execution, expertise, production—and a number of others in particular contexts. Each distinction makes its own point; but the common term is far from being a constant. One man includes within his box labelled 'administration' the phenomena which another man carefully separates from and contrasts with 'administration'; distinctions valid (by definition) in their own context are mutually incompatible when brought into the same context, but not always obviously so.

Sir Edward (later Lord) Bridges once began a lecture entitled 'Administration: what is it? and how can it be learnt?' by referring to the appendix at the end of Bryce's *Holy Roman Empire* on the ten different senses in which the term 'Burgundy' was used at different periods of its history (the territory, not the wine). 'It is rather the same with administration', Sir Edward suggested (Bridges, in Dunsire, 1956, 2). I am proposing, in the early chapters rather than an appendix, to list at least some of the meanings that

have been given to the term 'administration' in different periods of
its history, and I fear there are more than ten.

The main part of the present book, however, is concerned not
with the name given to the thing, but with its study—'administrative science'. Now in such a usage the word 'science' itself has at
least two meanings. The first just signifies 'branch of learning',
'the study of' something or other. The second signifies a particular
kind of study, not so much a field (what 'Science' meant at school,
the 'exact sciences', mainly physics and chemistry) as a method,
a rigorous way of gaining knowledge that has its rules of what
constitutes 'evidence' and 'proof'. Of recent years, some academic
students of subjects like Politics have been wary of calling themselves Political Scientists in case they were thought to be claiming
to be *that* kind of scientist—and, of course, some others of them do.
Some of the scholars of 'administrative science' during a flowering
in the 1960s were beginning to aim at such a claim, too. But for
most of the period we are concerned with, the term merely means
'the study of administration'.

One might suppose that this was a relatively new subject, without
much of a history. I think one would be wrong; and the second
quarter of the book is devoted to an account of its development,
from the seventeenth century to the early twentieth. The third
quarter outlines the various branches of the current subject; and in
the final quarter, some contemporary problems are discussed.

My grateful thanks go to Professor W. J. M. Mackenzie, and to
my colleagues Dr David Coates and Lawry Freedman, who read
parts of the manuscript and gave good advice. Its faults, however,
are all mine.

A.D.
December 1972

CHAPTER ONE

The Development of the Term

The several nuances in English usage of the term 'administration' seem to have evolved in something like the following way. The classical Latin verb, as used by Cicero for instance, had two apparently distinct senses: to help, assist, or serve—taking the dative; and to manage, direct, or govern—taking the accusative. In Cicero, the noun *administer* means a male attendant or servant; *administratio*, often simply 'the giving of help'. But he also has *administrare rempublicam provinciam, exercitum*; and *administrare bellum cum Cimbris, administrare leges et judicia*, used without a following dative (Marchant and Charles, 1941, 13). The most convenient translation for some of these would seem to be the semi-colloquial English usage, 'to run'—'to run the State, to run the war with the Cimbrians'. Caesar has *administrare navem*, translated as 'to steer', but 'run' often does here as well; *cf.* 'to run a true course', 'run a vessel into danger'. For *administrare leges et judicia*, however, 'to run the laws and judgements' is false: the translation (avoiding 'administer') is something like 'to carry out', 'to implement', 'to execute'. Here we have the hint of a combination of the two principal senses: 'directing' and 'serving' at the same time; completing a process someone else has started, or running someone else's show, or seeing to the consequence of someone else's purposes. Or, if not someone else's, then one's own, arrived at by some act that is not 'administration', as in Chaucer (*c.* 1374), 'He [God] amynstreth in many maneres and in dyuerse tymes by destyne, thilke same thinges that he hath disponed'; 'I ... desired to put foorth in execucion and in act of commen administracioun thilke things that I had learned'; Lydgate (1413), 'The government of a reame shold be admynystred and executed by suche as were of grettest bounte'. (These illustrations are from the Oxford English Dictionary, 1961, 117–18.)

Thus far, we have some evidence for three distinct senses of the term 'administration': a First Meaning,

(1) *'help'* or *'service'* *pure and simple* (with no notion of 'direction').

This is seen in English today only in the somewhat archaic use of the root verb 'to minister unto'—as in 'ministering angel'. A Second Meaning,

(2) *'direction'* or *'government'* *pure and simple*, expressed colloquially as 'running the show', with connotations of 'service' or 'help' entirely suppressed, or remote.

This sense is not unequivocally exemplified in the OED, unless in a late reference to Robertson (1769), 'In him was vested the sovereign administration of the revenues'; but that is ambiguous. However, we may later find usages where only the unencumbered Ciceronian or Caesarian sense gives an adequate reading. Illustrations have already been given for the Third Meaning,

(3) *'government'* or *'direction'* *in the implementation of a given purpose or end*; execution.

But the first sense of 'administer' that the editors of the OED give brings in another idea:

Administer [. . . . . .]
1. *trans.* To manage as a steward . . .

There is warrant in Cicero for the notion of stewardship, perhaps even that it is included in the meaning of the word 'administration':

For the administration of the government, like the office of a trustee, must be conducted for the benefit of those entrusted to one's care, not of those to whom it is entrusted. (*Cicero, De Officiis; quoted in Lepawsky, 1949, 89*).

'Office' itself has a sense in which it is the equivalent of 'duty' and 'trust', and Wyclif (1382) identified 'administration' with 'office': 'Therefore we havynge this administracioun, or office . . . faylen not.' The identification is probably implicit in the modern legal usage of 'administration' in connection with wills and the estates of deceased persons: 'Letters of Administration' give an 'executor' authority to manage or dispose of the goods and property of a deceased person, not in his or her own interest but in that of the heirs. Let me then set forth a Fourth Meaning,

(4) *'direction'* or *'execution'* *in the interests of someone else*; government as deputy or trustee.

I supposed earlier that the Third or 'implementation' sense may begin from the unencumbered 'directing' (Second) sense, adding a proportion of the root 'help' (First) sense; possibly the Fourth or 'trustee' sense goes a little further in this. There is a common, if now somewhat formal, English usage which may be seen to move the other way, as it were: starting from the 'service' sense and adding something of the 'directing' sense. 'To administer' the sacraments, or medicine, or justice (especially if as punishment), means 'to dispense' or 'serve' these things—but note how it is implicit that it is someone in authority who does the dispensing, to someone in a client or inferior station; to the betterment of the latter, perhaps, but only in the manner that the dispenser considers proper. Shoreham (1315): 'The signe hys of thys sacrament the bisschopes blessynge, Forth myd the admynystracioun'; Fisher (1509): 'And admynystre ryght and Iustyce to every party'; and, *via* Copland (1541) 'They that by reason and Methode admynyster the arte of medycyne...' to (1743) 'His Attendants should stand ready to administer the Dressings'—the same displacement as from 'administer justice' to 'administer the birch', and from 'administer the sacrament' to 'administer the cup'.

Since this sense is nowadays easily recognisable, and separate from those in which we are primarily interested, we need not consider it further, but designate a Fifth Meaning,

(5) *authoritarian service*; used in conjunction with 'of the sacraments', 'of medicine', 'of justice', and the like, or in imitation of that use.

The 'minister' becomes 'a servant in authority' in many contexts. And as in the *cliché* 'the administration of justice', more than one of these senses may be meant, or unconsciously implied, in the one use; *cf.* John Stuart Mill,

But, if the administration of justice, police and gaols included, is both so universal a concern, and so much a matter of general science independent of local peculiarities, that it may be, and ought to be, uniformly regulated throughout the country ... there is also business, such as the administration of the poor laws, sanitary regulation, and others, which, while really interesting to the whole country, cannot consistently with the very purposes of local administration, be managed otherwise than by the localities (*Mill*, (*1861*) *1910, 353*).

By the middle of the eighteenth century, the *cliché* phrase 'the administration of the realm' had undergone not only the displacement on to the 'things administered' but a further one, on to the 'persons administering', as a collective noun (*cf.* 'The Court', 'The Stage', etc.). OED cites (1731) 'A Defence of the measures of the present Administration'; and Cowper (1783), 'The deplorable condition of the country, insisted on by friends of administration, and not denied by their adversaries'; and Adam Smith has

> They remained for several years in quiet possession of this revenue; but in 1767, administration laid claim to their territorial acquisitions, and the revenue arising from them, as of right belonging to the crown ... (*Smith, (1776) 1812, 593*).

This usage, 'administration' with neither article nor capital letter, to signify 'Government' or 'Crown' (as other nations would use 'State') seems to have become obsolete; indeed, the more familiar usage, with an article or possessive proper noun and a capital ('the Gladstone Administration'), as an earlier generation used 'Ministry' and a later uses Cabinet ('the MacDonald Cabinet') or Government ('the Wilson Government'), seems now somewhat antique, though still in common use in the United States of America ('the Nixon Administration'). But the latter was the formal usage in the middle of the nineteenth century:

> ... Sir Robert Peel trusts that your Majesty will permit him to state to your Majesty his impression with respect to the circumstances which have led to the termination of his attempt to form an Administration for the conduct of your Majesty's service (*Sir Robert Peel to Queen Victoria, 10 May 1839; quoted in Hanham, 1969, 44*).

and the former was that employed by Alpheus Todd in the quotation given earlier with a date as late as 1869.

Obsolescence notwithstanding, it seems we must distinguish two separate eighteenth- and nineteenth-century displacements on to persons, for 'administration' and 'Administration'; a Sixth Meaning:

> (6) (lower case *a*) *collective noun for* '*the Crown*', or the King and his servants engaged in the government (or 'administration' in another meaning) of the realm.

and a Seventh,

> (7) (Upper Case *A*) *collective noun for the King's Ministers,* without the King; 'the Government of the day'.

Incidentally, there is a list of all these Meanings on page 229, for easy reference.

In the eighteenth century, the 'administration of the affairs of the realm', the 'administration of the laws', 'of justice', and so on, might very reasonably be subsumed under the same term; in England, there was almost no 'machinery' other than the judicial machinery available to Government, for the implementation of its intentions, or indeed those of Parliament (Barker, 1944, 32).

> The notion that government needed administrative machinery to enforce the law, outside certain fields such as the collection of the revenue, was foreign to the thought of eighteenth-century Britain. In the traditional view, law enforced itself through such agencies as common informers, grand juries and interested parties (*Parris, 1969, 164*).

The Government acted, as Dicey pointed out in respect of the revolutionary movements of 1795 and 1815–20, 'not by departmental action but by parliamentary legislation'—severely coercive measures, often: but with no content of 'machinery' for their implementation. Parliament passed a Prisons Act in 1791, but since there was no means of enforcing it, it was a dead letter from the start (Parris, 1969, 165). Municipal improvement, and much else of the effort to cope with the increase in manufactures, the growth of towns, and transport, was by private Act of Parliament. The nineteenth-century governments began to invent ways of making more sure that what Parliament said should happen, would happen: the Metropolitan and other police forces, the device of Crown (His Majesty's) Inspectors, the central government grant to local bodies, were ideas borrowed from the Continent and adapted to British conditions; and a 'civil service' began to take definite shape. With it, the nineteenth century began to appreciate a rather different sense of 'administering the government of the realm'.

Let me trace this development through citations from some of the major (and some of the minor) writers and statesmen of the century, beginning with perhaps the largest figure of all, a profoundly eighteenth-century man who had enormous influence on the outlook of the nineteenth: Jeremy Bentham (1748–1832).

Bentham and Taylor

Bentham's use of terms was at once precise and idiosyncratic. In his later years, he developed an obsession for uniqueness of meaning in the definition of key words, recognising very clearly the social significance of language. His last great work, the *Constitutional Code* (written mostly between 1820 and 1830) abounds in neologisms, and 'scientific' Latinisms and Graecisms. But he has no stipulative definition of 'administration' or 'administrative' that I have found; he takes for granted our Third and Fourth meanings, with occasional use of the Sixth. In the *Code*, however, 'Administrative' is used as a noun (as one speaks of 'the Executive'), signifying one of the four authorities in the hypothetical State for which the *Code* was designed: the *Constitutive*, referring to the 'popular sovereign', the electorate; the *Legislative*; then, not the 'Executive', as in other seventeenth- and eighteenth-century writing, but the *Administrative*; and the *Judiciary*.

> To the Administrative it belongs, amongst other things, to give execution and effect to the ordinances of the Legislative in so far as regards the persons and things placed under its special direction, by the Legislative: to wit, in so far as litis-contestation has not place (*Bentham, (c. 1820) 1843, IX, 154*).

The relationship of these terms to others in common use is ingeniously expressed thus:

> Taken together, the Legislative and the Administrative compose the Government; the Administrative and the Judiciary, the Executive; the Legislative and the Executive, what may be termed the Operative, as contradistinguished from the Constitutive (*1843, IX, 154*).

Very much earlier, in a book called *Of Laws in General*, substantially completed in 1782 but never published by Bentham (it was discovered only in 1939), he had distinguished between a *law* and

> a temporary order issued by any magistrate who is spoken of as exercising thereby a branch of *executive* power, or as exercising the functions belonging to any department of *administration*. But the executive power is continually mentioned as distinct from the legislative; and the business of administration is as constantly opposed to that of legislation. Let the Board of Treasury order a sum of money to be paid or issued to such or such a person, let the Commander-in-Chief order such and such a body of troops to march to such a place, let the Navy Board order such or such a ship to be fitted out, let the Board of Ordnance order such or such a train of artillery to be dispatched to such a destination—Who would ever speak of any of these orders as acts of legislative power, as acts of legislation? (*Bentham (1782); Hart, 1970, 4*).

It is striking that, although the distinction is one we understand perfectly today, Bentham went to the 'Defence' field for most of his illustrations, whereas it would not occur to us to do so, having so many other fields to choose from.

In his scheme for an Encyclopaedia, appended to the *Chresto-mathia* (1816), Division 18 concerns Politics and Government (a footnote reads: 'By the word *Government*, the practice, and thence the art, seems to be more especially signified: by the word *Politics*, the corresponding branch of science'). Politics is divided into *Esoscopic* and *Exoscopic*, or Internal Politics (or Government) and International Politics. Internal Government and Politics is divided again:

> In so far as it is by the establishing of laws that the business of government is carried on, it is carried on in the way of *legislation*; in so far as it is carried on otherwise than by the establishing of laws, it is carried on in the way of *Administration* (*Bentham*, (*1816*) *1843*, *VIII*, *94*).

'Administration' is then divided into 'Administration in the more common import of the term', or *Aneristic* administration, and *eristic*, or contentious, administration—viz. Judicature. Common administration is thus twice defined negatively: it is not law, and it is not litis-contestation. There is a long footnote to the contrast with 'law', of which the following condensation retains the sense:

> A law is a discourse—conceived mostly in general, and always in determinate, words—expressive of the will of some person or persons to whom ... the members of the community addressed are disposed to pay obedience. ... Of the mode and degree of generality necessary to distinguish a *law* from a order of administration, no description is to be found anywhere: and any description on the subject would be here out of place.
>
> Scarcely, perhaps, will the few lines that follow find excuse.
>
> Of the hands by which political power—whether of the administrative or the legislative cast—is exercised, the situation may be either supreme or subordinate. In common speech, however—so indistinct are the conceptions commonly held ... —the terms *legislation* and *legislators* are wont to be employed [as if the power involved were always] supreme. Accordingly and in consequence, [wherever a power used is regarded as being subordinate], the discourses in and by which their will stands expressed are ... wont to be spoken of as being ... administrative.
>
> Between such discourses as are regarded as being the results or products of the exercise of legislative power, and such as are not regarded in that light ... the line of separation remains,

> even to this day, altogether unsettled and indeterminate.
> Among the terms employed ... the greater the proportion of
> those which ... are of the generic cast—being names of *sorts* of
> persons or things, the more likely ... the discourse is to be re-
> garded as ... legislative ... (*Bentham*, (*1816*) *1843, VIII, 95*).

Men talk in their loose way, Bentham is saying, as if laws were
never made by subordinates, and that all that subordinates did were
necessarily administration. But that gives no real distinction between laws and administrative orders; the nearest we can come to
that, is to note that laws are usually expressed generally, administrative orders more particularly. Here is a warning against a 'laws/
administration' dichotomy being identified with a hierarchical
distinction, that is more than a century ahead of its time.

But Bentham's *Code*, which contains hundreds of pages of im-
mensely detailed and systematic recommendations on 'administration', was not available to his contemporaries. So it is perhaps
reasonable for the Colonial Office official Sir Henry Taylor, who
published in 1836 a compilation of (for the most part) light-hearted
essays entitled *The Statesman*, to say in his Preface:

> Amongst the writers on Government whose works my limited
> opportunities of study have enable me to examine, I have not
> met with any who have treated systematically of *Administrative*
> Government as it ought to be exercised in a free state. ...
> whilst the structure of communities and the nature of politi-
> cal powers and institutions were thus extensively investigated,
> the art of *exercising* political functions, which might seem to
> be no unimportant part of political science, has occupied
> hardly any place in the speculations of its professors (*Taylor*,
> (*1836*) *1958, 23*).

And in his 'Conclusion' Taylor refers to the 'couplet of Mr Pope's,
which has obtained such singular celebrity'—

> For forms of government let fools contest;
> Whiche'er is best administered is best.

He does not subscribe to that thought, but nevertheless concludes
the book with his motive for writing it,

> to divert the attention of thoughtful men from forms of
> government to the business of governing (*Taylor*, (*1836*) *1958,
> 159*).

The term 'business', in the later eighteenth century and early nineteenth, had all the most general of the meanings it still has, such as
contrasting 'business' with 'pleasure', or 'business matters' with

'private matters'; but it held then a basic meaning more general than we now use it for, almost the root meaning of 'busy-ness', signifying the daily comings and goings, the transactions and practical decision-making of public men with one another, in any walk of life. A great landowner, or a party leader, or churchman, would have a 'man of affairs', or 'man of business', who was confidential secretary, agent, and impresario (as is the 'manager' of today's pop star, or prize fighter). On the other hand, 'business' had not yet become primarily identified with one sector of public life; when Taylor says

> The engagements which have deprived me of literary leisure and a knowledge of books, have, on the other hand, afforded me an extensive and diversified conversancy with business; and I hope, therefore, that I may claim from my readers some indulgence for the little learning and for the desultoriness of these disquisitions, in consideration of the value which they may be disposed to attach to comments derived from practical observation (*Taylor*, (*1836*) *1958, 26*).

he does not at all mean, as we would mean, that he had been much in contact with merchants, bankers, and industrialists ('businessmen'). Taylor, who was thirty-six years old when he published the book, had first joined the civil service at the age of sixteen; he meant that he knew a lot about practice, even if he were deficient in academic learning. Instead of 'the business of governing', he might have written 'the practical daily details of governing'.

But it is very noticeable that these include for Taylor what we should call 'the business of being a politician' as well as what might now be thought of as 'the business of a department'. There are, accordingly, 'worldly' essays on when to marry, the arts of winning advancement, and so on, as well as avowedly more serious matter, on the internal organisation of a Minister's office and such topics, written as part of a debate on colonial government and the operation of the Colonial Office (Murray, 1965, 219).

Taylor uses the actual term 'administration' but a score or so times in the whole book; most of them are the ambiguous commonplaces 'the administration of the law', of justice, and of patronage; one refers to the Government of the day; and only two or three are significant for this survey. One of these is:

> For administrative regulations, like other laws, require to be frequently revised and codified, as the experience of their operation is extended (*Taylor*, (*1836*), *1958, 69*).

The content of that is interesting in itself, as we will note later; but note now the usage 'administrative regulations' (not 'administrative orders' of a particular nature, as in Bentham), which are laws like others. The second significant use is one of only two appearances of the term in the essay entitled 'Reform of the Executive' (the other is quite unremarkable):

> Till a wise and constant instrumentality at work upon administrative measures (distinguished as they might be from measures of political parties) shall be understood to be essential to the government of a country, that country can be considered to enjoy nothing more than the embryo of a government—a means towards producing, through changes in its own structure and constitution and in the political elements acting upon it, something worthy to be called a government at some future time. For governing a country is a very different thing from upholding a Government (*Taylor*, (*1836*) *1958, 106–7*).

He is talking about acts of Parliament, and distinguishing between a party measure and an 'administrative' one. Without 'administrative measures', we have but the potentiality of government; and what 'administrative' measures are is made clear later, in a truly remarkable passage:

> It is not only necessary that the legislature should make provision in the laws for their due execution; it is also desirable that the executive agency should work towards new legislation on the same topics. For the execution of laws deals with those particulars by an induction of which the results to be aimed at in legislation are to be ascertained; and the generalisation from those particulars can only be well effected when the lowest in the chain of functionaries is made subsidiary to the operations of the highest in a suggestive as well as in an executive capacity—that is, when the experience of the functionary who puts the last hand to the execution of any particular class of enactments is made available for the guidance of the legislature.
>
> But in most cases this cannot be accomplished to any useful purpose otherwise than by a system of filtration. The lowest classes of functionaries, whilst they may be assumed to have the largest knowledge of facts, must also be taken to have the least power to discriminate and to generalise. They cannot be expected to distinguish barren from fruitful facts; those which are mere specialties from those which lead to general conclusions. What is wanted is that the crude knowledge collected in the execution of the laws should pass upward from grade to grade of the civil functionaries intrusted with their administration, more and more digested and generalised in its

progress; and, lastly, should reach the legislature in the shape of a mature project of law, whereby what was superfluous in the legislation in question might be abrogated; what was amiss might be amended; what was insufficient, enlarged; what was doubtful, determined; what was wanting, added (*Taylor*, (*1836*) *1958, 128–9*).

The bare idea of the 'meliorative-suggestive function' is in Bentham; but Taylor has a complete understanding of how it must work, on what we might call 'feedback' principles: 'crude' information generated by operative action at the 'lowest' levels must be collected, filtered for 'noise', and summed or 'generalised' in successive stages until it results in an error-correcting 'measure' at legislative level. Once more, this is a hundred years and more before its time. But for present purposes, we must rather note that Taylor is filling in the gaps in Bentham's rather negative account of what it is to 'carry on government' other than by making laws or bringing court cases: it requires 'machinery', and it requires knowledge of 'the real world' of basic operational fact. This is what 'administrative measures' are about, and it indicates what 'administration' can mean to a man like Taylor: something much more precisely articulated than a mere idea of 'implementation' or 'execution' of the laws, and involving the creation and maintenance of a structured hierarchy of tasks, of which the 'highest' is legislative in nature and the 'lowest' is executive in nature, of the kind which makes changes in the world and not simply proposals for change. It is surely difficult to deny that this understanding is implicit in the passages quoted from Taylor; and though it may not be 'common sense' yet in 1836, we may see that such a meaning for 'administration' is necessary shortly after, to make sense of certain usages. Let me, therefore, list now an Eighth Meaning,

(8) '*implementation of laws by non-judicial machinery of civil offices*'; the creation and maintenance of such machinery, and the provision of information generated by it for legislative purposes.

Ministers and their servants

By the time Taylor wrote, what was even then being called the 'permanent civil service of the Crown' had taken on the greater part of its modern meaning. The lower levels of clerks in Government offices were not subject to removal on a change of political fortunes in the House of Commons, fees had largely been replaced by salaries and superannuation introduced under Treasury control; and the line between positions compatible with membership of Parliament, and positions where this was an anomaly, was hardening (Cohen, 1941; Parris, 1969; Hanham, 1969). The eighteenth-century politicians had been interested in reducing the number of 'placemen' (officials) in the Commons; by 1830, the business of a department was becoming voluminous enough and complex enough for specialisation in one career or the other to be necessary. It was still true that

> The most striking feature of British administration in the first quarter of the nineteenth century was the extent to which the work of government departments was performed by the ministers themselves (*Young, 1961, 1; see Parris, 1969, 24*).

But in their departments, Ministers needed a 'man of business' who had grown up through the department, as well as one they could trust with their purely Parliamentary and party business. The two kinds of business were not always clearly distinguished, and a man might alternate between the two—shifting from being the (precursor of the) 'parliamentary secretary' to what we would now call the 'permanent secretary'. Taylor does not differentiate consistently between the emergent roles: both are 'statesmen', but some are 'closet statesmen' (Taylor, (1836) 1958, 106), or 'a species of indoor states-men' (1958, 116). Inside the department, the distinction between 'intellectual' and 'mechanical' work was already visible (1958, 109). When Taylor himself had joined the Colonial Office staff in 1824, it was not for 'routine' work, but as a junior 'closet statesman'.

Lord Palmerston, a good example of the statesman who was almost as permanent an official as any 'permanent civil servant' (he was in Ministerial office from 1809, with only short gaps, until 1865) had been the kind of man who thought it his duty *not* to delegate detail to any closet statesman. He read and answered every despatch and letter that came into the Foreign Office. As he explained to the Queen:

> The ministers who are at the head of the several departments of the state are liable any day and every day to defend themselves in Parliament; in order to do this they must be minutely acquainted with all the details of the business of their offices and the only way of being constantly armed with such information is to conduct and direct those details themselves.

If a Minister delegated to his subordinates, then he was no better than the Ministers in France, Austria, Prussia, and Russia, whose

> leaning on their subordinates ... gives to those subordinates ... real influence. This class of subordinate men has, from the fact of its being possessed of so much power, been invested with the title of 'bureaucratic' (*Benson and Esher, i. 136, dated February 25, 1838; quoted in Parris, 1969, 108–9; see also Hanham, 1969, 322–3*).

Palmerston at this period used his Under Secretaries as mere clerks (Parris, 1969, 109–10). But by 1854, he had been forced by sheer quantity of work to abandon these principles, and to adopt instead the principle of having in each department

> a permanent secretary, not belonging to any political party, not swayed by passion or feeling ... but a man who, being the depository of the lore and knowledge belonging to the particular department was able ... to give the newcomer into that office information as to past events, as to the principles regulating the department, as to the knowledge of individuals, and as to the details of transactions, without which it was impossible for any man, let him be ever so able and ever so expert, to perform his duties with satisfaction to himself and advantage to the public (*Roberts, 1960, 127; Parris, 1969, 110*).

Edward Ellice, writing to Lord John Russell in 1850, rationalises the change; subordinates, even if 'more able', have not a Minister's 'qualifications' (one must pass over his supposition that Ministers in earlier time dealt *less* with detail):

> It is a bad habit for statesmen to mistake their avocation of directing an administration for that of undertaking the details of its execution—a habit increasing sadly of late years—and which savours more of jealousy, and want of confidence in subordinate instruments (often more able than themselves) than of the greater qualifications required for their high station (*Public Records Office, Ellice to Russell, June 16, 1850; quoted in Parris, 1969, 117–18*).

And a few years later, George Arbuthnot, commenting on the Northcote-Trevelyan Report of 1854, puts the reverse point—civil servants should not aspire to doing Ministers' work:

> The officers of our Civil Service cannot in ordinary cases aspire to become statesmen, and to carry out systems of policy. Their humble but useful duty is, by becoming depositaries of departmental traditions, and by their practical acquaintance with the working of those laws, by which constitutional jealousy has guarded the Civil administration, as they affect their own

departments, to keep the current business in due course; to warn Ministers of the consequences of irregular proceedings into which they might inadvertently fall; to aid in preparing subjects for legislation; and possibly to assist by their suggestions the development of a course of reform ... Such is the complicated character of our institutions, that, without such division of labour, no man could obtain that intimate acquaintance with details, and the bearing of those details upon general principles, which constitute the distinction between the permanent executive officers and the members of Government who are charged with the duty of administration (*Hanham, 1969, 327*).

It is clear from both quotations that 'statesman' by now has come to mean 'member of Government' solely, and that the distinctive tasks of the two classes of men are well enough seen: both writers link 'permanent executive officers' with 'details of execution', and 'administration' with Ministers. However, a few lines later Arbuthnot is saying:

It is true that in most offices there is a large amount of mere copying work, which when not of a confidential character may be entrusted with advantage to an inferior class of clerks.... In some few departments, also, the duties of the administrative or directing functionaries are so distinct from those of the clerks who carry into effect the routine duties, that the line of demarcation is easily drawn. But in the great mass of the Revenue departments a thorough acquaintance with forms is so essential to a full comprehension of the business to be carried on, that to fulfil the superior offices satisfactorily a previous apprenticeship in the inferior classes is essential. In order to direct details effectively, an officer ought to know how to do them himself ... (*Hanham, 1969, 328*).

Arbuthnot is speaking here of a line between two kinds of permanent civil servant, not between Ministers and civil servants; and he calls the 'superior' kind 'administrative or directing', which indicates that, although 'administration' is seen as something Ministers are charged with, the superior class of civil servants can be seen as doing it also.

Mill and Bagehot

John Stuart Mill (1806–73) was, like Bentham, Taylor, and others, concerned with another line, that between Parliament and those who 'have charge of administration':

But a popular assembly is still less fitted to administer, or to dictate in detail to those who have charge of administration. Even when honestly meant, the interference is almost always injurious. Every branch of public administration is a skilled business, which has its own peculiar principles and traditional rules, many of them not even known, in an effectual way, except to those who have at some time had a hand in carrying on the business.... No one who does not thoroughly know the modes of action which common experience has sanctioned is capable of judging the circumstances which require a departure from ordinary modes of action.... Besides, an assembly never personally experiences the inconveniences of its bad measures until they have reached the dimensions of national evils. Ministers and administrators see them approaching, and have to bear all the annoyance and trouble of attempting to ward them off (*Mill*, *(1861) 1910, 231–3*).

The tone and content of this passage is probably completely acceptable to modern ears. But 'administration' has a quite general (Third or Fourth Meaning) sense, or could have; the only noteworthy points for the present purpose are the easy use of the phrase 'branch of public administration', and the *possible* separation of 'Ministers' from 'administrators'—unless the 'and' is conjunctive, as in 'an officer and a gentleman'. If a distinction is intended, it is clear that 'administrator' refers to people who 'have charge of administration' and yet are not Ministers; i.e., the superior grades of the permanent civil service.

A few years later, it is just as clear that Walter Bagehot (1826–1877) is using the word to refer to Ministers:

... That event is a change of Ministry. All our administrators go out together. The whole executive Government changes— at least, all the heads of it change in a body... (*Bagehot*, *(1867) 1964, 183*).

But Bagehot may here be utilising the ambiguity of the word to get a point across: later he says:

This conception of the use of a Parliamentary head shows how wrong is the obvious notion which regards him as the principal administrator of his office. The late Sir George Lewis used to be fond of explaining this subject. He had every means of knowing. He was bred in the permanent civil service. He was a very successful Chancellor of the Exchequer, a very successful Home Secretary, and he died Minister for War. He used to say 'It is not the business of a Cabinet Minister to work his department. His business is to see that it is properly worked. If he does much, he is probably doing harm. The permanent staff of the office can do what he chooses to do much better, or if they cannot, they ought to be removed (*Bagehot*, (*1867*) *1964, 200*).

Whether or not 'administrator' here is meant to convey 'permanent head', or merely 'head', is not clear, even if the distinction of function between Cabinet Minister and permanent staff of the office is plain enough. Ambiguity is present again in another section:

> ... no man would select the cadets of an aristocratic house as desirable administrators. They have peculiar disadvantages in the acquisition of business knowledge, business training, and business habits, and they have no peculiar advantages.
>
> Our middle class, too, is very unfit to give us the administrators we ought to have... The sort of education which fits a man for the higher posts of practical life is still very rare; there is not even a good agreement as to what it is. Our public officers cannot be as good as the corresponding officers of some foreign nations till our business education is as good as theirs (*Bagehot*, (*1867*) *1964, 207–8*).

'Officer' need not signify permanence; in succeeding paragraphs, the Lord Chancellor and the First Lord of the Treasury are instanced as 'principal English officers', and Ministers later are called 'Parliamentary officials'. On other pages, again, 'the administration' clearly means 'the Government of the day', which has a majority in both Houses (1964, 290) and can be 'turned out' by the public (1964, 302) but 'our administration' or 'English administration' can mean 'the way we do business in our public departments', or a collective term for the complex of these departments, otherwise 'public administration' (Bagehot, (1867) 1964, 183, 212, 206).

It is obvious that the risk of anachronism, in using a quotation from Bagehot in illustration, is severe. If there is, by the seventh decade of the nineteenth century, a fairly clearly accepted distinction between the qualifications and work of Ministers and the qualifications and work of permanent civil servants, both kinds of work may still be thought of as and called 'administration'. There is, however, general acceptance of a distinction between 'administration' and the work of a Parliamentary assembly (even where both are to do with legislation), on the one hand; and on the other, between 'administration' and routine or 'mechanical' clerical work. Perhaps we are justified in listing a Ninth Meaning.

(9) *work of directing, or establishing the principles of, the execution or implementation of the laws, or of public policy,* as contrasted with both the determination of those laws

or that policy, and the detailed or routine stages of such execution or implementation.

A Tenth Meaning would be a narrowing of the Sixth; a collective term for a body not as wide as 'the Crown' or 'the King and all his servants', but embracing the 'civil offices' named in the Eighth Meaning,

(10) *collective noun for the non-judicial machinery of civil offices*, the complex of government departments headed by Secretaries of State, other Ministers of the Crown, or Boards, and staffed by permanent civil servants or their like; 'public administration'.

CHAPTER TWO

The Term in the Civil Service

The evolution of several of the remaining modern connotations of the term 'administration' follows the evolution of the British Civil Service; and although this is not the place for a complete (or even a coherent) account of the history of the Civil Service (see Cohen, 1941; Bourn, 1968; Parris, 1969; Fry, 1969; etc.), a bare outline is unavoidable for the present purpose.

The intellectual First Division

The basic principle that underlay the several recommendations of the Northcote-Trevelyan *Report on the Organisation of the Permanent Civil Service* (presented in 1854) was their version of Sir Henry Taylor's distinction between 'intellectual' and 'mechanical' functions (Taylor, (1836) 1958, 109). It was to be a distinction between kinds of work; but they saw the distinction carrying over into methods of recruitment, examination, posting, and promotion, since the men who were able only for 'mechanical' work would be transferable between offices (this had begun to happen already), while the young men destined for 'intellectual' labour would, of course, have to learn the 'skilled business' of their own particular 'branch of public administration', as Mill put it, by continuous service in one department:

> We consider that a great step has been taken by the appointment in several offices of a class of supplementary clerks, receiving uniform salaries in each department, and capable therefore of being transferred without inconvenience from one to another, according as the demand for their services may be greater or less at any particular time; and we expect that the

movable character of this class of officers, and the superior standard of examination which we have proposed for the higher class, will together have the effect of marking the distinction between them in a proper manner (*C. 1713, 1854; reprinted in 'Fulton' Report, Cmnd. 3638, 1968, vol. I, App. B, 115*).

In spite of this clarity, Northcote and Trevelyan were obliged, in response to criticism, to emphasise that they had 'nowhere suggested or even hinted at the idea of transferring men from one office to another in cases where the business is not of a cognate character' (Parl. Papers 1854–55, xx. 421; see Bourn, 1968, 427; Fry, 1969, 47n.). Their recommendation that clerks should be moved around inside a department, 'so that each may have an opportunity of making himself master of the whole of the business before he is called upon, in due course of time, to take a leading position' ((1854) 1968, 116) likewise refers, in context, only to clerks of the 'inferior' class.

The view that the differences between the businesses of the several departments were such as to make transfer between them of the 'higher' class civil servants an impossibility remained orthodoxy well into the twentieth century. The Playfair Commission (1874–1875) distinguished four groups of civil servants according to method of recruitment: 'Staff Officers', the highest ranking, often brought in from outside the Service; the Higher Division, recruited by the examination for university graduates established in 1870; the Lower Division, recruited by the examination for the inferior officers established in 1870; and the group of 'Writers' recruited without examination, mainly for copying. Playfair recommended that these groups should be officially recognised, and work inside departments allocated accordingly, thus making the groups into service-wide classes as the Lower Division already was in principle, and as it became by Order in Council of 1876; and they thought that there was a case for transfer between departments in the early years of service in the Higher Division, though they recognised that there is 'a great deal of work in public offices special in its character, and requiring much study and care to master, the performance of which would therefore be seriously embarrassed by frequent transfers' (Cd. 1113, 1875, 19; Bourn, 1968, 433).

The Ridley Commission (1887–90), too, recommended that all those entering the civil service should be liable to work in departments other than the one they joined on entry, and that uniformity of pay and grading should be introduced into the Upper (or Higher) Division (which they proposed should be renamed the First Division;

the Lower, the Second Division). The Treasury rejected both principles, on the grounds of lack of homogeneity in the work of the Upper Division (1894; Fry, 1969, 48). The MacDonnell Commission (1912–15) proposed a special division of the Treasury with the duty (*inter alia*) of securing that 'in cases where it would be to the advantage of the Service that transfers should be made from one Department to another, such transfers shall take place' (Cd. 7338, IX, para. 101; Bourn, 1968, 444).   But the Permanent Secretary to the Treasury, in evidence to the MacDonnell Commission, stated succinctly the current position: 'The Class I man is certificated to his office; the Second Division man is in the Service at large' (question 35, 942; Fry, 1968, 48).

'Class I' referred to the examination taken by those entering the Higher or Upper Division, which never was officially named 'First Division' as Ridley had recommended, although the Lower Division became officially the Second Division in 1890. Playfair (1875) had used the term 'Staff Officer' for the highest ranks of all: Mac-Donnell, first distinguishing between clerical classes, departmental classes, and professional and technical classes, divided 'the clerical classes' further by method of entry into six, the highest of which were the 'Secretaries, Assistant Secretaries, Heads and sub-Heads of Divisions'; the second of these classes was the 'First Division', then an 'Intermediate' class and the 'Second Division', followed by the classes of Assistant Clerks and Boy Clerks. But the Permanent Heads of major departments, appointed directly by the Crown, were above even the highest of these classes.

MacDonnell proposed to tidy up this structure by reducing these classes to three, on the 'broad principle of gathering the natural fruits of the educational system of the country in its various stages as they mature' (Cd. 7338, III, para. 6; Bourn, 1968, 441); namely, a 'junior clerical' class recruited from boys at about the age of sixteen; a 'senior clerical' class recruited from boys at about the age of eighteen; and an 'administrative class' recruited in the main from university graduates.

Administration is as Administrative does

There is an interesting reservation to the Report about this. The signatories to this reservation agreed that the 'administrative class' should be small, but thought that its definition should be wide enough to include men recruited other than by the Class I examination system—for example, District Auditors:

> We believe that if the term 'Administrative Class' were used as a description of the work done by the members of the class, instead of as a 'nomenclature . . . based on the normal method of recruiting' that class, a considerable proportion of these important and highly paid officials would be classed as 'administrative' and that the rest could be classed as 'professional' in the sense in which that term is used in Clause 7 of the Order in Council, and we are of opinion that such a classification should be made (*Philip Snowden, Graham Wallas and others, Cd. 7338, 1914, First Reservation; Bourn, 1968, 446*).

This signalled recognition of an ambiguity that has remained ever since: the 'administrative class' might be a class of those who did 'administrative work', whatever that might be taken to mean; or it might be the name (more or less arbitrarily chosen as the successor to Superior Grades, Higher Division, First Division and so on) of a class recruited by the Class I examination from university graduates of a high educational calibre, and other desirable qualities, whatever their work might be called.

There is plenty of evidence in the MacDonnell Report that the Commission had a clear idea of the type of person they hoped to recruit into this class, to do the kind of work they saw as required. They endorsed many of the Macaulay principles enshrined in the Northcote-Trevelyan Report about the value of a good education as such, no matter what its subject-matter (but it is worth remarking that whereas Northcote and Trevelyan, and Macaulay, were speaking of an *entrance* examination to civil service training in the 'business of government', MacDonnell has more than a hint of the belief that an honours degree course *is* the training: 'The best education taken in conjunction with the training: and formative influence of University life produces the best type of public servant' (Cd. 7338, III, para. 42; Bourn, 1968, 442. See Parris, 1969, 293)). They also thought that competitive examinations were the best method of securing candidates 'giving the greatest promise of administrative capacity' (Cd. 7338, III, para. 42; Bourn, 1968, 442).

As to what 'administrative capacity' meant: there is no doubt that the Commission were considerably influenced in their thinking by the character of the new tasks that had been laid on the civil service in the previous decade—Old Age Pensions, National Insurance, Labour exchanges—which had required not only a considerable expansion in numbers, and in organisational structure, but also a considerably higher participation by senior civil servants in the business of devising the legislative provisions themselves, and the regulations required for their implementation: as

> the Civil Service is now being called upon to take a larger share in carrying out the policy of the legislature than has been usual in the past, the burden of administration is certainly heavier now than it has ever been before in the history of this country (*Cd. 7338, III, para. 4; Bourn, 1968, 441*).

Now 'carrying out the policy of the legislature' is what 'administration' has always been for; the 'burden of administration' has clearly increased because the legislature has been passing more of a particular kind of legislation; the significant point is that the Civil Service has been taking a 'larger share' of the work—and it can have been taking it away only from Ministers. So 'administration' here cannot mean 'implementing the laws' or 'execution' or the like in the entirely general sense; it means 'ministerial work', corresponding to our Ninth Meaning—from the drafting of the legislation in the first place, to the devising or adaptation of the 'machinery' for its implementation, and the setting of that machinery in motion; and corresponding to the Ninth Meaning also in being clearly distinguished from 'routine':

> there is no worse training for the real duties of administration, which requires freshness of mind, individuality and judgement, than a long period of routine work, however faithfully performed; if, therefore, a man has sufficient capacity to fit him for administrative work, his fitness should be ascertained as early as possible in his career (*Cd. 7338, VIII, para. 23*).

'Administrative capacity', thus, is the capacity to take on the work of a vice-Minister, at the head of a department, in all its aspects save that of being the actual Parliamentary spokesman. It is worth noting that, even in 1914, it is not assumed that 'administration' is exclusively the work of civil servants; 'administration' is a name given to work which is like that of Ministers—or at least, like that of Ministers who would follow the precepts of Ellice and the later Palmerston in the 1850s, rather than the earlier Palmerston.

This understanding is made concrete in the 1920 Interim Report of the Joint Committee on the Organisation of the Civil Service set up by the Civil Service National Whitley Council. Drawing upon MacDonnell and the reports of other committees, this so-called 'Reorganisation Committee' (composed entirely of civil servants) first followed Northcote and Trevelyan in finding two broad categories of civil service work:

> The administrative and clerical work of the Civil Service may be said, broadly, to fall into two main categories. In one category may be placed all such work as either is of a simple mechanical kind or consists in the application of well defined regulations, decisions and practice to particular cases; in the other category, the work which is concerned with the formation of policy, with the revision of existing practice or current regulations and decisions, and with the organisation and direction of the business of Government (*Report, 1920, para. 16; Bourn, 1968, 448*).

Not much there about 'depositories of lore and knowledge' or of 'departmental traditions'; by 1920, all that is in the files.

The Reorganisation Committee then divided the total of this 'administrative and clerical work' into four, appropriate to separate classes of officer (the classes which, on adoption by the Government, lasted for nearly the next half century): a writing assistant (clerical assistant) class, for the simple mechanical work, and a clerical class for the application to particular cases; an executive class, to handle difficult individual cases, initial investigations of matters of importance, internal organisation and control, and the responsible conduct of important operations; and an administrative class, whose duties were envisaged as

> those concerned with the formation of policy, with the coordination and improvement of Government machinery, and with the general administration and control of the Departments of the public service. (*Report, 1920, para. 43; 'Fulton' Report, 1968, vol. 4, 16; Bourn, 1968, 449*).

The interpretation of this nomenclature is complicated, but is important for our purposes, since once given, the name of the class (as already hinted) came to be applied to the work done by its members, and that only.

First, then, the whole of the work of the relevant sector of the Civil Service (presumably, laying aside the departmental specialists, professional, and technical sectors) is called 'administrative and clerical'. MacDonnell had called this work simply 'clerical work', including in that the work of the highest civil servants under the Permanent Heads. It is, of course, ambiguous to say that all of x is a and b: it could mean that every part of x is both a and b, or that x consists of the sum of what is a and what is b. But whatever 'administrative and clerical' really meant for the Committee when they used the words in that sentence, after the Report was adopted 'clerical' for ever after signified (within this sector) the work of lowest importance. It would be hard for an Under Secretary to think of his own work as 'clerical' in nature, even if MacDonnell had perfectly intelligibly called it that in 1914.

'Executive' underwent a similar process. Historically 'executive' had applied to the work of 'executing' legislation or policy, and had been interchangeable with 'administrative' in many contexts. Now, it was desired to make a contrast between work that was internal organisation and control of a department, and work that was inter-departmental organisation; between work that was the settlement of difficult cases under existing rules, and work that was essentially the devising of new rules—and a number of other such contrasts, alluded to in the Reorganisation Committee's Report. The Committee perhaps saw this distinction as that between work that was predominantly 'executive' in the general sense, and work that was essentially policy formation; though they also made statements indicating that they saw both of the higher classes as taking part in policy work. Whatever they had in mind, it came to pass that 'executive' was identified with work of a less exalted nature, higher than 'clerical' but lower than that of the remaining term of the trilogy.

The description of the work of the Administrative Class is of the form: work of type *a*, type *b*, and type *c*. Type *c*, however, is 'the general administration and control of the Departments of the public service'. Clearly, one ought not to designate the *whole* of the work of the Class as 'administration', since one part of it is so named specifically (in the unencumbered Ciceronian Second Meaning sense, of 'running' things); if one were logical, and the Committee had been consistent, type *a* work and type *b* work ought to be excluded from 'administration'. In any event, what has happened in the years since 1920, to the enormous confusion of readers of polemic, is that what 'administration' is has become identified with what the Administrative Class does. Fry asserts that Treasury witnesses before the Priestley Commission (1953–55) went further, claiming that if the Administrative Class does not do it, it is not 'administration':

> For example, *Priestley Evidence*, questions 4114–15. The Treasury maintained: 'The case put by the Society depended very largely on the proposition that the Executive Class is engaged in administrative divisions in departments and that is true of a small minority of the Class, and one gets perhaps a

little misled if one only looks at that minority.' It was difficult to give an accurate figure, but the Treasury estimated that 'more likely under rather than over 10 per cent of the Executive Class are employed in administrative divisions' (*Priestley Evidence*, question 3263). An 'administrative division' being one in which the Administrative Class was employed: the implication was that 'administration' was not performed elsewhere (*Fry, 1969, 171n.*)

What the Treasury men meant there depends upon what they meant by 'an administrative division', and Fry may or may not be right on that. Fry then goes on to contrast this with the words of another Treasury man to a Commons Select Committee in 1964: Sir Lawrence Helsby said that

> as the size of the Administrative Class was only about one half per cent of the total Civil Service, it would be 'quite wrong to assume that any large proportion of all administrative work in the general sense could possibly be done by such a small group'. He added: 'The great weight of the day-to-day administration in the Service is carried by the Executive Class, by the Scientific Officer Class and by the senior grades of the number of other Classes who provide the aggregate of probably something around ten per cent of staff engaged in administration in the broad sense, which is necessary in this kind of organisation' (*Fry, 1969, 172*).

What might Sir Lawrence have meant by 'administration' in this passage? Clearly not merely 'the work of the Administrative Class', as Fry points out; nor, either, 'clerical' work in the broadest Mac-Donnell sense, since Scientific Officers do it; it is, however, work for *senior* grades, which argues that it is used in an early Ciceronian 'running things' sense. But it is 'day-to-day', which argues something of a routine character—we have not yet found a Meaning which *identifies* 'administration' with routine, yet Sir Lawrence certainly seems to be engaged in creating that impression. Later (I quote Fry again)

> As to the relationship between the duties of the Executive and Administrative Classes, Sir Lawrence argued that there should continue to be 'a small Administrative Class remaining separate from the general service Class responsible for the day-to-day run of administration'. The Administrative Class was responsible, not for administration, but 'for somewhat special-ised functions which seldom had any precise counterpart in out-side organisation, particularly in the industrial and commercial sphere, until you get right up to board level' (*Fry, 1969, 172*).

This kind of verbal sword-play, in which the participants manipulate the senses of a word in conscious or unconscious creation of
ambiguity, is found throughout the skirmishing between representatives of the Executive Class and of the Administrative Class, and
between the Professional, Scientific and Technical Classes on the
one hand, and the Administrative (with the Executive sometimes
in alliance) on the other, that has marked the growing dissatisfaction with the 1920 settlement; culminating in the Evidence to the
Fulton Committee on the Civil Service (1966–68), and the latter's
Report—which has been sufficiently reviewed elsewhere (Ridley,
1968; Fry, 1969; Parris, 1969; Brown, 1970; etc.). Gellner puts the
general point thus:

> ... nothing is more false than the claim that, for a given asser-
> tion, *its use is its meaning.* On the contrary, its use may depend
> upon its lack of meaning: its ambiguity, its possession of wholly
> different and incompatible meanings in different contexts, *and*
> on the fact that, at the same time, it as it were emits the im-
> pression of possessing a constant meaning throughout....
> *(Gellner, in Wilson, 1970, 45).*

Leaving Sir Lawrence Helsby aside for a moment: we are bound,
I think, to add another to the list of meanings that are necessary to
make sense of a usage of the term 'administration' in a particular
context: an Eleventh Meaning,

> (11) work concerned with the formation of policy, with the co-
> ordination of and improvement of Government machinery,
> and with the general [administration and] control of the
> Departments of the public service; *the duties of the
> Administrative Class* (1920).

Generalists and specialists

A quite distinct development to that just discussed occurred about
the same time, the end of the 1914–18 War and the succeeding
decades. We saw successive Royal Commissions and Committees of
Inquiry into the civil service recommending a measure of trans-
ferability between Departments for members of the Upper Division
(Class I entrants) as well as for Second Division men, and the
Treasury resisting on the ground that the work of the several
Departments was so different that transferability would mean a

waste of acquired experience, and a gap in the usefulness of the transferred officer while he learned his new job. By 1920, the Treasury had changed its view rather; by 1929, entirely.

Fry considers that, in the stress on the role of the Higher Division as the Minister's personal advisers, there was a 'latent cult of versatility' even before it became manifest; and that the experience of the 'National Insurance adventure of 1911–12', and the other developments of these years of the Asquith Government, when young men from 'all over the First Division' were brought into the Treasury to 'help with the passage and implementation of this bitterly contested social advance' began to convert some (Fry, 1969, 48; and see Addison, 1924, 21); others were influenced by similar experiences during the war of 1914–18, when the numbers in the civil service doubled and many new Departments had to be rapidly created 'out of nothing', as it were—which meant, by transferring a certain number of experienced Higher Division men, used to the ways of the civil service and of Ministers and Parliament, to the top positions, and bringing in 'large numbers of people with commercial and industrial experience . . . usually on a temporary basis, to help with these tasks' of manpower deployment and the production of war material (Bourn, 1968, 446; and see Chester and Willson, 1957, chapter 1; etc.); and then recruiting lower ranks wholesale from wherever they could be found. In respect of the higher officers, this 'mobilisation of the best brains of the departments' had, according to Lord Salter, 'profound consequences for the future development of the Civil Service':

> It was interesting to see when the great test of the Civil Service came with the War a few years later, that a Civil Servant, whether of the First or Second Division, who had had the educative experience of work with the Insurance Commission, was regarded as a jewel beyond price by the departments which had to expand rapidly for the new tasks (*Salter, 1961, 70; quoted in Fry, 1969, 49*).

But mobilisation, such was the need, had perhaps to go beyond the 'best' brains; Lloyd George, seeking experienced Higher Division men for the new Ministry of Munitions, was 'more than thankful when the Admiralty could not see their way to lend him any of their staff' (Smellie, (1937) 1950, 268).

The third influence (besides the 'National Insurance adventure' and the War) towards acceptance of the doctrine of transferability for Higher Division officers was the need to 'unify the civil service', as it came to be called. The long process of creating true 'service-wide' classes, advocated by all the major Commissions and Committee on the Civil Service since 1854, had meant for the later of them centralisation of supervision, over matters of placement, pay, and conditions of service; the obvious place for such power being the Treasury. Very gradual moves in this direction (which had begun as early as 1816) were somewhat disrupted by the enormous expansions before and during the 1914–18 War—indeed, a massive move in the opposite direction took place perforce, which by its obvious extravagance and dangers even of corruption (MacDonnell Report, Cd. 7338, 1914, 22–3; Chamberlain, 1936, 441) perhaps reduced departmental opposition to Treasury hegemony. This then came in a series of steps in 1919 and 1920, setting up an Establishment Division and a standing Committee of Establishment Officers from the various other Departments, designating the Permanent Secretary to the Treasury 'Permanent Head of the Civil Service', to advise the Prime Minister on Civil Service appointments and decorations (a designation that gave rise to much controversy), and decreeing that the Prime Minister's consent was necessary for the appointment or removal of any Permanent Secretary, Deputy Secretary, Principal Establishment Officer, or Principal Finance Officer in a Department. In practice, this meant the centralisation of selection for these key posts—treating the entire service as a single promotion pool. This move was seen by the Government as necessary in any case, in the special conditions of 1919, when 'a most extraordinarily rich crop of great Civil Servants' at the head of several Departments were all approaching retiring age together (Fry, 1969, 55, quoting Geddes, House of Lords Official Report 1942–43, vol. 125, cols, 284–291).

These three factors set the Treasury pendulum swinging away from opposition to the transferability principle for Administrative Class officers. But the pendulum did not stop at mid-point; it was given a decided push towards the other extreme, which has been variously described in the pre-Fulton controversy as 'the cult of the enlightened amateur', the 'superiority of the all-rounder', the 'generalist on top'. There are two main aspects of this doctrine: the first, which has already been noticed, concerned the relationship between the work of the Administrative Class and the work of the Executive Class, particularly the question of class-to-class promotion; the second concerned the relationship between 'generalists' and 'specialists' as advisers to Ministers, the 'specialists' being mainly the professional, technical, and (after 1931) scientific classes. We cannot here go into the details or the merits of these controversies, which have been fully treated in the plentiful literature which preceded and followed the setting up of the Fulton Committee on the Civil Service in 1966 (see Chapman, 1963; Sixth Report of the Estimates Committee, 1964–65, H.C. 308; Shonfield, 1965; Shore, 1966; Nicholson, 1967; Ridley, 1968; Evidence to the Committee, Cmnd. 3638, 1968, vols. 5(1)–(4); Fry, 1969; Brown, 1970; Chapman, 1970; etc.). It is necessary only to illustrate the development of the term 'administration' which they occasioned.

The 'problem of the specialist' only appeared, of course, with the growth in the numbers of those recruited into the civil service other than by the normal examination methods laid down in 1870. Their existence was barely noticed by the Playfair Commission in 1874–75, alluded to by the Ridley Commission of 1886–90, and regarded by the MacDonnell Commission, according to Bourn, as 'outside the main stream of Departmental work' (Bourn, 1968, 443). Employment of professional and technical officers had been sparsely regulated by Section IV of the Superannuation Act of 1859 and subsequent Orders in Council, applying exemptions from examination and age rules to persons filling situations for which the necessary qualifications were 'wholly or in part professional, or otherwise peculiar, and not ordinarily to be acquired in the Civil Service'; the consolidating Order in Council of 10 January 1910, which 'became, in effect, a Civil Service code of regulations' (Bourn, 1968, 439), added nothing of significance to the Order of 4 June 1870 allowing the Civil Service Commissioners to grant their certificate if satisfied that 'the said person is fully qualified in respect of age, health, character and knowledge and ability' (Clause 7, p. 7). By 1930 their greatly increased numbers were still relatively unorganised, so that there were more than 500 distinct grades, each a 'watertight compartment' with its own methods of recruitment and conditions of service (Fry, 1969, 199; Institution of Professional Civil Servants' evidence to Tomlin Commission, Cmd. 3909, Minutes of Evidence App. XI, paras. 15–18).

In a paper read to the then recently-founded Institute of Public Administration in 1923, entitled 'The Sphere of the Specialist in Public Administration', Sir Francis Floud, Permanent Secretary to the Ministry of Agriculture and later of the Board of Customs and Excise and the Ministry of Labour, and a member of the Administrative Class throughout his career (Bourn, 1968, 458n.), put both sides of the case. He referred to the 'large and increasing army of specialists concerned with almost every form of human endeavour and drawn from almost every profession' who had come into the service with the pre-war and wartime expansions, as technical advisers; and gave his opinion that

> ... if specialists are to be mainly employed as advisers I consider that there are certain conditions which they are entitled to demand. In the first place they have a right to demand that their advice should be sought. I have known cases in which administrative officers have come to decisions on technical questions without ever consulting the technical advisers of the Department (*Floud, 1923, 122*).

Moreover, it was indefensible that, once sought, technical advice should be set aside. (It was presumably recognition of this problem that led Sir Robert Morant, the first Permanent Secretary to the Ministry of Health, to ensure that its Chief Medical Officer should have direct access to the Minister, by giving him the same status and salary as the Permanent Secretary himself (Bourn, 1968, 454; Newman, 1939, 112).)

But Sir Francis was in no doubt that the technical adviser should not himself be the 'administrator': in the characteristic partial misreading of Macaulay that has become so familiar since, he held that the essential quality of 'adaptability' was

> more likely to be found in men who have had a good general education and have been initiated at an early age into the daily routine of civil administration than in men who have become specialists in one particular branch of knowledge (*Floud, 1923, 124*).

The 'ordinary non-technical Civil Servant' acquired a 'great capacity for seeing both sides of a question'; the specialist 'may be described as seeking for absolute truth, whereas the lay Civil Servant looks for something which will work'. It followed that 'the sphere of the specialist should be mainly advisory rather than executive', for

> The specialist is rightly so enthusiastic about his own particular work that he is in danger of lacking that sense of proportion and that recognition of political, financial, and practical limitations which every administrator must learn to possess (*Floud, 1923, 125–6; quoted in Fry, 1969, 236*).

This is a remarkably complete and succinct statement of what was perhaps implicit in the 1920 settlement, but became explicit orthodoxy during the decade.

The man who was appointed head of the Treasury and hence of the Civil Service in 1919 was Sir Warren Fisher, who had made his reputation 'during the Insurance episode' (Fry, 1969, 49n.). His evidence to the Tomlin Commission (1929–31) became the authoritative *locus classicus* for the doctrine of the generalist administrator (Cmd. 3909, 1931; Minutes of Evidence):

> Let us guard ourselves against the idea that the permanent head of a department should be an expert; he should not be anything of the kind (*question 18,805*).
>
> My own conception of the permanent head of a large Government department is that he is not (except by accident) a specialist in anything, but rather the general adviser of the Minister, the general manager and controller under the Minister ... (*question 18,846*).
>
> If you ask my folk [in Inland Revenue, his former department], I hope they would say I was not a bad fellow, but I think that they would also say that I knew very little about their technicalities (*question 18,848*).
>
> The Permanent Secretary is a general manager rather than an expert. His duty is to shopwalk the department and to see that the Minister gets the best technical advice (*question 18,849*).

The new orthodoxy is reconciled with the old, in the evidence of the Association of First Division Civil Servants to Tomlin, describing the duties of the Administrative Class:

> The volume of official work which calls for decisions affecting the public is nowadays such that it is physically impossible for the Minister himself to give the decision except in the most important cases. And further, even when the issue is one which can and must be submitted for the Minister's personal decision, it has to be fairly and fully presented to him so that the material facts and considerations are before him. The need for services of this kind is present in every department which has a political head ...
>
> Almost any administrative decision may be expected to have consequences which will endure or emerge long after the period of office of the Government by which or under whose authority it is taken. It is the peculiar function of the Civil Service, and the special duty of the Administrative Class of that Service, in their day-to-day work to set these wider and more enduring considerations against the exigencies of the moment, in order that the Parliamentary convenience of today may not become the Parliamentary embarrassment of tomorrow. This is the primary justification of a permanent administrative service. Vacillation, uncertainty and inconsistency are conspicuous symptoms of bad administration. The formation of policy in this limited sense—subject always to the control of the Minister and to the supreme authority of Parliament—is typical of ad-

ministrative work in all departments and in relation to all subject matters whether of greater or of lesser importance . . .

These, we conceive, are the common characteristics of all
administrative work, whatever the subject matter. In each particular branch of that work other characteristics will also be
found, but they are special to those branches. For example, in
the Board of Education and Ministry of Health, the important
function of maintaining good relations with the autonomous
Local Authorities, while securing in general the application of
those standards of local administration which Parliament desires, is a type of work which is not found in a Department like
the Customs and Excise or the Admiralty. Similarly, in some
branches but not in others one of the functions of administration is the determination of policy in the light of technical
advice, which has to be weighed and balanced against other
non-technical considerations, such as financial conditions or the
state of public opinion (*Statement submitted by the Association of First Division Civil Servants, pp. 5–6; Cmd. 3909, 1931,
Evidence, App. VIII*).

In these passages 'administration' is used in several of the senses
we have isolated; but there is also what amounts to a new definition:
the function of 'administration' is to assign weights to the several
factors in a decision, to combine technical advice and other considerations in due proportion, to balance the short-term pressures
against the longer-term consequences, and fairly and fully present
the relevant material for decision. This is not offered as a description of the work of the Administrative Class, but of 'administration'.

The Tomlin Commission broadly accepted both this implicit
definition of 'administration' and the associated assertion that only
non-specialists, recruited and trained in the manner of the Administrative Class, were fully capable of discharging the function. In
the following year, the Bridgeman Committee of Inquiry on the
Post Office, while being willing to accept the definition of the
function, denied (a) that civil servants brought up in the traditional
Administrative Class manner were fully capable of discharging it—
they did not have enough engineering experience or knowledge to
be able to apportion due weight to engineering advice; and (b) that
civil servants recruited through a professional channel were incapable of discharging it—there should be no bar to a technical
officer holding an administrative post 'provided he has shown himself to possess administrative ability' (Cmd. 4149, 1932, para. 122;
Bourn, 1968, 453). These are basically the positions occupied by
the disputants throughout the following quarter-century, in evi-

dence to various Committees and Comissions, including the Priestley Commission of 1953–55 and the Fulton Committee (Fry, 1969, chap. 5).

In the First Division Association's evidence to Tomlin, the pre-1914 claims that differences between departments precluded transferability for Upper Division men were diluted into a distinction between those aspects of 'administrative work' which are common to all departments and those aspects which are special to particular departments. There is an extreme position of this doctrine, also; Sir Warren Fisher characteristically went a little further himself—a Permanent Secretary, he said, who

> has been running one of these huge businesses under inconceivable difficulties can run any of them (*Cmd. 3909, Minutes of Evidence, question 18,809*).

This is a version of a theory of Walter Bagehot's, about the similarity of mountain tops, which will fall better for discussion in a later section rather than this: it is a thought (that there are 'principles of administration' applicable in any kind of enterprise) that was endemic in the 1920s and early thirties, though possibly Sir Warren would not have wanted to go so far as did Bertrand Russell in 1932; we might quote him here to illustrate the extreme of the 'transferability' doctrine.

> A man who has a position of power in a great organisation requires a definite type of ability, namely, that which is called executive or administrative: it makes little difference what the matter is that the organisation handles, the kind of skill required at the top will always be the same. A man who can organise successfully (let us say) the Lancashire cotton trade will also be successful if he tackles the air defences of London, the exploration of Central Asia, or the transport of timber from British Columbia to England. For these various undertakings he will require no knowledge of cotton, no knowledge of aerial warfare, and no acquaintance with forestry or navigation. His helpers in subordinate positions will, in the several cases, require these several kinds of skill, but his skill is, in a sense, abstract, and does not depend upon specialised knowledge (*Russell, (1932) 1951, 240*).

The qualities of the administrator

The doctrine of the generalist administrator in the civil service received its finest expression in the lectures of a later Permanent

Secretary of the Treasury, Sir Edward (later Lord) Bridges; including the Rede Lecture of 1950, *Portrait of a Profession*, and the one already mentioned entitled 'Administration: what is it? and how can it be learnt?', given in a series commemorating the centenary of the Northcote–Trevelyan Report in 1954. In this latter, he began in the Floud–Fisher tradition:

> The administrator is a layman rather than a specialist; or at least he has about him something of the qualities of a layman.

This is 'consistent with the general pattern of things', since in public affairs, or in commerce, it is essentially lay bodies of electors, Members of Parliament, and shareholders, who must approve the proposals of specialists before they can get started; and a 'strong lay element in the work of administration, which represents the top layer of direction of any organisation' is only to be expected. Yet the experienced administrator is a layman only by contrast with the technical expert; by contrast with the true lay amateur, he has a skill or expertise of his own (Bridges, in Dunsire, 1956, 2–3).

This expertise is of two kinds: the one is gained by departmental administrative experience, which 'varies greatly in the degree of its specialisation'; the other by 'general administrative experience', which grows out of the first, would not exist but for it, and is developed from it. Sir Edward here follows the First Division Association line, rather than the 'general principles of administration' line; but nevertheless, generalised skills exist—

> What then are the qualities of a general administrator—by which I mean the qualities which a man will acquire in his work, and will find of use if sent to do a job about which he knows nothing, and starts from scratch? . . .
>
> First I would put the power of rapid analysis. He must be able to grasp all the facts in a complicated situation; to sort them out and to set them in their proper relationship one to another, and to present the whole to his Minister in the fewest possible words.
>
> Closely allied to this power of analysis, there is the capacity to recognise the essential points in a situation. However complicated the facts may be—however much your junior may try to persuade you that there are seventeen arguments in favour of one course and fifteen in favour of the exact opposite, believe me, in four cases out of five there is *one* point and one only which is cardinal to the whole situation . . .
>
> Next, I would put the sense of timing. Often enough in administration the difficulty lies not so much in finding a solution which is intellectually sound . . . as in . . . [knowing] when the moment has come . . .

Next, I put the capacity to think much less in terms of things as they are today, but in terms of what is going to happen . . . He seems always to be two or three moves ahead. . . .

If these qualities are to be effective there must also be the capacity to hold an even balance between principle and expediency . . . The really wise administrator shows a fine discrimination about the points he can concede and the points on which he must stand firm . . .

Finally, I must not forget the personal qualities which a man in such a position needs: imagination and perseverance needed to work out and carry to a conclusion large measures in reforms; the capacity not only to understand people but to lead them—to be the conductor of the orchestra.

If this adds up to an 'impression of a man who can see round corners and through brick walls', or black magic—

. . . as with most pieces of magic the explanation is quite simple once you know it. I am told by those who are good linguists that when you have learnt about five languages, the sixth, seventh and eighth become quite easy to master and the ninth and tenth are child's play. It is as though the essence of all syntax of language had got into their blood stream. And something rather like this is, I believe, true of many administrative problems. Nearly every problem bears a family resemblance to something which the experienced administrator has seen and handled before. To him it is not some entirely new problem which he is asked to solve at short notice: it is the old wolf in a new-look sheepskin. Something in the shape of the thing strikes him as familiar. His experience tells him where the point of entry will probably be found; or warns him of the difficulties ahead which others, without his training, would not see.

But let me repeat my warning. This type of administrative skill is no substitute for departmental experience: and no man has ever attained it without having made himself the master of at least one branch of work (*Bridges, in Dunsire, 1956, 12–15*).

The 'qualities of the administrator' approach, here exemplified in the words of Bridges, provided an entire *genre* of writing on the Administrative Class of the British Civil Service—academic, polemic, *belles lettres*, and fictional—from the twenties until the sixties, the most renowned names perhaps being Wallas (1928), Laski (1933), Dale (1941), Munro (1952), Sisson (1959), and the 'Lewis Eliot' sequence of C. P. Snow's novels *Strangers and Brothers*. The more careful writing emphasises, as does Bridges, the extent to which the Administrative Class civil servant has a particular job to learn, one that is only partly similar in different departments, and for the rest has both different content and different 'style' (see Griffith, 1966). The popular appreciation, however, stresses the claims to general competence, as if the experience of the substance of departmental work made no difference and as if this competence came from the university background and high educational qualifications. While the British Administrative Class was regarded by the world as a model for emulation, as it undoubtedly was until the 1950's, this basic misunderstanding mattered little; when the British themselves turned against their Administrative Class, it became crucial, and even a weapon to be exploited by the unscrupulous with acceptable taunts about 'gifted amateurs', 'the arrogance of the Oxford First in Classics', and so on. It is one of the heaviest of the many criticisms that have been levelled against the first chapter of the Fulton Report, the result of that popular revulsion, that in this respect it is fundamentally unhistorical.

This is not to say, of course, that the Fulton Committee's conclusions and recommendations were erroneous, or that the criticisms of the Executive Class, the Professional Civil Servants, and so many others, were without merit. One does not wish to enter the controversy about avenues of recruitment, selection, promotion, status, and remuneration, but to make the distinction Snowden, Wallas and their co-signatories of the First Reservation to the MacDonnell Report wanted to have made in 1914—between all that (and particularly, educational entry-points), and the description of kinds of work. The Administrative Class can be charged, rightly in my opinion, with being too ready to run these two things together. But they did not themselves define the *work* in the terms charged against them by some of the critics.

By the midle of this period, nevertheless, a meaning had been given to 'administration' in English that persists, even outside the civil service; one that goes considerably beyond the Ninth, and can be seen as an expansion of the first phrase of the Eleventh ('work concerned with the formation of policy')—a Twelfth Meaning,

> (12) *work of analysing, balancing, and presenting for decision complex policy considerations*; assigning due weights to each factor (technical, financial, political, etc.), balancing short-term considerations against long-term considerations; to be contrasted with the work of giving specialist advice on any one factor;
> *work of persons trained and experienced in this task*, as distinct from the work of persons trained in a specific professional capacity or technical expertise before entry and employed in such capacity.

We may also note, without actually incorporating it into a separate meaning, that at some point in the protracted debate about the structure of the civil service, it came to be assumed that, whatever its proper content might be, and whoever should be doing it and not doing it, 'administration' was something done by permanent civil servants first and foremost, if not exclusively. To describe the work of Ministers as 'administration' might today be a little puzzling, unless consciously archaic.

CHAPTER THREE

The Term in other Settings

We do not have an adequate account of the evolution of the term 'administration', or an adequate list of its common meanings, without taking note of an entirely different train of development from that which the term took in the civil service context; but perforce, more sketchily. Men in other walks of life—local government, industry, the armed services, the Church, universities, and so on—tend today to use the term rather differently from the usage described in the last few listed Meanings, and more consistently with one another than with civil service usage; in so far as one can trace it, the divergence begins to appear clearly only in the closing years of the nineteenth century.

As we have seen, from the earliest times the term 'administration' has had two curiously opposite elements in its meanings: the element of 'serving', and the element of 'managing' or 'directing'; a connotation of inferiority, and a connotation of superiority. According as one or the other element is dominant in a particular context, the meaning appears to vary quite considerably: the 'administration of the realm' can be the aspect which is subservient to the sovereign will of the king, or it can be the name of the ruling group. One and the same man, called an 'administrator', may be a powerful figure at the head of his office, or a subordinate carrying into effect the policies of the person or body to whom he himself is accountable. Administration can be seen as relative detail, the mere devising of means to given ends; or it can be concerned with the formation of policy and the direction of a nation's destiny. As the perspective alters, so does the apparent object. Administration wears the two faces of Janus, not only looking in the two directions through different eyes, but *seeming* different from each direction: as must the 'first servant' of any lord, in any walk of life.

We have seen also, how 'administration', applied first to certain aspects of the activity of the King in his Court or household, became attached to the whole activities of those ('Ministers') who, as government became more complex, specialised publicly in those aspects, the 'household' retreating into a form of privacy. As government became more complex still, the name was applied to certain aspects only of the activities of those persons; and later, came to be applied to the work of other people who specialised in these aspects—'civil' 'servants', although not until much later did it cease to apply at all to Ministers; meanwhile, with specialisation among the civil servants, the term came to apply to certain aspects only of their activities. Specialisation of meaning followed emerging specialisation of function.

Commerce and industry

In commerce and industry, the main distinctions that emerged between, say, the sixteenth century and the beginning of the nineteenth, were first, the distinction between the work of the 'entrepreneur' and that of the 'manager'; and second, the distinction between the work of production (using 'product' in a wide sense, to include all services to customers, clients, and the outside world generally), and the commercial work of an undertaking, mainly accounting (Pollard, (1965) 1968; Urwick and Brech, 1946).

The distinction between 'ownership' and 'management' may have been, as Urwick and Brech suggest, known in 1688: J. Hill's treatise on accounting, *The Exact Dealer*, spoke of 'those that manage or are the proprietors of manufacture' (Urwick and Brech, 1946, II, 18). But the recognition of a distinction between the roles of 'entrepreneur' and manager took as long to emerge as did that of the distinction between 'statesman' and 'civil servant'. Pollard, noting that

> The concepts of entrepreneurship and management do themselves change with the changing structure and purposes of industry (*Pollard, (1965) 1968, 12*).

chooses a definition (of G. H. Evans Jun.) which he thinks appropriate for the early nineteenth century; entrepreneurs have the

> task of determining *the kind of business to be operated* ... the kinds of goods and services to be offered, the amounts of these to be supplied, and the clientele to be served.
> ... Other 'top level' decisions become essentially management

decisions—that is, decisions designed to achieve the goals set
by the entrepreneurial determination of the kind of business to
be operated (*Pollard*, (*1965*) *1968, 14*)

—a distinction which is close to that between 'legislation' and
'execution' as generally appreciated in the eighteenth century.
What was still then in flux, whether in industry or in government
(as Bentham suggested), was whether the line between these roles
was identifiable with a line between different classes of individual.

The other distinction, between 'manufacture' as such and the
monitoring of manufacturing processes so as to maximise the aims
of the entrepreneur, had also to be learned. The practices of financial 'book-keeping' were well enough known, though not all entrepreneurs either had the skills or saw the necessity—many such
happy-go-lucky 'ventures' ending in bankruptcy. But pre-industrial
accounting was based on the needs either of large landowners, to
check the stewardship of their bailiffs, or of bankers and merchants,
to calculate the return on individual ventures by the shipment; each
resulted in a different system of accounts, neither immediately suitable for factory accounting, where service of capital was a much
more significant factor. Each of them, too, resisted a distinction
between 'managing an estate' and 'acting as steward', or 'lending'
and 'calculating the risk'; it was this kind of distinction that had to
be learned.

The eighteenth century was an era of invention in this field,
therefore, as much as in methods of manufacture; one of the most
significant being the discovery that records of 'output and input', as
we might now say, could result in measures of performance that
were much more what the entrepreneur needed than the accounting
of invoices and receipts. Pollard notes:

> Thus the Stanley (Copper) Co., controlled from Anglesey,
> returned fortnightly details of output, sales and salaries on
> regular printed forms; Coalbrookdale began regular four-weekly
> returns of production, consumption of raw materials, labour
> and wages from about 1718 onwards; ... the Shrewsbury work-
> house steward was required to keep thirteen sets of books in the
> 1790s, beside journal and waste book; the Soho Foundry, in its
> heyday of early control, used twenty-two; ... (*Pollard*, (*1965*)
> *1968, 253*).

By the early nineteenth century, methods of cost estimating of considerable sophistication were fairly well-known (though the same
could not be said for *ex post facto* accounting, keeping track of
what actually happened—Pollard, (1965) 1968, 257); the writings

of the early economists were closely concerned with correcting simple ideas about cost analysis, and in 1832 a Cambridge Professor of Mathematics, Charles Babbage (1792–1871) published *On the Economy of Machinery and Manufactures*, in which he extended Adam Smith's celebrated illustration of the division of labour in a pin-making factory by observing the time required for each of the operations of pin-making, putting it together with hourly wages, and calculating the price of making each part of a single pin, in millionths of a penny (Urwick and Brech, 1945, I, 25). The concept of controlling the process of manufactures, as distinct from specifying its technical content, was clearly received.

This consciousness of the power of proper accounting did not escape the politicians, of course; it is the background to 'Economical Reform', and Burke's famous speech in 1780, when he criticised the antiquated and wasteful organisation of the royal household, the maladministration of royal property, the inefficiency of the Exchequer, the retention of large balances by paymasters and other public accountants, and the utter uselessness of some entire departments (Keir, (1938), 1953, 384). It was a manner of thinking which greatly appealed to the Utilitarians: a section of Bentham's *Constitutional Code* is given over to the minute specification of the books that should be kept by public departments (see below, p. 60). But the question of monitoring government operations for 'efficiency', as distinct from ensuring cheapness, avoidance of waste, and financial probity, is one that still exercises experts today.

The history of industrial accounting, and other 'book-keeping', in the nineteenth century would take us too far from the central purpose: let it only be noted that, in the use of the term 'administration' or 'administrative', eighteenth- and nineteenth-century industrialists appear to have been no different from 'statesmen'; the range of meanings employed falls within the first eight Meanings we have listed. Not until the end of the century, when the first text-books in 'commercial management' for managers (as distinct from textbooks in accountancy for accountants) appear, does the usage of 'administrative' began to take on a distinctive colouring. J. Slater Lewis in *The Commercial Organisation of Factories* (1896), speaking of the 'duties of the manager', says

> As regards the technical details of the business, he should be a thoroughly practical all-round man. He need not necessarily have an intimate acquaintance with the mathematical or other minutiae of each branch of the business, but must have a strong capacity for administrative work.

What might be meant by 'administrative work'? The passage goes on:

> He should have an instinctive knowledge of what his custo-
> mers really require, and know the smartest and cheapest way of
> supplying their wants. He should be quite at home in modern
> office routine, in accounts kept by double entry, in the handling
> of large bodies of men, and in the application of modern
> machinery to all classes of engineering work (*Slater Lewis,
> quoted in Urwick and Brech, 1946, II, 82*).

Later, he speaks of 'an administrative routine sufficiently pliable'
to be able to respond to suggestions arising from a 'precise and
accurate representation of daily operations and a system of registration and accounts equal to the exhaustive demands of modern
industrial conditions'. But precisely what 'administrative' means is
not clear.

By 1920, however, usage had settled down almost as firmly in
industry as it had in the civil service—but differently. The title of
another pioneering work in 1914 was *Factory Administration and
Accounts* (E. T. Elbourne). Urwick and Brech, in a chapter entitled
'The Administrative Training of the Engineer 1847–1935', quoted
a Lieut.-Colonel W. A. J. O'Meara in February 1919, who 'reminded his audience how in the past education and training for the
British electrical engineering profession had been built up on a
tacitly assumed distinction between the "technical" and "administrative", whereas in other countries the professional training had
included the "business aspects"' ... and continued:

> Instruction in the appropriate subjects dealing with the com-
> mercial and administrative problems with which the engineer is
> confronted almost daily should find a place in the curriculum
> of every engineering course in the schools and colleges of this
> country (*Urwick and Brech, 1946, II, 127*).

Manchester University established a Department of Industrial
Administration in 1918; the University of Bristol in 1919 'included
in their Engineering Degree Course a series of lectures on administration, costing, and so on' (Urwick and Brech, 1946, II, 129).

Although the meaning of 'industrial administration' in such
usages could, of course, be a quite general one—'the running of
industry'—it is noticeable even in this brief selection how often
'administration' is coupled with 'accounts', 'commercial', 'costing',
and so on. It is inescapable that by 'administration' in the industrial
context users sometimes mean to convey a sense far removed from

that connected with 'the formation of policy', for instance. As to what they do mean to convey, let me rest on the opinion of one of the two authors just quoted, E. F. L. Brech, in a successful textbook first published in 1953. Noting that the chief ambiguity arises from the influence of the usage of the public departments, and that

> In some of the larger commercial organisations and the nationalised industries the term 'administration' has been imported to refer to some activities of the higher level of management centred at Head Offices; generally speaking, no analytical reason lies behind this, but it can often be traced to the whim of a particular individual, or possibly to a mistaken notion of prestige

he goes on to say that the term 'administration' is sometimes applied

> to the offices or staffs that are engaged in the control activities; for instance, one sometimes finds the name 'Administrative Block' given to the office sections of the buildings of the large combines

and asks

> Has, then, the word 'administration' any part to play? In any sense that is synonymous with management the answer is 'no'. Equally, in any sense that suggests a superior process restricted to the upper executive structure, the answer had also best be 'no'. Popular usage does suggest that the main significance of 'administration', wherever it is used, centres on the procedures which form the tools of management, i.e. the techniques or routines of planning and control. To this extent the term 'administration' can be a useful label to these aspects of the total process (*Brech*, *(1953) 1963, 23*).

In this, Brech is parting company with Urwick, who preferred the distinction between 'administration' and 'management' that was suggested by Sheldon (1924),

> *Administration* is the function of industry concerned with the determination of the corporate policy, co-ordination of production, finance and distribution, the settlement of the compass of the organisation and the ultimate control of the executive . . . *Management* is the function of industry concerned with the carrying out of policy within the limits set up by administration and the employment of the organisation for the particular objects set before it (*quoted in Urwick, 1929, 115–16*).

This distinction is almost equivalent to that between 'entrepreneurship' and management; and if adopted, would indeed have been a departure from the course of the term's evolution, to equate 'administration' and 'entrepreneurship'. There is a passage in Urwick and Brech which imputes to a speaker in 1913 a

> distinction—now voiced for the first time—between the administrative and the executive, between the directors and the managers (*Urwick and Brech, 1946, II, 122; and see also Urwick, 1969*)

but this is highly dubious in the context actually quoted. In any case, although traces of this attempt to harmonise industrial usage with civil service usage can still be found, there is no doubt that, as a reporter of popular usage in 1953, Brech is right: 'administration' in industry is distinguished both from the 'determination of corporate policy', the activities of directors, and from the 'production' aspects of manufacturing or providing a service to customers. In this it is similar to the Ninth Meaning that emerged in the middle of the nineteenth century to help distinguish a Minister's 'proper' work from what some of them were too inclined to indulge in, the actual detail of the office; but whereas from this point the civil service usage moved closer to the 'policy' pole, industrial usage registered a 'functional' rather than a hierarchical differentiation, and came to signify the essentially domestic or internal housekeeping specialisation, concerned at its mundane level with book-keeping, recording, registration, accounting, budgeting, estimating and costing, and at its reflective level with statistical inference and similar abstracting of basic information, with layout and timetabling, scheduling, programming, planning and so on. The manipulation of feedback information derived from internal 'paper' of this sort is, of course, a prime 'tool of management decision', and as such, contributory to corporate policy-making. But in industry, it is 'management' and 'direction' that does the assigning of weights to decision factors, the balancing of short-term and long-term considerations, and the like: not 'administration'.

Military administration

To turn to another field: the reorganisation of the War Office in 1904 was a matter of 'public administration' and not of industry or commerce; yet the Esher Committee was able to use without explanation a distinction between 'administration' and something else that does not make sense in terms of the distinctions we have noted so far in the public service. It is perhaps plain enough in the context what they meant; the passage now quoted follows their recommendation of an Army Council of seven members (six besides the Secretary of State), with individual responsiblities for Operations of War, Personnel, Supply, Armament, Civil Business, and Finance:

> For the exercise of effective action, the sphere of the Commander-in-Chief, as at present understood, is far too wide; while for administrative purposes he may be sometimes not the most efficient, and sometimes too fine an instrument. In order to secure effective control, a Commander should be in constant touch with the units of his command. Owing to the wide extent of the King's Dominions, this necessary condition cannot be fulfilled by a Commader-in-Chief. ... We, therefore, consider that it is imperative to abolish the Office of Commander-in-Chief, which was only revived as late as 1887, and we urge the divorce of administration from executive command, and the decentralisation of the latter (*Cd. 1932, 1904, 10; Hanham, 1969, 371*).

This would appear to be another variant of the Ninth Meaning, distinguishing 'administration' from 'the exercise of effective action'. But whereas the Ninth Meaning did so by regarding 'administration' as 'the directing, or establishing the principles of' such action, the Esher usage clearly envisages that as the task of the Commander in the field; 'administration' is something else entirely—possibly, the 'logistic support' functions of the five members of the Army Council other than 'Operations of War' (Personnel, Supply, Armament, Civil Business, Finance). None of our listed civil service Meanings, at any rate, would make adequate sense of this passage; while the industrial usage would at least convey its 'drift', the connotation of 'the paperwork' or 'Admin. Block' functions inseparable from, but quite distinguishable from, large-scale military operations themselves.

Local government

Local government provides another illustration of ambiguity introduced by infection from civil service usage. A thumbnail sketch of the evolution of local authorities in the nineteenth century would show something like the following differentiation of roles. After the uniformity of internal structure induced by the sweeping away of all the old (and diverse) forms (Webb, 1908; 1922) by the Municipal

Corporations Act of 1835, large elected councils formed committees of their own number 'for administration'; then employed a single full-time official, more or less professionally qualified in the field of work of the committee, for each branch of their responsibilities; the single officer became a 'department' of such officers, with a head or 'chief officer', and supporting clerks; then the technically-qualified or 'professional' officers became specialised in smaller sections of the work of the department, either becoming heads of section or of new separate departments, each with his own subordinate 'qualified' staff and supporting 'unqualified' or 'lay' staff; and finally, in the middle twentieth century, the 'lay' staff differentiated into senior or more responsible officers and junior or 'clerical' officers, the senior coming to be called 'administrative' (See Webb, 1922, 428ff; Keith-Lucas, 1958; Rhodes, 1967; Smellie, 1946; Warren, 1952; etc.).

The Committee on the Staffing of Local Government under Sir George Mallaby, and the Committee on Management of Local Government under Sir John Maud (later Lord Redcliffe-Maud), were the local government equivalent of 'Fulton' in the reform climate of the 1960s. The Mallaby Report began with an account of the present diversity of work performed by local government officers, in terms not only of the various different professions and technical skills, but also 'vertically', in the hierarchy of responsibility: from 'senior staff' advising the authority on the development of its services, and 'supervising their execution', through officers 'organising' the provision of these services, to the 'great majority' of officers

> engaged in executive work in providing services or the machinery of administration, for example in the collection of revenue, and in accounting and recording operations necessary to support the services and functions of the authority (*Mallaby, 1967, para. 16*).

The Report distinguishes between work that is little different from that in other forms of employment, and that which requires an understanding of the procedures and constitutional workings of a local authority—such as the work of solicitors, treasurers, 'lay administrative officers', heads of departments and their deputies, who 'advise elected members collectively in council or committee and who provide information and help to members individually' (Mallaby, 1967, para. 18). It is in a footnote to this paragraph that the ambiguity first seriously appears:

Officers qualified in a number of professions undertake administration in its broadest sense, particularly at the senior levels of a department. To avoid confusion we have used the term 'lay administrative officers' to denote those officers who are normally known as 'administrative officers' or 'administrative assistants'. We do not imply that the work of lay administrative officers is not professional work (*Mallaby, 1967, 8n.*).

Here the Committee wrestles not only with a civil-service-inspired use of 'administration in its broadest sense' (by which they mean not that at all, but something like our Eleventh or Twelfth Meaning, or 'the duties of the Administrative Class') contrasted with 'administration' as popularly understood in local government and by themselves two paragraphs earlier, as a middle-level set of responsibilities; but also with the conventional local government sense of 'professional', meaning holding a degree-level qualification in one of the established regulated professions such as law, accountancy, engineering, and so on, set against the susceptibilities of those who, having gained similar-level qualifications in municipal administration, public administration, or management studies, wish to be regarded as equally professional.

What the Committee saw as the province of the 'lay administrative officer' is given in the following passage:

In the departments of a local authority there is an important element of administrative work to be done at varying levels of responsibility which does not require professional judgement. While there is a shortage of professionally qualified men, this administrative work should be done by lay administrative officers who may be general graduates. This work can take many forms:
(a) specialist work in, for example, management services, and in personnel and establishment control;
(b) the drafting of reports and memoranda and the organisation of the flow of work in the department's headquarters offices;
(c) consultation and co-ordination with other sectors of the authority's activities;
(d) executive responsibility with powers for action in non-professional fields (*Mallaby, 1967, para. 233*).

But for the headship of a department, the Committee considered that in many of them, at least, 'there is no substitute for professionally qualified principal officers', and recommended that the career of the 'lay administrative officer' should take him to the second or third tier position in a department, with equality of salary and status with his qualified colleagues at those levels (Mallaby, 1967, para. 234)—except for the Clerkship:

> The Clerk in any authority, whatever its size and responsibilities, spends much time in administration, in the servicing of its committees, in the co-ordination of its many activities where this is necessary to prevent over-lapping or confusion of plans, and in general provision of management services. These are in fact high administrative tasks requiring distinctive gifts of personality and leadership. Men in any profession, including the profession of administration, may possess these gifts. The lay administrator should have an equal chance with members of other professions to become the Clerk of an authority (*Mallaby, 1967, para. 236*).

Here again we can see the (undoubtedly deliberate) manipulation of ambiguity in what 'profession' implies, and what sort of tasks 'high administrative' ones are. (If there *is* a 'profession of administration', surely it should have the *monopoly* of this kind of Clerkship, at least, as other professions have the monopoly of 'their' departmental headships? Opposing that argument entails exposing the truth that the words merely, as Gellner put it, 'emit the impression of possessing a constant meaning throughout.')

Universities

The Mallaby Committee's recommendations on the work of the 'lay administrative officer' correspond more nearly with Brech's understanding of the role of 'administration' in industry than they do with the 'duties of the Administrative Class'. Examples of convergence in the senses of 'administration' conventional in other fields could be multiplied: in railways and other public corporations, the health services, and so on. In a British university, 'the administration' is a separate corps from both 'the academic staff' or 'faculty' and 'the domestic staff', leaving aside servants, such as porters and groundsmen. The senior ranks of 'the administration' enjoy equality of status with the professors; but the monopoly of the academic staff over the direction and control of 'production'—teaching and research, 'what the university is there for'—is jealously guarded, within a budget whose amount is fixed outside the university altogether, and budgetary distributions in which they have a representative voice, along with 'the administration' and the university version of the 'lay' element, who are eminent local personages and local authority appointees on the University Council, the formal 'governing body'. The tasks of the 'administration', are, at the higher end, the provision and maintenance of 'plant' and 'manpower', the 'logistic support' of the prime functions of the university; and at the lower end, the clerical operations of recording, registration, accounting and so on.

Within that structure, however, the academic staff are themselves accustomed to differentiate their work into, usually, three parts: teaching, research, and 'administration'. In the last category come matters such as the selection of first-year students, the preparation of syllabuses and reading lists, examining, termly assessments and other reports, references for employers, and a number of other such activities, little of which can be shifted on to other shoulders, since although it is analytically distinguishable from the teaching of one's subjects, it is inseparable from it in the present conditions of university teaching. In addition, there is for most teachers participation in 'policy making' at faculty board or departmental board level, and for some, participation in the university-wide Senate and its committees, participation in college affairs, and in professional bodies of university teachers with a national constituency. A few who hold the position of departmental head may consume a very large proportion of their time in running a department, comprising a dozen to twenty academic staff and two or three secretaries on average, including appointment of staff, co-ordination of teaching programmes, departmental finance, and so on; and it it often the same persons who are most occupied with the committee formulation of University policy.

All this non-teaching and non-research activity may be called 'administration', or differentiated into 'university government' and 'departmental administration'; but there is no uniformity of nomenclature beyond the basic trichotomy. What is a trichotomy in university work can be recognised, as a dichotomy, in many other walks of life; *mutatis mutandis*, in local government, in the surgery of the general practitioner, in the architect's drawing office, in the vicarage, and so on, the same distinction may be expressed, between two kinds of a single man's work; particularly when the man in question is employed as a 'professional', or was originally trained and recruited as such. The one kind, his professional or vocational work, frequently called 'what he is paid for', is regarded as primary (there may be an assumption that it 'ought' to be his sole work, to take up 100 per cent of his time); the other kind, usually called 'the paperwork', is seen as secondary and often resented, the assumption there being that it is dispensable and imposed by 'them' for no good reason (the usual explanation being in terms of 'bureaucracy'). Of course, to use professionally-remunerated labour for simple clerical operations is, as Mallaby pointed out, a gross waste of scarce resources; but there is a category of 'clerical' (as distinct from technical or professional) work which cannot be entrusted to non-professional labour, because it requires professional judgement, or experience in the professional post, for its completion: and this category, however small it can be made, will always comprise an irreducible minimum proportion of a professional man's total time—whether it be 'imposed' by a man's employers or by the circumstances of self-employment. There is an inseparable 'administrative' element (for that is the term commonly used to name it in more formal speech) in all 'professional' work, and this is so without taking into account any increase in its proportion consequent upon 'promotion' to be head of an organisational section, or the like.

Meanings reviewed

The usages briefly described in this chapter, in industry, the armed services, local government, universities, and in individual 'professional' work generally, might generate a considerable range of additional Meanings for our list; but to avoid over-complication, I propose to identify only two, a general one and a particular one; and to include their associated collective terms in the Meaning. So, a Thirteenth Meaning,

(13) *ancillary housekeeping and 'office' or 'desk' work in an organisation,* or part of the work of an individual, contrasted with but inseparable from the work of producing the goods or services whose production defines the public role of the organisation or individual; work of logistic support, structuring and programming, procedural record and control, contrasted with direction of production, and making of corporate policy, as well as productive operations;
collective noun for persons engaged in such work in an organisation.

Within this more general Meaning, however, there are found usages which have to be explained by a more particular sense, a Fourteenth Meaning,

(14) *work of book-keeping, registration, accounting, and other internal communication of record*; 'clerical' work, as contrasted with the use of such records in control or in policy-making;
collective noun for persons engaged in such work.

Of all the Meanings we have listed, these are perhaps closest to the First Meaning, 'service pure and simple', with less connotation of 'direction' or 'government' than any of the others; lacking both the notion of 'execution of purpose' and the participation in policy decision, though the strong implication of connection with internal records and procedures undoubtedly comes from association with the forms of 'implementation of laws by non-judicial machinery' found in the public service at an earlier stage of the term's evolution. It is worth emphasising, therefore, that it is these usages and understandings which are the most widespread, and probably would convey the generally-accepted meaning of the term 'administration', if it were not for the great prestige of the somewhat specialised civil service usage.

It would be foolish to suppose that these fourteen Meanings cover all of the present or possible usages of the term 'administration' in English. Further development, by sub-division of these senses, or re-grouping, or special reasoning in special circumstances, has been going on and will go on; conventions change. What was formerly an Americanism, designating a particular government department or agency 'an Administration' as we might call it 'an Authority', as in the Federal Food and Drug Administration and many others, has now been adopted in Britain with the 'Overseas Development Administration'. Perhaps this should be listed as a Fifteenth Meaning, a narrowing of the Sixth and Tenth still further; but I forbear, since there is no end to the process, and the point is not to compile an exhaustive lexicon but to illustrate how various are the senses in current use, and to conjecture how it came so.

What is a little astonishing in the face of such variety is how life manages to continue in relative order, people communicating what they mean by 'administration' through the context in which they use it as they do with so many other words, deliberate ambiguity being relatively infrequent. If it is not whim or search for prestige, as Brech suggested, it must be a special reasoning that, for instance, gives the title General Administrator to the chief executive of one theatre, General Manager to that of another, and General Director to that of a third. Brech describes how in the late 1940s a 'serious-minded thinker and practitioner in management ... could in all sincerity prepare to plead at the High Court for an injunction to withhold the publication of the new translation of Fayol—on the sole ground that the translator had rendered Fayol's French title *Administration* into English *Management* (Brech, (1953) 1963, 23n.). If one scans the Appointments pages of the heavier newspapers it becomes apparent that, not only 'Administrator', but also 'Director', 'Manager', and above all 'Secretary' are all deeply ambiguous titles; one must read the smaller print and guess from the salary offered what kind of a job is meant—there are fewer levels of job than there are titles for them. Rules of thumb emerge: an 'Administrative Officer' is of lower status than an 'Administrator', just as 'Executive Officer' in a job title usually indicates a less exalted rank than does 'Executive'. It requires skills suitable for the appointment to understand what the advertiser is looking for— a version of those advertisements written in computer code or (in English newspapers) in Arabic. For some colleagues of mine, the advertisement of a post as that of 'College Manager' was opposed on the grounds that 'managers' are what prize-fighters or pop-groups have; 'College Administrator' implied too clerical a post; 'College Bursar' was finally approved. I am not scoffing; it was a perfectly proper discussion to have, and this that we have just had has been of the same nature.

CHAPTER FOUR

European
Administrative Science

Having thus traced the evolution of the use of the term 'administration' and its cognates over the last two hundred years or so, I should like to turn now to a superficially similar but quite different evolution: that of the study of administration, or administrative science. In surveying the English literature of the field in the eighteenth and nineteenth centuries, one had no opportunity to consult a contemporary textbook of administrative science, because as Taylor and others said, none exists; yet, if the language had been either French or German, one would have had opportunity in plenty of doing so. This surely needs explanation.

One fairly obvious hypothesis to explain the absence of English textbooks on administrative science would be the absence of English students to use them. It was not necessary, in England, before becoming a public servant, to have had a technical training in appropriate subjects; in some continental countries it was.

It is a historical commonplace that the centralising 'absolute monarchy' phase of European political development in the sixteenth and seventeenth centuries was not nearly so marked in England as it was in most of the continental kingdoms. The same forces were at work, perhaps; the expansion of trade, the creation of royal standing armies, the royal monopolising of justice, the decline of ecclesiastical and the rise of royal eleemosynary and sumptuary regulation, the personalisation of relationships with foreign powers. The development of machinery that this extension of royal activity required was paralleled in each country; and indeed, one sovereign copied another's innovations—a committee system from Spain, the Secretary of State from Elizabethan England, revenue collection from France, organised recruitment and training of functionaries from Prussia—where centralisation of all authority had gone farthest (Barker, 1944, 2; Chapman, 1959, 17).

Prussian cameralism, French rationalism, and English self-government

Beginning by tightening control over the administration of the royal estates and the military, the Prussian monarchs from the Great Elector onwards (Frederick William of Brandenburg, 1640–88), and especially Frederick William I (1713–40), established a strong corps of professional public servants responsible directly to the King, on the pattern of Colbert's *intendants* in France, in order to break the power of the landed aristocracy and the provincial towns. This apparatus, covering all the Prussian dynastic estates and territories in a single pattern, unified economic and military regulation in a system of provincial Boards of War and Domains (*Kriegs-und-Domänenkammer*), under a central General Directory headed by four ministers who were 'supervisors, not directors of the state's bureaucratic activity' (Rosenberg, 1958, 39). To ensure the adequate training of his public officials, Frederick William I established chairs in the universities of Frankfurt and Halle, for what, in English, we might call 'Council Studies'—Cameralistics, or the cameralistic sciences. These included such technical subjects as agriculture and forestry, for the working of the royal estates themselves (and 'domain management' is a root meaning of 'economics'), and also the sciences of finance and taxation, statistics, and 'administration'. By the middle of the eighteenth century it was virtually impossible to obtain a high official post in the Prussian royal service without a qualification in these subjects (see Chapman, 1959; Rosenberg, 1958; Lepawsky, 1949; Small, 1909).

As is clear from the extensive selections made by Small from the lectures and writings of a number of the professors of cameralistics, there is not a great deal that is 'scientific' in the positivist modern sense in these works; they described current institutions and practices, and were badly recommendatory of what was considered good practice. But in two respects the movement was remarkable enough: it was wholly concerned with what Taylor in England a century or so later noted the lack of: the 'art of *exercising* political functions', of *Administrative* Government; with what we now should certainly call 'administrative studies'—or on the Continent, 'the administrative sciences'. Secondly, it was rooted in what we should now recognise as an 'economic' mode of thinking, rather than a legal. That might be anachronistic; rather did 'economics' come out of this eighteenth-century mood of

Aufklärung, as Barker said, 'with its creed of superior benevolence and its utilitarian levelling rationalism' (Barker, 1944, 2), than the other way round. Jeremy Bentham was the English father of utilitarianism, but he himself acknowledged his indebtedness for his methods to the European *philosophes*, particularly Helvetius, Beccaria, Maupertuis, and D'Alembert (Mack, 1962, 107–9). The cameralistic writers shared the definitional and analytic spirit of the *philosophes*, the conviction of having discovered the 'natural' systems underlying reality, of which only men's blindness, or self-interested short-sightedness, or slothful habits, prevented the realisation.

'Prussian' centralisation, and to a degree the special recruitment and training of officials also, was adopted in Austria, in France, and to a somewhat modified extent in the Low Countries and Scandinavia. But for a variety of reasons, centralisation in England was inhibited. The monarchy was never as absolute, especially in the control of financial resources; there were many 'centres of countervailing power', collectively represented by a strong Commons, uniting burgesses of the cities with knights of the shires, who had broken the power of the royal sheriffs two centuries before. The Justices of the Peace were centrally-appointed officials, indeed, carrying out a great variety of 'administrative' duties as well as dispensing petty justice; but there was no machinery for controlling them. They were, in sixteenth-century French terms, *officiers* not *commissaires* (Rosenberg, 1958, 17); office-bearers, not executive agents. In a splendid passage, Barker puts it thus:

While France was insisting, by the Revocation of the Edict of Nantes, on unity of religion, England was becoming a home of Free Churches, which influenced deeply her political life, alike by the genius of their inner spirit and by the challenge which they steadily offered to all policies of conformity. While France was seeking to control all economic life by a central controller-general and his *intendants*, England was practising a system of voluntary economic activity, which promoted more than any other cause the rapid growth of her commerce and industry. Finally, while the nobility and gentry of France were powerless before the *intendant*, and, destitute of local authority, were content to exact dues from their peasantry in order to lead a satellite life at Paris, the English nobility and gentry were masters of Parliament at Westminster, and the governors, through quarter sessions, of their shires. But the converse of this picture, and a converse which may well inspire us with modest reflections, is that while France (and, we may also add, Prussia)

'made a science of the service of the State', England 'considered it a task for intelligent amateurs' (Professor Pollard, in
the *Camb. Mod. Hist.*, x, 353). (*Barker, 1944, 29.*)

This system was the one celebrated by the nineteenth-century
German historian Rudolf Gneist in the somewhat-misunderstood
term 'self-government' (Gneist, 1857–60; Redlich and Hirst, 1903,
II, 384). He applied it to a decentralised state, ruled not from one
seat of government through officials owing all their position and
power to the ruler, but from a thousand seats of government, each
an independent personage with his own standing in his own village
or town: a 'squirearchy', the same person often being the major
landowner, a considerable local employer, patron of the church
living, Justice of the Peace, possibly assessor or collector of taxes
as well (Finer, (1932) 1946, 1288ff.; Parris, 1969, 22), appointing
his own assistants and enjoying a profit on what he collected.
Gneist was not applying the term to elective municipal councils,
which indeed he saw as a form of betrayal of the true principles
of local self-government—false or 'commercial' self-government;
instead of being moved by duty and social obligation, the burgess
was moved by the local interest of a majority of the voters; instead
of governing in the interest of England, the new 'boards' (councils)
were busied with the commercial interest of local combinations.
Gneist was no democrat.

'English self-government'—or rather the accounts of it given by
French and German writers (Redlich, 1903, I, xii)—along with the
accounts of English Common Law and the English Constitution
based largely on Blackstone, became in their turn a matter of
admiration and emulation among Continental liberals, particularly
after disillusionment with the increasingly rigid and degenerating
Prussian system had set in, in the early decades of the nineteenth
century. John Stuart Mill, Walter Bagehot, and a score of statesmen
and writers in the reviews, were not being merely self-satisfied, or
even patriotic, when they contrasted the 'freedom' that all agreed
existed in England with the evils of what they had learned to call
'bureaucracy' on the continent. In the English system, no greater
burden of 'State business' had been placed on any of the thousands
of unpaid, honorific and locally-domiciled public dignitaries, who
kept going the English administrative machinery in the shires, than
the ordinary educational attainments of the English country gentleman had been able to bear; and the same was true of the incum-
bents of official positions in the London offices, being so often the
relatives of these same squires. Thus, not only had England avoided

bureaucracy, it had also avoided schools for public servants; and with them, administrative science textbooks.

Pollard, in an interesting chapter on the parallel question concerning the 'strange absence of management theory' in the Industrial Revolution and, indeed, during almost the whole of the nineteenth century, does not use this argument as an explanation (Pollard, (1965) 1968, 296). He gives three reasons for it: first, one must be able to isolate something one can call the 'managerial' function, from out of the heterogeneous activities of the entrepreneur as 'capitalist, financier, works manager, merchant, and salesman'—all these not so much by turns as at the same time, indistinguishably. Secondly, in a period dominated not only by basic structural revolution in so many different technologies but by the hegemony of the founders, innovators, and pioneers—whose success seemed to depend so much upon 'character' and happy accident—'such questions as the structuring and management of firms must have seemed too individual, too unclassifiable, to repay further generalised study'. Thirdly, a fundamental element in general management theory would have to be a consensus on the treatment of 'labour'; but on this, there were two distinct poles of thought (Pollard, (1965) 1968, 296-7). Yet, as Pollard himself shows convincingly, there was a great deal of writing, about the 'principles' of their actions in developing their own firms and empires, by several astonishingly 'advanced' industrialists such as Boulton and Watt, Arkwright, Robert Owen, James Nasmyth, and others; writing which, for want of collecting and drawing together at the time, was in fact 'lost' until the middle years of the twentieth century.

What was lacking, perhaps, was the *incentive* to collect and draw together and generalise from this kind of material, in textbooks; the incentive is present when there is a demand for teaching or training, and the demand for that only emerged when the accustomed methods of supplying enough trained recruits, or recruits sufficiently trained (in this instance, succession of sons and nephews, coupled with 'on-the-job' informal apprenticeship) began to fail to supply the changing needs of English industry—towards the end of the nineteenth century.

In the public service of the Prussian king, the demand began to obtain in the middle of the seventeenth century. In the public service of the British Queen, there may be controversy over whether it fully obtains in the third quarter of the twentieth century, so apparently successful was the adjustment made to the whole provision of national higher education in the mid-nineteenth century to meet the then demand for 'trained men', that arose when the grandsons of the eighteenth-century squires were sent out to administer India, and were found wanting.

Bentham's 'Code'

Yet the half-century around 1800 in Britain cannot, after all, be said to be devoid of serious and 'quasi-scientific' writing on administrative science: for it was the heyday of Jeremy Bentham. Bentham's grand ambition, according to Mack, was

> a panoramic art-and-science of morals and legislation analogous less to Newtonian physics than to the art-and-science of medicine in all its branches—anatomy, physiology, pathology, surgery: curative and preventive. He hoped to create a logic of the will, a monumental and fully articulated structure rising from a foundation of fact, individual pleasures and pains, through ever-ascending orders of generality to the crowning abstraction, the normative Greatest Happiness principle. The propositions of this logic were presented in his codes—of procedure and evidence, civil and penal, international and constitutional law. This was a dazzling vision, and he never once lost sight of it (*Mack, 1962, 3*).

His prime interest was reform of the legal system, and he had practised law, whereas he knew politics and administration only at second-hand, through his patron and his brother. But in his last great work, the *Constitutional Code* (a work of enormous imagination, not a codification of English law at all, but an 'ideal' Code for an 'ideal' republic), of the total of 500 closely-printed double-column pages in the 1843 Bowring edition, at least half are unequivocally concerned with 'administration'—the structure and procedures of government departments; and another 150 are about the 'administration of justice' in the same pragmatic structural and procedural sense. The formal arrangement into a 'Code', with some reflection of Parliamentary drafting practice and the fiction of 'enactment', is little more than a vehicle for Bentham's zeal for, first, definition and classification and second, reforming polemic. Most of each page is straight argument and persuasion, with every now and then a long footnote comprising a self-contained essay. The apparatus of the *Code* so restricts the 'readability' of the work, and its usefulness to even the indefatigable reader, as to deny it the character of 'scientific' writing even in the eighteenth-century sense.

Yet a sympathetic editor might certainly draw out of the *Code* a coherent and fully-developed theory of administration as Bentham understood it: its aims, principal and collateral (the latter being 'exclusion of delay, vexation, and expense' (Bentham, 1843, X, 214)); and means (or 'subend'), beginning with a logical distribution of portfolios, as a later age would have said, among Ministries (thirteen of them, for Elections, Legislation, Army, Navy, Preventive Service, Interior Communication, Indigence Relief, Education, Domain, Health, Foreign Relation, Trade, Finance), and an account of the tasks that are common to all Ministers in the several Departments (*executive, directive, inspective*; a group we might call 'staffing'—*locative*, covering recruitment and selection, appointment, posting and promotion, *dislocative*, covering dismissal, transference, and demotion, and *suppletive*, covering the provision of deputies, part of a rather odd scheme of Bentham's for ensuring the collateral aims; a group dealing with the procurement, security and movement of supplies—*procurative, custoditive, applicative, reparative, transformative, and eliminative*; a group concerned with information—*statistic, recordative, publicative,* and *officially-informative*; and finally, reform and efficiency, the *meliorative-suggestive* function). The nomenclature is somewhat barbaric, but this too, like so many other things about Bentham, is deliberate and in pursuance of principle—one that we need not go into (see Mack, 1962, 152ff.). For each of these functions, rules are worked out in great detail: some derived from common sense, as when he recommends names of offices above the door, and the name of each officer on his door or desk; some derived from practices abroad, particularly what he likes to call 'the Anglo-American United States', as in his specification of an Official Calendar containing the names and other details of every civil, military and naval 'officer and agent' as was done in the US in 1817 (Bentham, 1843, X, 236); and others derived from middle-range theorising of his own, as in this passage about the number of persons necessary for the discharge of each of the functions of departments listed, and conversely, the number of functions a single official might be able to discharge:

> Correspondent and opposite to the case of the union of divers persons in one official situation, is that of the union of divers official situations in one person. Cases in which a demand for this union may have place are the following—

CASE I. For the business of several situations, the applicable time of one individual sufficient.

Of causes of demand in this case, examples are—

1 On the part of all—need of the service of one and the *same subordinate* or set of subordinates, at the same time.

2 Saving of the *time* necessary for *conveyance* of appropriate information from one to another, in so far as information, necessary to all, is, in the first instance, received by any number less than all.

3 Saving of *expense*: more particularly expense in remuneration.

CASE II. By reasons of the smallness of the local field of service and the logical field taken together [as we might now say, division by area and division by function respectively] —unfrequency of the individual instances of demand for the exercise of the functions belonging to the several situations. [For example] . . . In the situation of *Local Headman*, number of functions belonging to the Administrational Department, eleven; to the Judicial Department, five; total, sixteen: many of them widely dissimilar.

Thus it is—that, at the top and at the bottom of the official climax [stairway—we should say 'scalar chain' or 'hierarchy'], the greatest scope for the union of functions of different natures has place: at the top, because there the functions are chiefly of the *directive* kind; and to the directive function, exercise may, in minute portions of time, be given to the operations of functionaries in indefinite number: at the bottom, because, for the performance of the functions, though of the executive kind, the demand of performance will generally be so unfrequent (*Bentham, 1843, X, 218*).

'Directive' functions of differing nature can be combined in one person not so much because 'direction' in all fields is of the same kind, but because each exercise of it takes so little time; 'executive' functions of differing nature can be combined in one person only if the demand for each kind is very small.

There is no doubt that this is 'administrative science' as it was understood at the time on the continent; and the *Code* is full of it. Bentham went much further, into what we might call 'administrative technology': in laying out the 'statistic' function of departments, he specified the titles and subjects of all the books that should be kept: Register books, divided into Service books and Loss books; Service books divided again into Outset books (inventories) and Journal books; Outset books divided again into Original and Periodical books; each Original Outset Service book into 'specific' books, in the four categories Personal, Immovable,

Movable, and Money books; and likewise for the periodical Outset books and Loss books; and Journals for the same four categories plus an Occurrence book; and then, each of these 'specific' books into 'sub-specific' books, the Entrance book, the Continuance book, and the Exit book. This programme of books to be prepared covers several pages of the *Code*; and then he specified the kind of entry that should be made in each book, covering several pages more.

A little later, he is to be found advising on methods of store-keeping; how to mark out a storeyard into a grid of equal squares, like a map of Paris he had once seen, so that the reception entry in the Journal book can be annotated with the grid reference indicating where the article is stored, and a drawing of the yard annotated to show that that location is occupied. A few pages on, he gives lists of the causes of deterioration of stocks of various kinds, classifying for several purposes—chemistry was one of his early delights (Bentham, 1843, X, 248). This eclectic mish-mash of polemic, reminiscence, traveller's tales, good armchair theorising, and amateur science is not at all untypical of even 'scientific' writing of the period; but as 'administrative science', the much that was extravagant and even foolish in the *Code* must have made it unusable as a textbook without rewriting; and there was no one to do that. The age, *pace* Taylor, was more taken up with forms of government.

In two respects, however, Bentham is entitled to be placed by a historian squarely in the Cameralistic tradition: for his concern for specialised training and examinations for public officials, and for his espousal of monocratic or single-headed administrative structures as against conciliar or 'Board' direction.

In the *Code*, Bentham proposed that all official situations whatsoever, including those of Minister, should be open only to those who had attended courses of instruction and taken appropriate examinations. Following the American example, every situation would be listed in *The Office Calendar*, and arranged under three heads: situations of *talent*, situations of *simple trust*, and situations of *trust and talent* (Bentham, 1843, X, 272). The first group were those requiring special knowledge and ability, the second those requiring none but *moral* aptitude, and the third, 'talent' positions with responsibilities either for large numbers of subordinates or for high-value equipment. Then followed a table of the departments, with the special talents appropriate to each, expressed as subjects of instruction. For the Army Minister and his subordinates, for example,

Mechanic and Chemical Art and Science, various branches. Mathematics, in so far as subservient thereto. Fortification. Military Tactics. Medical Art and Science, in most of its branches. Judicature, as applied to Army Service.

For the Domain Minister 'according to the nature of the several domains'—

Agriculture, Geology, Mineralogy, and the several branches of Mechanical and Chemical Art and Science subservient thereto.

for the Indigence Relief Minister, 'Political Economy'; and so on (Bentham, 1843, X, 273).

True to principle, Bentham envisaged that instruction would be given by undertakers successful at tender; he set out how the advertisements for instructors should be drafted, how they should be selected, what accommodation, board, clothing and lodging for pupils would be necessary, and how the candidates would be examined—in the greatest detail; some of it Bentham's improvements on the practices at the East India Company, at the Woolwich Academy (the Government military school), at the University of Glasgow, and at 'the Health sub-department at Berlin', each acknowledged in a footnote. He concluded the section with an essay on the benefits of such a system of 'appropriate instruction', which though designed for the instruction of officials, would operate as a system of *national* instruction, 'not to speak of education in other respects'. He warned that every sort of obstacle would be put in its way, but that, once the public examination system was installed, 'the sceptre of arbitrary power' would be swept away by 'the influx of tried minds, whose aptitude has been made manifest to all eyes' (Bentham, 1843, X, 293).

Collegium and 'Einheitssystem'

In an earlier very well-known work, *Panopticon, or the Inspection-House* (1791) containing his complete specification for a new type of building to make supervision of prisoners, paupers, patients and so on economical and efficient, Jeremy Bentham had distinguished between 'contract-management' and 'trust-management'—the latter being equivalent to 'management by one holding an office or duty to do so':

Economy, it has been already shown, should be the ruling object. But in economy, everything depends upon the *hands* and upon the *terms*. In what hands, then? upon what terms? These are the two grand points to be adjusted, and that before anything is said about regulations. Why? Because, as far as economy is concerned, upon these points depends, as we shall see, the demand for regulations. Adopt the contract-plan—regulations in this view are a nuisance: be there ever so few of them, there will be too many. Reject it—be there ever so many of them, they will be too few.

Contract-management, or *trust-management*? If trust-management, management by an *individual* or by a *board*? Under these divisions, every possible distinct species of management may be included. You can have nothing different from them, unless by mixing them. In an economical concern like this, contract-management, say I—Board-management, says the act: which says right? ...

This 'early' Bentham style, while repetitious, is much more readable. The passage also illustrates his method, of 'exhaustive bifurcation':

By whom, then, shall we say, ought a business like this to be carried on?—by one who has an interest in the success of it, or by one who has none?—by one who has a greater interest in it, or by one who has an interest not so great?—by one who takes loss as well as profit, or by one who takes profit without loss?—by one who has no profit but in proportion as he manages well, or by one who, let him manage ever so well or ever so ill, shall have the same emolument secured to him? These seem to be the proper questions for our guides: where shall we find the answers? In the questions themselves, and in the act! (*Bentham, (1791) 1843, IV, 125*).

This has the air of Adam Smith, and Bentham did know *The Wealth of Nations* and its discussion of partnerships, regulated companies, and joint-stock companies (Smith, (1776) 1812, 586ff.).

In the same section of the *Panopticon*, Bentham set out at considerable length his views about individual management versus board management. It is a theme he returns to again and again; in the *Rationale of Evidence* (1806):

A board is thus a rampart of defence, behind which each of its members finds a place of security against all attacks of the nature of those of which responsibility in the burthensome sense is the result ... (*Bentham, (1806a) 1843, VI, 557*);

in the *Reform of Scotch Justice*, perhaps the most celebrated of his aphorisms on the subject:

A board, my Lord, is a *screen*. The lustre of good desert is obscured by it; ill-desert, slinking behind, eludes the eye of censure ... (*Bentham, (1806b) 1843, V, 17*);

again in the *Radical Reform Bill* (1819), memorably:

What is everybody's business is nobody's business; what is everybody's fault is nobody's fault; by each one the fault is shifted off upon the rest ... (*Bentham (1819), 1843, III, 57n.*);

and again and again in the *Constitutional Code*.

Divided responsibility was not the only charge Bentham brought against boards at the head of departments. As one would expect, there was a finely divided catalogue of them: boards were a pretext for multiplication of situations, and hence corruption; they wasted time, they were given to ridiculous compromises, and so on. But he did not condemn boards *as such*: there was a place for them in government, particularly in the constitutive and legislative authorities, and there were also places where they did no harm (Bentham, (1806a) 1843, VI, 558n.).

The relative merits of boards (or councils—German, *Kammer*) and single-headed hierarchies had been a staple topic for discussion in Cameralistics, though I can find no evidence that Bentham had read the Prussian professors—he had little German, and the reference noted to the Berlin sub-department of Health was from a secondary source in English. On the other hand, he was well acquainted with French and with events in France; and on this topic, the most formative influence on European thought in the early nineteenth century was not Prussian administrative science but French administrative reform.

When Napoleon Bonaparte took control in Paris in 1799 and dissolved the Directory, it can be seen as the first expression of a style which he continued in all his reforms, even in the drafting of, for instance, the family law provisions of the great Civil Code, which so influenced Bentham. Napoleon had an extreme dislike for and distrust of 'divided responsibility':

With the hard logic of the military mind Napoleon insisted on the personalisation of authority. ... insisted that even if advice was the function of several, responsibility for every action should be taken by one man who could be clearly distinguished; the emperor for the affairs of state, the ministers for the affairs of their ministries, the prefects for the affairs of the communes (*Chapman, 1959, 27*).

The Napoleonic reforms of national administration are well

known in outline, though there are few detailed studies in English (Chapman says that 'undoubtedly the clearest exposition of the Napoleonic system of government is Alejandro Oliván, *De la Administración publica con relación a España*, first published in 1843' —Chapman, 1959, 29n.). Resembling the administrative system of the Roman empire, but above all of the Roman army, the Napoleonic state had the military features of a clear hierarchy of command and clearly defined allocation of duties and responsibilities, and was characterised by the careful articulation of division of labour at the centre and at the operating bases in the localities through the 'field command post' of a single official in each area—an area chosen on purely 'rational' (i.e., non-traditional) criteria. Hippolyte Taine writing in 1890 about the Napoleonic regime produced the natural metaphor, an architectural one:

It forms one unique, vast, monumental block, in which all branches of the service are lodged under one roof; in addition to the national and general services belonging to the public power, we find here others also, local and special, which do not belong to it, such as worship, education, charity, fine arts, literature, departmental and communal interests, each installed in a distinct compartment. All the compartments are ordered and arranged alike, forming a circle around the magnificent central apartment, with which each is in communication by a bell; as soon as the bell rings and the sound spreads from division to sub-division, the entire service, from the chief clerk down to the lowest employee, is instantly in motion.

Nowhere in Europe are human lives so well regulated, within lines of demarcation so universal, so simple, and so satisfactory to the eye and to logic: the edifice in which Frenchmen are henceforth to move and act is regular from top to bottom, in its entirety as well as in its details, outside as well as inside; its stories, one above the other, are adjusted with exact symmetry ... the structure is classic. For the first time in modern history we see a society due to ratiocination and, at the same time, substantial; the new France, under these two heads, is the masterpiece of the classic spirit (*Taine, 1890; reproduced in Lepawsky, 1949, 161–2*).

The 'national and general services' were grouped under four Ministries, of Finance, Foreign Affairs, War, and Justice. The fifth Ministry, which looked after the 'local and special' services, was that of the Interior. Each Ministry was organised into divisions and sections; and throughout, each official was responsible not only to his superiors but to the *law*, for the correct discharge of his appointed tasks. Napoleon had inherited the *Ecole Polytechnique*, the training school for engineering and other specialists, from which came an élite corps of expert civil servants and army officers; he extended the system, creating the basis of the present higher civil service, the 'Grand Corps', entry to which was based on intellectual merit and conferred high prestige (see Barker, 1944; Finer, 1946; Chapman, 1959; Ridley and Blondel, 1964; Ridley, 1966; Anderson, 1970).

Although the ideas were not novel, the potency of the *fact* of this highly centralised national administration was soon evident throughout Europe. In Prussia, 1806 marked the defeat by Napoleon of Frederick William III, who was obliged to send again for the Minister whose internal reforms he had long opposed, Carl vom Stein (1757–1831). Barker called this period, 1807–10, 'the Prussian revolution'—'a revolution not directed against the administration, but achieved by it' (Barker, 1944, 24). It was not a revolution of the people, as had been the French, and vom Stein's reforms, although Napoleonic in some respects, were anti-monarchical without being populist. Serfdom was abolished, municipal government was instituted partly on the 'self-government' principle so as to re-involve the property-owning classes; the army was reformed as 'the nation in arms' rather than as the instrument of royal will; and the axe was laid at the root of the absolutism, the way the king had kept the reins of state in his own hands by taking advice not from his Ministers, or from the formal Council of State, but from 'private advisers'. Vom Stein reorganised the collegiate General Directory (which had already begun to differentiate into departments) into five distinct Ministries, each headed by a specific Minister, and subdivided into sections each with a personally responsible head. These five Ministers formed the *Staatsministerium* or Government, from which the king was then obliged to 'seek advice'.

The single-head system was in Prussia, not surprisingly, known as *Einheitssystem*; the allocation of precisely defined duties to departments and sections was known as *Burosystem*. The major administrative change in Prussia during those years could therefore be characterised as a shift from *collegium* to *Einheitssystem*, from *Kammer* to *Buro*. The debate between the two systems had begun long before Cameralism; and Bentham's strictures on the collective head had been anticipated in English writing, not only by Bacon (*Essays*, No. 25) in the seventeenth century, and his imitators, but by Hamilton in America a few years before Bentham wrote (Hamilton, *Federalist* No. 70, March 18, 1788). The discussion can be found in practically all the language of Europe, and recurs throughout the nineteenth century in English official papers (see Schaffer, 1957; Willson, 1955; Parris, 1969); it is found in reference to the Scottish Departments in the Report of the MacDonnell Commission in 1914 (Cd. 7338, 77–9; Hanham, 1969, 354), in the report of the Haldane Committee on the Machinery of Government in 1918 (Cd. 9230), in the evidence by the professional civil servants to the Tomlin Commission (Cmd. 4149, 1932, para. 122; Bourn, 1968, 453); and, in somewhat altered guise, in the Report of the Maud Committee on Management in Local Government (1967)—as we may see later. It seems never to lose its relevance, or its interest; and the arguments change very little.

Centralisation and 'bureaucracy'

Burosystem must be distinguished from 'bureaucracy'. That term had been coined in the early eighteenth century by the French physiocrat, de Gournay (Albrow, 1970, 16), to signify what was certainly not a new idea then, a form of government which was neither monarchy, aristocracy, nor democracy, but 'bureau'-cracy—desk-government, rule by officials, the self-interested tyranny of jacks-in-office. From this point of view, therefore, Prussia had had 'bureaucracy' for long enough, since the Great Elector had begun his replacement of the barons by his own functionaries; nor did the 'Prussian revolution' alter things, in the view of vom Stein himself. He wrote in 1821, in retirement, a bitter critique of Prussian officialdom—but of their lack of spirit, of civic involvement, rather than of (in French style) their petty tyranny:

> We are governed by salaried, book-learned, disinterested, propertyless bureau people . . . These four points sum up the spirit of our own and similar lifeless governmental machines. Salaried, so they strive to maintain and increase the number of the salaried; book-learned, living in the printed, not the real world; without cause to support, for they belong to no class of citizens that constitute the State, they are a class in their own right—the clerical caste; without property, so they are unaffected by its fluctuations. Come rain or sunshine, let taxes rise or fall, let ancient rights be destroyed or preserved, it makes no difference to them. They draw their salaries from the Treasury and write, write, write, in silence, in their offices behind closed doors, unknown, unnoticed, unpraised; and bring up their children to be just as useful writing machines. There is the ruin of

our dear Fatherland . . . *(see Albrow, 1970, 19; and Finer, 1946,
II, 1211. Version here is amalgam of both translations)*.

It was Honoré Balzac, in his novel *Les Employés* (1836) who
summed up the French criticism of 'bureaucracy'—its penchant for
minute regulation, fussiness, and delay. Albrow dates the reception
of the term into English at around 1830; some of the early accounts
were 'perfunctory', but not all: some were extremely sophisticated—

> Many of them anticipated points upon which whole theories
> have been centred. An essay of 1836 on the French educational
> system observed that, for any defect in bureaucratic machinery,
> the remedy always took the form of further machinery. In 1842
> J. S. Blackie, a commentator on the German scene, considered
> that the way in which the Prussian bureaucracy monopolised
> the intelligence of the nation was detrimental to energy and
> enterprise outside it, and resulted in submissiveness and ser-
> vility *(Albrow, 1970, 21)*.

This last point was taken up by Mill in both the *Principles of
Political Economy* (1848) and *On Liberty* (1859), and by Toulmin
Smith and others; it had an oddly potent influence on English
thought.

Discussions of the relative merits of individual and collegiate
heads of departments, and of the effects of a system of government
upon the personalities of officials or the character of the nation,
can of course be distinguished analytically from discussions of the
relative merits of centralised government and decentralised government, rule from one seat and rule from ten thousand seats. But
by the time information about French, Prussian, and Russian systems had filtered across the Channel, and been absorbed by the
reading public so that, for instance, Mill and Bagehot could assume
familiarity with them, the term 'bureaucracy' had come to stand,
not for a malfunctioning of their ancient forms of government that
continental critics could see for themselves, but for the root of these
forms as the English saw it—the existence of paid, permanent,
centrally-appointed officials in the localities, instead of 'local self-
government'. But 'local self-government' for the English did not
mean what it meant for vom Stein or Rudolf Gneist: it meant the
system of popularly elected local councils which had replaced the
'old corporators' of municipal government after 1835.

The most articulate extremists on each each side of the native
English debate on centralisation and decentralisation were Edwin
Chadwick and Toulmin Smith, the one a fiercely independent-

minded civil servant, campaigner for poor law reform and public
health, the other a radical lawyer and antiquarian, who conducted
a pamphlet debate covering the middle years of the century; which,
in the opinion of Redlich (or more probably Hirst), although it
'never played any great part in English politics', neither Tories, nor
Whigs, nor Radicals being

> willing to be identified with the extreme views of either
> doctrinaire—of Chadwick, to whom a Central Board was
> everything, or of Toulmin Smith, who could see no good thing
> outside a common law vestry... is interesting because it is the
> only important *theoretical* dispute upon the subject of internal
> administration which has taken place since the era of reform
> (*Redlich and Hirst, 1903, II, 413*).

Let me quote a few sentences only, from each side; first, from
Toulmin Smith's *Local Self-government and Centralisation* (1851):

> There are two elements to which every form of Government
> may be reduced. These are, LOCAL SELF-GOVERNMENT
> on the one hand, and CENTRALIZATION on the other.
> According as the former or the latter of these exists more or
> less predominant, will the state of any nation be the more or
> less free, happy, progessive, truly prosperous and safe...
> LOCAL SELF-GOVERNMENT is that system of Govern-
> ment under which the greatest number of minds, knowing the
> most, and having the fullest opportunities of knowing it, about
> the special matter in hand, and having the greatest interest in
> its well-working, have the management of it, or control over it.
> CENTRALIZATION is that system of Government under
> which the smallest number of minds, and those knowing the
> least, and having the fewest opportunities of knowing it, about
> the special matter in hand, and having the smallest interest
> in the wellworking, have the management of it, or control
> over it.... The wholesome adjustment of practical arrange-
> ments suited to the exigencies of the times, and the satisfactory
> management of administrative functions, must depend upon the
> vital activity of Institutions which give every freeman the full
> opportunity of discussing, and hearing discussed, all the ques-
> tions which, directly or indirectly, concern him.... Men cannot
> discuss without having first paid some attention to the subject
> matter of discussion. As long as everything is done *for* them
> they have no occasion to think at all, and will soon become
> incapable of thinking. But the moment they are thrown on
> their own resources... they wake from their torpor, put forth
> their energies, and rouse their faculties...
>   The fundamental idea of Centralization is, *distrust*... Cen-
> tralization is only Communism in another form. Its object is, to

take away the free action of every man over his own property;
to stay the free use, by every man, of his own resources, his own
ingenuity, and his own free action and enterprise. . . . Servility,
sycophancy, selfiishness, and apathy, are the moral qualities
which it is the necessary effect of Centralization to engender . . .
(*Toulmin Smith, 1851; Hanham, 1969, 377–8*).

Chadwick was never inhibited by his position as a civil servant
from holding and publicly stating his views on any subject; according to Finer, he was 'headstrong, importunate, and impatient of
delay and opposition' (Finer, 1952, 2); and he was at the centre
of 'anti-centralization' storms for much of his career. He summarised his views on 'local self-government' in 1885, thus:

> The term, 'local self-government', signifying as it does the
> direct individual knowledge of the local affairs of the local unit
> of administration and the participation of the ratepayer in the
> expenditure of his own money, is in the majority of cases a mis-
> chievous fallacy . . . what means are there of his knowing any-
> thing about them—although they really affect the purity of his
> water supplies, and his health and life, and his relief from the
> excessive burden of the sickness and other rates? If he could
> be made aware of them, by reading reports . . . what are his
> prospects of bringing that knowledge of his own affairs—with
> which the political theory of self-government credits him—by
> the application of his twenty-thousandth share of the adminis-
> tration as a voter?
> Besides science, chiefly sanitary science, to be applied, there is
> administrative science to be acquired. Besides the demand for
> such sciences, to effect large economies in local administration,
> there is required, moreover, business or administrative science
> to insure their application . . .
> . . . it must be for you, the advocate of decentralisation and
> disunity, to say whether you prefer disease and premature
> mortality and waste with what is called local self-government,
> to health and strength, and economy with centralisation . . .
> In regard to the effect of superior legislation produced by the
> attainment of unity, by doing everywhere the same thing in the
> same way, as closely as may be, choosing the best, I would point
> to . . . the Code Napoleon. (*Chadwick, 1885; Hanham, 1969,
> 383–4*).

'Self-government'—of either kind—had political attractions for
central Government in a Parliamentary democracy, however; showing sound grasp of political reality as well as administrative science,
Sir Charles Wood wrote in 1850:

> There is nothing in the world which I think is so much to be
> deprecated in this country as discouraging country gentlemen

in the performance of those duties which they now execute throughout the country ... This tendency is most dangerous. We have hitherto been for the most part locally governed ... In old times if twenty overseers starved twenty paupers, they were corrected or punished: but nothing was shaken of the administration of the country. It was quite right to mend this. But how much unpopularity attached to Melbourne's government on account of the new Poor Law administration? ... We should [provide] as few fields for attacking the government of the country as we can help. Heaven knows there are plenty, and the universal disposition now, is to hold them responsible for matters hitherto beyond their province altogether. This is ... the black cloud on the horizon, that we are gradually approaching the state of Continental countries; where the government is responsible for everything, for whatever goes wrong the government is blamed. ...

If country gentlemen are not to have some power and responsibility, they will not act ... A far better race of justices now do the work, but they are actuated by a desire to do the duty of the business of the counties, and have naturally the pleasure and enjoyment of the exercise of power, but if you supersede them in this you will leave them no motive for mere routine, and you will have then to administer the counties by *prefets* and *sous-prefets* and the bureaucratic [machinery] which prevails abroad (*PRO 30/22/8. Wood to Russell, December 31, 1850; Parris, 1969, 208*).

John Stuart Mill, in *Representative Government* (1861), paid much attention to what we might now call the effects of structure upon administrative behaviour. There is a passage which succinctly sums up many of his findings—some of them echoes of Bentham, some of them pregnant with future development:

... in regard to the constitution of the executive departments of administration. Their machinery is good, when the proper tests are prescribed for the qualifications of officers, the proper rules for their promotion; when the business is conveniently distributed among those who are to transact it, a convenient and methodical order established for its transaction, a correct and intelligible record of it after being transacted; when each individual knows for what he is responsible, and is known to others as responsible for it; when the best-contrived checks are provided against negligence, favouritism, or jobbery, in any of the acts of the department. ... The ideally perfect constitution of a public office is that in which the interest of the functionary is entirely coincident with his duty (*Mill, (1861) 1910, 194*).

As to what distribution of business may be convenient:

It may be sufficient to say that the classification of functionaries should correspond to that of subjects, and that there
should not be several departments independent of one another
to superintend different parts of the same natural whole; as
in our own miltary administration down to a recent period,
and in a less degree even at present (*Mill*, (*1861*) *1919*, *331*).

Mill was as much against 'boards' in executive positions as was
Bentham:

> As a general rule, every executive function, whether superior
> or subordinate, should be the appointed duty of some given
> individual. It should be apparent to all the world who did
> everything, and through whose default anything was left un-
> done (*Mill*, (*1861*) *1910*, *372*).

His writing on 'bureaucracy' was both perceptive and influential,
for he espoused 'local self-government' without going all the way
with Toulmin Smith; 'parliamentary' democracy rather than any
of its more extreme forms; and the institutional control of a
skilled, paid, permanent civil service rather than its condemnation.
He was satisfied that the Russian and Austrian Governments, 'and
even the French Government in its normal condition', although
technically monarchies, were oligarchies of permanent officials:

> The work of government has been in the hands of governors
> by profession; which is the essence and meaning of bureau-
> cracy (*1910*, *245*).

And, although a bureaucratic government has some important
advantages—

> It accumulates experience, acquires well-tried and well-con-
> sidered traditional maxims, and makes provision for appro-
> priate practical knowledge in those who have the actual conduct
> of affairs (*1910*, *246*)

it has fatal flaws also:

> The disease which afflicts bureaucratic governments, and which
> they usually die of, is routine. They perish by the immutability
> of their maxims; and still more, by the universal law that
> whatever becomes a routine loses its vital principle... (*1910*,
> *246*).

The conclusion is:

> Government by trained officials cannot do, for a country, the
> things which can be done by a free government; but it might be
> supposed capable of doing some things which free government,

of itself, cannot do. We find, however, that an outside element of freedom is necessary to enable it to do effectively or permanently even its own business. And so, also, freedom cannot produce its best effects, and often breaks down altogether, unless means can be found of combining it with trained and skilled administration. There could not be a moment's hesitation between representative government, among a people in any degree ripe for it, and the most perfect imaginable bureaucracy. But it is, at the same time, one of the most important ends of political institutions, to attain as many of the qualities of the one as are consistent with the other... (*Mill*, (*1861*) *1910, 247*).

For this we need to recognise the separation between the work of government, the doing, and that of 'selecting, watching, and, when needful, controlling the governors'. But 'the democracy' will have to recognise that 'the work which requires skill should be done by those who possess it'. In other words, although we do not want 'bureaucracy', we must recognise that we cannot do without trained, permanent, salaried, non-political, 'professional' civil servants.

Bagehot's doctrine

Walter Bagehot's *The English Constitution* (1867) can be read, as Crossman points out in his Introduction to a new edition, as a commentary on, and in some respects a reply to, this book of Mill's. Both Mill and Bagehot compared the British system not only with the continental one, but also with the United States, where it was known that officials were elected, or else went out of office with a change of party in government:

The scale of the financial operations of the Federal Government is now so increased that most likely in that department, at least, there must in future remain a permanent element of great efficiency; a revenue of £90,000,000 sterling cannot be collected and expended with a trifling and changing staff. But until now the Americans have tried to get on not only with changing heads to a bureaucracy, as the English, but without any stable bureaucracy at all. They have facilities for trying it which no one else has. All Americans can administer, and the number of them really fit to be in succession lawyers, financiers, or military managers is wonderful (*Bagehot*, (*1867*) *1964, 193*).

Bureaucracy, it was generally conceded, was at least 'efficient'. But Bagehot demurred:

> Just now, the triumph of the Prussians—the bureaucratic people, as is believed, *par excellence*—has excited a kind of admiration for bureaucracy, which a few years since we should have thought impossible (*1964, 194*).

But intelligent and liberal Prussians saw well its faults: an 'obstinate and bigoted official sets at defiance the liberal initiations of the Government', and guilty officials 'as in France, in all conflicts with simple citizens' are 'like men armed *cap-à-pie* fighting with defenceless' (1964, 195); and the faults that produced such behaviour were inherent:

> It is an inevitable defect, that bureaucrats will care more for routine than for results ... to think the routine of business not a means, but an end—to imagine the elaborate machinery of which they form a part, and from which they derive their dignity, to be a grand and achieved result, not a working and changeable instrument (*1964, 195*).

It was the system Frederick the Great had established—'a good system for his wants and his times'—which in a different age and in a new competition, had brought his country to ruin—a 'dead and formal' system, to be contrasted with the living French post-Revolutionary system.

> Not only does a bureaucracy thus tend to under-government, in point of quality; it tends to over-government in point of quantity. The trained official hates the rude, untrained public. He thinks that they are stupid, ignorant, reckless—that they cannot tell their own interest—that they should have the leave of the office before they do anything ... A bureaucracy is sure to think that its duty is to augment official power, official business, or official members, rather than to leave free the energies of mankind; it overdoes the quantity of government, as well as impairs its quality (*Bagehot, (1867) 1964, 197*).

The cure was the importation of one of the 'most sure principles' of the 'art of business':

> The truth is that a skilled bureaucracy—a bureacracy trained from early life to its special avocation—is, though it boasts of an appearance of science, quite inconsistent with the true principles of the art of business ... One of the most sure principles is, that success depends on a mixture of special and non-special minds ... The success of the great joint-stock banks of London—the most remarkable achievement of recent business—has been an example of the use of this mixture.

These banks are managed by a board of persons mostly *not* trained to the business, supplemented by, and annexed to, a body of specially trained officers, who have been bred to banking all their lives. . . . it is found that the board of directors has greater and more flexible knowledge—more insight into the wants of a commercial community—knows when to lend and when not to lend, better than the old bankers, who had never looked at life, except out of the bank windows. Just so the most successful railways in Europe have been conducted—not by engineers or traffic managers—but by capitalists; by men of a certain business culture, if no other. These capitalists . . . manage far better than any of the different sorts of special men under them. They combine these different specialities— make it clear where the realm of one ends and that of the other begins, and add to it a wide knowledge of large affairs, which no special man can have, and which is only gained by diversified action. But this utility of leading minds used to generalise, and acting upon various materials, is entirely depen- dent upon their position. They must be at the top. A merchant's clerk would be a child at a bank counter; but the merchant himself could, very likely, give good, clear, and useful advice in a bank court. The merchant's clerk would be equally at sea in a railway office, but the merchant himself could give good advice, very likely, at a board of directors. The summits (if I may so say) of the various kinds of business are, like the tops of mountains, much more alike than the parts below—the bare principles are much the same; it is only the rich variegated details of the lower strata that so contrast with one another. But it needs travelling to know that the summits *are* the same. Those who live on one mountain believe that *their* mountain is wholly unlike all others (*Bagehot, (1867) 1964, 198*).

This is very close to the expression of a theory that there are common elements in the direction of enterprises of all kinds, a theory that goes back to Socrates' dialogue with Nicomachides in the fifth century B.C. (Xenophon, *Memorabilia* and *Oeconomicus*; George, 1968, 15); and which, as we have already seen, had a flowering in the British civil service in the decades after 1920—at least, as it might apply between branches of the service: the Admini- strative Class was certainly not of the mind that imported business- men could do their job, or they theirs, as a consequence of merely having been 'at the top' elsewhere. It is, in fact, necessary to note that Bagehot wrote the above in a chapter entitled 'On Changes of Ministry'; that he was referring to Ministers when speaking of 'non- special minds', and that for him the permanent civil servants would count as 'special men'.

If such English writing as this, from Bentham to Bagehot, on the structure of the administrative sector of government, on individual management and board management, on centralisation and decentralisation, and on the character and control of bureaucratic behaviour, does not qualify as 'administrative science' as it was known on the Continent, it must be because it was not done by university professors in the academic style with classrooms in mind, but by philosophers writing for a more general public, dealing with these themes more or less *obiter*, and by pamphleteers. That no professor thought to bring this material together into an administrative science textbook, as several did for constitutional law and political science, may be (as I suggested in respect of management science for industry) a function of the demand for the creation of the 'subject' in colleges, which was certainly low throughout the nineteenth century in England, and depressed further by the dominating opinions of Macaulay, Jowett, and the other great names of higher education, as to the proper training for 'intellectual' work in government.

CHAPTER FIVE

The Study of Bureaucracy

On the Continent, meanwhile, the demand for 'administrative science' that had formerly existed was beginning to decline. Both in France and in Prussia, the absolutist state had given way to something more 'democratic', one in which the rights of citizens against the State were beginning to be formally recognised and protected by special systems of law. The rapid development of administrative law gave a different emphasis to the training of officials, and the cameralistic tradition in Prussia was almost entirely eclipsed— 'dissolved into other sciences', as the greatest name in nineteenth-century German administrative studies, Lorenz von Stein, lamented (Molitor, 1959, 27)—the other sciences being, as well as politics and law, the new science of sociology.

Von Stein, Le Play, and Saint-Simon

Von Stein (1815–90—no connection with the Freiherr, Carl vom Stein) was a professor of Government at Vienna who combined socialist ideas derived from Saint-Simon with Hegelian views on the nature of the state and the citizen. His early work was a history of the class struggle in France; but after arriving in Vienna he devoted himself to the systematic study of public administration and finance in France, England, and Germany. His major work, *Die Verwaltungslehre* ('The Study of Administration') appeared in three volumes between 1865 and 1868 (Roth, 1968, 257). He was perhaps rather the last great name in the earlier tradition of German administrative science, than a precursor of the modern; but Molitor suggested that his influence is still felt in German academic circles, where a 'return to Stein' has been the keynote of certain attempted reforms in administrative science during the last ten years (*Molitor, 1959, 30*)

—possibly the expression of a wish to reverse the emphasis on administrative law. Stein's principal themes were those we have already noted, the contrast between the centralising systems and 'self-government' (Gneist acknowledged his debt—Redlich, 1903, II, 393n.), and the development of 'bureaucracy'. On this, any discussion must now begin from Albrow's excellent essay (1970). The old debate about *collegium* and *Einheitssystem* took a new twist, as criticism of bureaucracy as 'rule by officials' increased: the new post-1806 system was widely seen as giving more power to a single official, compared with the *collegium*; hence *burosystem* was quickly identified with '*bureakratie*':

> In every branch of administration bureaux or offices have multiplied, and have been accorded so great a power over citizens that in many countries a veritable bureaucracy, rule by offices, has developed. This bureaucracy becomes increasingly dangerous as the previous custom of conducting business through *collegia* falls into disuse (*Brockhaus Encyclopaedia, 1819 (5th edn), II, 158; Albrow, 1970, 28*).

Historically, in Prussia, the civil service of the Hohenzollerns had followed the military organisation of the Prussian army: Görres developed the idea in *Europe and the Revolution* (1821), showing how bureaucracy was based on the same principles of discipline, promotion, group honour and centralisation, and that it had succeeded in extending its own internal principles of subordination to the citizens, who then only counted as numbers (Albrow, 1970, 20). Karl Heinzen, a socialist critic of the régime, assumed a definition of 'bureaucracy' as

> an administrative structure where a single official controls the administration, as opposed to the collegial structure where several officials work under a head, but with definite rights to participate in administration on a collective basis (*Heinzen, 1854, 12; Albrow, 1970, 28*)

but then linked this technical meaning with all the connotations of arrogance and usurpation of power. In the first academic analysis of the use of the term, in 1846, von Mohl, professor of political science in Heidelberg, distinguished between 'burosystem' and the pejorative senses of 'bureaucracy', which were different according to the interest of the complainer: distilling what was common to all such complaints appeared to leave the idea of a false conception of the tasks of the state, implemented by a numerous body of professional officials (*Von Mohl*, (*1846*) *1862, 108; Albrow, 1970, 29*).

But von Mohl's catalogue of bureaucratic abuses, familiar enough to us—excessive form-filling, arrogance, delay, and so on—was of popular appeal, and since these abuses were liable to appear under any system of administration, led to the use of the term 'bureaucracy' for describing any organisation of officials, a usage it has had in some quarters ever since.

In opposing local variety in the provision of governmental services, Chadwick, we saw, spoke of 'unity' instead of centralisation. 'Unity of the state' was for Germans a real problem, and the root of their own centralisation. In a book called *Die Verfassung Englands* (1862) ('The English Constitution'), Eduard Fischel argued that centralisation, the securing of a sufficient degree of uniformity, was not incompatible with 'self-government' on the English pattern—the English gentry were not lawless, on the contrary they were law-abiding, in spite of the lack of authoritarianism and of strict official subordination. The real incompatibility was between *bureaucracy* and 'self-government' as methods (Albrow, 1970, 24). Fischel's book was translated and published in English in 1867.

Le Play (1864) also sharply distinguished 'bureaucracy' from centralisation. To the French, 'bureaucracy' had in particular meant a kind of official behaviour, which was not so much an abuse as an inevitable concomitant of 'the system'; Le Play gave this approach a definite statement. To him 'bureaucracy' was noticeably a phenomenon of the middle ranks of functionaries—who owed their position entirely to their knowledge of the rules; who were intent, therefore, upon creating more complication rather than less, and suppressing initiative towards change. (The structural explanation of behaviour in organisations was the theme of another major French contribution to the study of *La Phénomène Bureaucratique*, nearly one hundred years later—by Crozier).

In the nomenclature of academic departmentalism of the middle twentieth century, Le Play would be thought of as a 'sociologist', in a line of succession that begins with Saint-Simon (1760–1825), passes through Comte (1798–1857) and Spencer (1820–1903) and continues into the twentieth century with Durkheim (1858–1917) and Max Weber (1864–1920), to mention only the most illustrious of those usually considered primarily as sociologists. These men had the whole of human social behaviour as their field, and there can be no attempt here to give any account of their work. But it is a plausible judgement that would see the administrative science tradition on the Continent overwhelmed by the development of administrative law in the nineteenth-century explosion of government, until the contribution of the sociologists to what would now be called 'theory of organisations' had been assimilated into the *new* tradition of administrative science, social and behavioural—a consummation that did not come about until the fifth decade of the twentieth century, and whose effects are still working out.

Saint-Simon is in the succession because of his espousal of the possibility of a positive 'science of society' (his phrase), and because Auguste Comte was undoubtedly a disciple for a time (Gray, (1946) 1947, 138). In his *Worker's Political Catechism* (1820) he initiated the idea developed more familiarly by Engels: as the laws governing human social relations become known, so society will pass from a *régime gouvernementale* to a *régime administratif*. In Comte, one can find the first modern statement of a synthetic system of thought embracing all positive science, as well as a clear understanding of the hypothetical method and appreciation of what were later called 'structural-functional analysis' and 'general systems theory' (Fletcher, 1971, I, 174, 185).

Spencer, Schmoller, and Weber

Herbert Spencer's work is parallel to Comte's in many respects, but adds to the understanding of human social structures a detailed analysis of 'organisation', by which in biological metaphor he means the differentiation of parts and their consequent specialisation:

> As its parts assume different functions they become dependent on one another, so that injury to one hurts others; until, in highly-evolved societies, general perturbation is caused by derangement of any portion. This contrast between undeveloped and developed societies arises from the fact that with increasing specialisation of functions comes increasing inability in each part to perform the functions of other parts (*Spencer, 1876, I, 582*).

'Complication of structure accompanies increase of mass', Spencer said; and conversely, there will not be growth unless there is 'changeableness of structure' (Spencer, (1882) 1883, 261). But 'any arrangement stands in the way of rearrangement':

> The stones composing a house cannot be otherwise used until the house has been pulled down. If the stones are united by mortar, there must be extra trouble in destroying their present combination before they can be recombined. And if the mortar has had centuries in which to consolidate, the breaking up of the masses formed is a matter of such difficulty, that building with new materials becomes more economical than rebuilding with the old ...
> ... And this, which is conspicuously true of an individual organism, is true, if less conspicuously, of a social organism. Though a society, formed of discrete units, and not having had its type fixed by inheritance from countless like societies, is much more plastic, yet the same principle holds. As fast as its parts are differentiated—as fast as there arise classes, bodies of functionaries, established administrations, these, becoming coherent within themselves and with one another, struggle against such forces as tend to modify them. The conservatism of every long-settled institution daily exemplifies this truth ... the dominant aim of each is to maintain itself ... the result being that when the function is needless, or even detrimental, the structure still keeps itself intact as long as it can (*Spencer, 1883, 253–255*).
> Nor is this all. Controlling and administrative instrumentalities antagonize growth by absorbing the materials for growth ... Where the abstraction of private means for public purposes is excessive, the impoverishment leads to decrease of population (*Spencer, 1883, 262*).

It was on grounds like these that Spencer, in many pamphlets, articles, and books, opposed the extension of State activity in England, and the centralisation which he saw going with it. But his main interest for the present purpose is his anticipation of so many later contributions to administrative theory; in theory of organisation, with his enunciation of the relationship between size and complexity, growth and adaptation; in the comparative method—

> Though it has become a commonplace that the institutions under which one race prospers will not answer for another, the recognition of this truth is by no means adequate (*Spencer, 1883, 232*).

No, indeed. In understanding 'authority':

> Implying, as this [that the uncivilised do not know naturally how to combine their several actions] does, that co-operation

can at first be effective only where there is obedience to peremptory command, it follows that there must be not only an emotional nature which produces subordination, but also an intellectual nature which produces faith in a commander. That credulity which leads to awe of the capable man as a possessor of supernatural power, and which afterwards, causing dread of his ghost, prompts fulfilment of his remembered injunctions ... is a credulity which cannot be dispensed with during the early stages of integration (*Spencer, 1883, 271–2*)

and in the highly developed sociology of 'Political Forms and Forces', where by the use of his comparative method he suggests that political discussion takes place among three parts, or classes, in any society: the chief or leader, his immediate circle of advisers or elders, and the main body of participant followers; the remainder of the society making a 'passive class excluded from their deliberations—a class at first composed of the women and afterwards containing also the slaves or other dependants' (Spencer, 1883, 311– 317). A modern sociologist, of course, might find fault with much of both Spencer's methods and his conclusions (though he is stoutly defended against some of the attacks that have been made on him by a recent historian of sociological thought—see Fletcher, 1971, I, 250ff.). The purpose here is to illustrate the basis of Spencer's considerable influence on European thought.

This model of the three political classes in any society had a particular influence. Relations between the three political classes will vary, said Spencer, with circumstances—war, for instance; and

... a despotism, an oligarchy, or a democracy, is a type of government in which one of the original components has greatly developed at the expense of the other two (*Spencer, 1883, 317*).

The analysis of political forms is intended to apply to all kinds of society—nations, joint-stock companies, public meetings even (chairman, platform, audience); and

Where the members of the mass beside being much interested in the transactions, are so placed that they can easily cooperate, they hold in check the select few and their head; but where wide distribution, as of railway share-holders, hinders joint action, the select few become, in large measure, an oligarchy, and out of the oligarchy there not infrequently grows an autocrat: the constitution becomes a despotism tempered by revolution (*Spencer, 1883, 328*).

Gustav Schmoller, in a history of the Prussian administrative system written in 1894, developed Spencer's model of the association as comprising always a leader, his staff, and the mass followers, and was himself (as Albrow shows, 1970, 53) an obvious influence on the German sociologist with whom 'bureaucracy' scholarship started afresh, as it were (the earlier writing being eclipsed by the power of his synthesis): Max Weber. That Spencer helped also to form, whether directly or indirectly, the contributions of Robert Michels and Gaeto Mosca to bureaucracy theory can hardly be doubted, though we cannot trace this here (but see Albrow, 1970).

Weber himself can be seen as in the cameralistic tradition: he was concerned with the distinction between the single-headed and the collegial structures, for instance, and kept clear the distinction between a kind of structure (*Burokratie* in *his* terminology) and the problem of rule by officials (*Beamtenherrschaft*) (Albrow, 1970, 47). But more fundamentally, he was a sociologist, concerned with the principles of a social science: his ideas about administration are more fully developed than were those of Comte or Spencer, but they are set in a similar framework of universal concepts. I shall draw heavily upon Albrow in the following summary account (see also Henderson and Parsons, 1947, 329–41; Gerth and Mills, (1946) 1961, 196–244; Bendix, 1960; Diamant, 1962; etc.).

Weber's basic concept of 'the organization' (*Verband*) built on Spencer, Mosca, and Michels; the term could cover the State, a political party, a church, an industrial firm, and any other such purposive association; and its defining characteristics were the presence of a leader or leadership group determining the direction of activity, and an administrative staff (*Verwaltungsstab*) maintaining the structure in being, both itself governed by the 'administrative order' or ground-rules of the organisation (*Verwaltungsordnung*), and ensuring that this was complied with by the remainder of the members of the organisation. Thus an organisation *by definition* consisted for Weber of a leader, an administrative staff, and the mass of the membership.

The most important of these ground-rules were those which distributed authority—a concept to be distinguished from the mere *power* to enforce one's will, because authority was derived from the belief of the subordinate in the *legitimacy* of the commands of the superior. Weber identified three bases of such a belief: first, the sacral nature of the superior person, 'charismatic' authority; second, the inheritance of 'traditional authority'; third, that commands were derived from duties within a code of rules embracing both the superior and the subordinate, as well as the superior's superior and the subordinate's subordinate—'legal authority'. This is the type of authority found in a modern organisation.

The Weberian term 'bureaucracy' refers to the administrative staff of an organisation: it cannot refer to elected officials, only to appointed persons; and although Weber occasionally used 'bureaucracy' to refer to bodies of appointed administrative officials who were in effect slaves (in the Roman Empire, ancient Egypt, and so on), modern bureaucratic officials are necessarily salaried, not fee-paid or honorific. Thus we move to Weber's 'ideal-type' of a *rational* legal-authority organisational structure, one which would exemplify all the features, in their optimum degree, of an administrative order calculated to fulfil best the functions of such a structure in an organisation.

Within the meaning of 'legal authority' (resting on five assumptions—that the organisation exists in a law-abiding environment, that the laws are general in application, that the superior obeys an impersonal law as does the subordinate, that only as member of the organisation is the law binding on an individual, that obedience is to the law and not to the person of the superior), a rational administrative structure would be *routinised* (tasks organised in an on-going pattern), *specialised* (tasks distributed in functionally distinct sectors, each sector given the requisite authority), *hierarchical* (arranged in ranks or levels of authority, with the rights of one rank over or against another specified), *expert* (every person trained in the necessary skills or knowledge to enable obedience to technical or legal rules), *corporate* (the resources of the organisation kept distinct from those of members as individuals), *inappropriable* (the office holder cannot appropriate his office), and *documented* (all transactions by written record). However, a structure could be found exhibiting these qualities which was nevertheless not bureaucratic— it might be collegial, or honorific. But the bureaucratic organisation will always be technically superior; its administrative staff will have these characteristics (Albrow's version):

1 Staff members are personally free, observing only the impersonal duties of their offices.
2 There is a clear hierarchy of offices.
3 The functions of the offices are clearly specified.
4 Officials are appointed on the basis of a contract.
5 They are selected on the basis of a professional qualification, ideally substantiated by a diploma gained through examination.
6 They have a money salary, and usually pension rights. The salary is graded according to position in the hierarchy. The

official can always leave the post, and under certain circumstances it may also be terminated.

7 The official's post is his sole or major occupation.

8 There is a career structure, and promotion is possible either by seniority or merit, and according to the judgement of superiors.

9 The official may appropriate neither the post nor the resources which go with it.

10 He is subject to a unified control and a disciplinary system (*Albrow, 1970, 44–5*).

The works from which these and other such accounts of the Weberian ideal type are drawn were published in the years between 1911 and 1920 (in German: they were not generally available in English until the 1940s); and although the elements can very often be traced to earlier writing, the addition of the concept of the *rationality* of such a structure set thought in a new direction altogether:

> The decisive reason for the advance of bureaucratic organization has always been its purely technical superiority over any other form of organization. The fully-developed bureaucratic mechanism compares with other organizations exactly as does the machine with the non-mechanical modes of production.
>
> Precision, speed, unambiguity, knowledge of the files, continuity, discretion, unity, strict subordination, reduction of friction and of material and personal costs—these are raised to the optimum point in the strictly bureaucratic organization, and especially in its monocratic form. As compared with all collegiate, honorific, and avocational forms of administration, trained bureaucracy is superior on all these points. And as far as complicated tasks are concerned, paid bureaucratic work is not only more precise but, in the last analysis, it is often cheaper than even formally-unremunerated honorific service (*Weber, in Gerth and Mills, (1946) 1961, 214*).

Whether to expound, apply and extend, or criticise and rebut the ideas of Weber, students of administration have since the reception of these ideas based themselves at least to some degree on the understandings they inspired.

But between the flowering of this style of German thought on administrative science, in Michels and Weber in the first two decades of the twentieth century, and the reception of their ideas into English (delayed until the fourth, fifth and even sixth decades) there had come two developments: one, the burst of native English empirical research associated with the 'sociographers' Geddes, Booth, and Rowntree, and with the early Fabians, of which the most notable contributions from the present point of view are the massive histories by Sidney and Beatrice Webb of local government between 1689 and 1834 (*The Parish and the County* (1906); *The Manor and the Borough* (1908); *Statutory Authorities for Special Purposes* (1920); and on Highways, Prisons, Liquor Licensing, and the Poor Law (Webb, 1948, 152). And the second development in these decades: the rise of the American science of administration, which in turn had considerable influence in the Europe of the 1920s and 1930s.

CHAPTER SIX

The American
Science of Administration

In America, a Professor of Political Science had written in 1887 a paper of which he did not himself think a great deal, but which authorities agree marked a new beginning in American thinking on administration. This was Woodrow Wilson's 'The Study of Administration'.

The Americans had in fact, perhaps because of the continuous debate about constitutional forms that had led to the idea of separation of powers between legislative, executive, and judicial authorities becoming by 1788 'a hackneyed principle', or a 'trite maxim' (Annapolis pamphleteer, quoted by Vile, 1967, 153), been much more firm and consistent about what 'administration' might consist of. Alexander Hamilton wrote in 1788:

> The administration of government, in its largest sense, comprehends all the operations of the body politic, whether legislative, executive, or judiciary; but in its most usual, and perhaps most precise signification, it is limited to executive details, and falls peculiarly within the province of the executive department. The actual conduct of foreign negotiations, the preparatory plans of finance, the application and disbursement of the public moneys in conformity to the general appropriations of the legislature, the arrangement of the army and navy, the direction of the operations of war—these, and other matters of a like nature, constitute what seems to be most properly understood by the administration of government (*Hamilton, The Federalist, No. 72; March 21, 1788; Rossiter, 1961, 435*).

Wilson and the politics/administration dichotomy

Wilson's treatment a century later is reminiscent of Hamilton's, but in speaking of an *act* of administration is closer to Bentham's contrast between an administrative order and a law:

87

Public administration is detailed and systematic execution of public law. Every particular application of general law is an act of administration. The assessment and raising of taxes, for instance, the hanging of a criminal, the transportation and delivery of the mails, the equipment and recruiting of the army and navy, etc., are all obviously acts of administration; but the general laws which direct these things to be done are as obviously outside of and above administration. The broad plans of governmental action are not administrative; the detailed execution of such plans is administrative (*Wilson, 1887, 209*).

Like Sir Henry Taylor, but with considerably less justification, Wilson is sure that

The science of administration ... is a birth of our own century, almost of our own generation. No one wrote systematically of administration as a branch of the science of government until the present century had passed its first youth ... Up to our own day all the political writers whom we now read had thought, argued, dogmatized only about the *constitution* of government *Wilson, 1887, 198*).

Even now, Wilson says, it is a foreign science, developed by French and German professors. 'If we would employ it, we must Americanize it' (1887, 204).

To Americanise it, Wilson had to tackle the difficulty posed by the fact that both France and Germany had constitutions and political systems very different from those of the United States. Bagehot had held that the 'mountain tops' were similar, though the details of various businesses were different: Wilson stood this on its head— it is the administrative business that is similar, and the top direction that varies in its character. He begins from the premise that administrative matters have to do with 'special means', not the 'general plans' of government:

The field of administration is a field of business. It is removed from the hurry and strife of politics; it at most points stands apart even from the debateable grounds of constitutional study. It is a part of political life only as the methods of the counting-house are a part of the life of society; only as machinery is part of the manufactured product (*1887, 211*).

In other words, 'Administrative questions are not political questions'. This being so, foreign administrative methods can be abstracted from their political and constitutional settings: it is business *methods* that are common to different régimes:

When we study the administrative systems of France and

Germany, knowing that we are not in search of *political* principles, we need not care a peppercorn for the constitutional or political reasons which Frenchmen or Germans give when explaining them to us. If I see a murderous fellow sharpening a knife cleverly, I can borrow his way of sharpening the knife without borrowing his probable intention to commit murder with it; and so, if I see a monarchist dyed in the wool managing a public bureau well, I can learn his business methods without changing one of my republican spots. He may serve his king; I will continue to serve the people; but I should like to serve my sovereign as well as he serves his. By keeping this distinction in view—that is, by studying administration as a means of putting our own politics into convenient practice, as a means of making what is democratically politic towards all administratively possible towards each—we are on perfectly safe ground, and can learn without error what foreign systems have to teach us. We can thus devise an adjusting weight for our comparative method of study. We can thus scrutinise the anatomy of foreign governments without fear of getting any of their diseases into our veins; dissect alien systems without apprehension of blood-poisoning (*Wilson, 1887, 220*).

What many readers took out of this, however, was less the rationale of comparative administrative study, or even the transferability of administrative technique, than the appearance of theoretical support for a domestic programme of American administrative reform of the 'spoils' system; and Wilson may have meant it so. He was already a propagandist for civil service reform, in his book *Congressional Government* (1885), and as such in a line of Political Science professor-activists (Crick, 1959, 24). One of them, Dorman B. Eaton, published in 1880 a book, *Civil Service in Great Britain: A History of Abuses and Reforms and Their Bearing upon American Politics* (which led to the Pendleton Act of 1883, going some way to reform); the title is fully expressive of the purpose of many such comparative studies at the time. The same 'unabashed normativism' (Riggs, 1962, 9) informed Wilson's essay: to hold up to Americans some foreign models for their emulation. The other side of the coin was just as normative. The sentence which followed 'Administrative questions are not political questions' was:

> Although politics sets the tasks for administration, it should not be suffered to manipulate its offices (*Wilson*, 1887, 211).

Thus was to be set up a defended frontier between 'politics' and 'administration'.

The history of the 'politics/administration dichotomy', as it came to be called, has frequently been told (Waldo, 1948; Appleby, 1949; Lepawsky, 1949; and most general texts since). Waldo's point of departure was Frank J. Goodnow's book *Politics and Administration* (1900) rather than Wilson; Goodnow distinguished political functions into those analogous to the 'mental operations' and those analogous to the 'actions' of individuals—the expression of the state's will, and operations necessary to the execution of that will (Goodnow, 1900, 11). These two functions are respectively Politics and Administration; any system of government establishes more or less differentiated organs, and

> ... each of these organs, while not perhaps confined exclusively to the discharge of one of these functions, is still character- ised by the fact that its action consists largely or mainly in the discharge of one or the other. This ... is inevitable both be- cause of psychological necessity and for reasons of economic expediency (*Goodnow, 1900, 11*).

W. F. Willoughby (1919) made a distinction between 'direction, supervision and control, on the one hand, and execution on the other' (Willoughby, 1919, 229), which seems clear enough; he is making a further division of functions between 'executive' and 'administrative' functions, often, he says, confused. But it turns out that it is the *executive* function which is

> distinctly political in character. It involves the making of far- reaching decisions in respect to governmental policies. In res- pect to the actual conduct of government affairs it has to do with seeing that policies that are adopted, or lines of action that are decided upon, are properly carried into effect rather than in undertaking the work proper of putting these policies and programs into execution ... The latter function, the ad- ministrative, on the other hand, strictly speaking, involves the making of no decisions of a political character ... (*Willoughby, 1919, 385*).

So for Willoughby 'the executive function' is concerned with what he earlier called 'direction, supervision and control', and 'the administrative function' is concerned with what he contrasted with this, 'execution'. There would appear to be an attempt here to make the 'function' fit the traditional name of the Presidential office, the Executive, while 'administrative' occupies a lesser role—yet Wil- loughby, like Goodnow, warned against directly identifying 'func- tion' and institution of government.

In later treatments of what became the orthodoxy of the 1920s, the careful distinctions of the originators between analytic 'functions

of government' and the appropriate province of different governmental organs were not always kept. 'Politics' became synonymous
with 'politicians', the political parties, the legislature; 'administration' was shorthand for the staffs of Government departments in
Washington and in the field. A parallel, alternative, and occasionally synonymous dichotomy also appeared, between 'policy'—the
concrete expression of the 'will' of Congress or of the people—and
'administration', its putting into effect (as in the extract from Willoughby, where 'policy' is alternative to 'program'; or White,
1926, 3—'public administration consists of all those operations having for their purpose the fulfillment or enforcement of public
policy'). John M. Pfiffner expressed a number of these senses, as
they were employed in normative discussion, in the following
passage.

> Politics is ... an inevitable and necessary part of the process
> of government. It must, however, be controlled and confined
> to its proper sphere which is the determination, crystallization,
> and declaration of the will of the community. Administration,
> on the other hand, is the carrying into effect of this will once
> it has been made clear by political process. From these
> premises, therefore, is derived the keystone of the new public
> administration—the conclusion that politics should stick to its
> policy-determining sphere and leave administration to apply its
> own technical processes free from the blight of political
> meddling (*Pfiffner, 1935, 9*).

The words 'apply its own technical processes' indicate a second
strand in the success of the politics/administration dichotomy. As
well as the push given to the doctrine by the desire to get rid of
the 'spoils' system and its accompaniments, there was a pull, coming
from the possibility of emulating American industry in the introduction of 'scientific management'.

Scientific management

This too is an oft-told story (see Urwick and Brech, 1945, I for a
'committed' history; Waldo, 1948 for a social philosophy analysis;
George, 1968 for a list of titles by decade). Waldo noted that the
'movement' had similarities to the positivism of the mid-nineteenth
century (Comte), and to the 'utopian' socialism of Saint-Simon
(Waldo, 1948, 48). It also has forbears in eighteenth-century

Aufklärung and Benthamite utilitarianism, and the first of the 'Thirteen Pioneers' of scientific management in Urwick and Brech's pantheon is Charles Babbage (1792–1871), the inventor of the digital computer, whom we have noted for his *On the Economy of Machinery and Manufactures* (1832), in which he expressed warnings about the use of the stop-watch in 'time study' which were not always remembered by later practitioners—although his work was certainly known to them (Gilbreth, 1914, 2; 76).

The title of 'Father of Scientific Management' is usually, however, bestowed on Frederick Winslow Taylor (1856–1915), the engineer who wrote several papers on time and motion study and their relationship to piece-rate wage systems, but whose main asset was an articulate style, an evangelical fervour, and a choice of themes that set sympathetic chords vibrating throughout America. His first notable published work was *Shop Management* ((1903) 1910), and a series of articles under the general title 'The Gospel of Efficiency' was followed in 1911 by *Principles and Methods of Scientific Management*. Taylor set out his intentions thus:

> This paper has been written:
> FIRST. To point out, through a series of simple illustrations, the great loss which the whole country is suffering through inefficiency in almost all of our daily acts.
> SECOND. To try to convince the reader that the remedy for this inefficiency lies in systematic management, rather than in searching for some unusual or extraordinary man.
> THIRD. To prove that the best management is a true science, resting upon clearly defined laws, rules, and principles, as a foundation. And further to show that the fundamental principles of scientific management are applicable to all kinds of human activities, from our simplest individual acts to the work of our great corporations, which call for the most elaborate cooperation.
> One of the important objects of this paper is to convince its readers that every single act of every workman can be reduced to a science (*Taylor, 1911, 5–7*).

The 'stop-watch technique' aroused instant opprobrium, and indeed led to a House of Representatives inquiry, and a Congressional ban on the expenditure of military appropriation funds for 'time-study with a stop-watch or other time-measuring device', which has been continually re-enacted (Lepawsky, 1949, 121).

But 'efficiency' was a potent gospel, and the 'principles' were applied with crusading zeal to many other aspects of production, and indeed every other function of industrial management. One enthusiast, Mr (Justice) Louis D. Brandeis, before the Interstate Commerce Commission in 1910, exemplified the scope of the principles of scientific management:

> We will show you, may it please your Honours, that these principles, applicable to all businesses, are applicable to practically all departments of all businesses ... (*Lepawsky, 1949, 123*)

and another, Morris L. Cooke in an article on 'The Spirit and Social Significance of Scientific Management' (1913, 493) went further:

> There is nothing to prevent scientific management from becoming a nuisance [but] in my opinion, we shall never fully realize either the visions of Christianity or the dreams of democracy until the principles of scientific management have permeated every nook and cranny of the working world (*Waldo, 1948, 52; Lepawsky, 1949, 125*).

There was an apostolic response: George (1968, 183–8) lists seven works published between 1906 and 1910 on scientific management (none by Taylor), but 37 between 1910 and 1915, and 53 between 1916 and 1920.

This movement meant by 'science' something more than the eighteenth- and nineteenth-century writers on 'administrative science' (or indeed 'economic science' or 'political science') had meant by the word—something like 'disciplined study'; perhaps something less than a modern 'social scientist' might now wish the term to mean (e.g. Golembiewsky, 1964). For Taylor and his followers the use of the term implied the replacement of 'hunch' by observation and measurement, of 'traditional practices' by calculation and 'rational methods'. The matter of their science was, to begin with, at the level of 'mechanical' or 'routine' operations, in terms of earlier discussions. But their aspirations, as shown by Brandeis and Cooke, ran higher; and it was not long before Taylor's own ventures into 'management structure' (the 'functional foremanship principle') were being extended and superseded by applications (or alleged applications) of scientific management principles to organisation of an enterprise as a whole, to leadership, and to the realm of business policy.

These will be matter for later chapters; but it was these developments of scientific management doctrine, rather than improvements in workshop practice, that most affected the 'policy/administration dichotomy' literature, and indeed, university and college courses in public administration. Wallace Sayre summed up the underlying concepts of the formulation implicit in the textbooks of the 1920s (White, 1926; Willoughby, 1927; and several others):

1 The politics/administration dichotomy was assumed as a self-evident truth and as a desirable goal; administration was perceived as a self-contained world of its own, with its own separate values, rules, and methods.

2 Organisation theory was stated in scientific management terms; that is, it was seen largely as a problem in organisation technology—the necessities of hierarchy, the uses of staff agencies, a limited span of control, subdivision of work by such 'scientific' principles as purpose, process, place or clientele.

3 The executive budget was emphasized as an instrument of rationality, of co-ordination, planning and control.

4 Personnel management was stressed as an additional element of rationality (jobs were to be described 'scientifically', employees were to be selected, paid, advanced by 'scientific' methods) . . .

(*Sayre, 1958, 38*).

The twin ideas, of the politics/administration dichotomy and Scientific Management, gave a form and purpose, a self-confidence, to both the practice and the study of administration in the 1920s and early 1930s. They were the foundation stones of the City Manager movement (White, 1927), of a similar reform movement in State government (Lipson, 1939), of the municipal research bureau movement (Beard, 1926; Waldo, 1948, 33), and in the employment of professors of public administration as consultants to governments.

Gulick, Fayol, and Haldane

Everything seemed to point to the correctness of the outlook and method—the depression, the New Deal, the expansion of governmental activity, all made simply more relevant and urgent the cry for a clear, cogent and rational administrative technology, liberated from class, ethnic, or other social conflict. The 'new public administration' had its high-water mark in 1937, with the appointment by Roosevelt of the President's Committee on Administrative Management, to make a survey of the entire federal machinery, and make recommendations (they recommended a strengthening of the office of the President); and the publication by one of the members

of the Committee, Luther Gulick, along with the former Director of
the International Management Institute at Geneva, the English-
man Lyndall F. Urwick, of *Papers on the Science of Administration* (1937), containing eleven essays constituting now the *locus
classicus* of the orthodoxy: some American, some European, some
concerned with public administration exclusively, most with 'business administration'; but all confident of a science of administration which transcends frontiers, and time, and purpose.

The American movement was, it is probably fair to say, much
more influential in Europe than it was itself aware of developments in European administrative science. The 'bureaucracy'
scholarship of the pre-Weberians and Weber himself, the English
psychology of politics—such as Graham Wallas' *Human Nature in
Politics* (1908)—and of industry (Seebohm Rowntree's *The Human
Factor in Business* (1921)), the work of Henri Fayol (1841–1925), a
French industrialist who urged men in high position in all walks of
life to set down what they regarded as the sound principles of their
own success, for the guidance of others; these did not make the
rapid impact across the Atlantic that 'Taylorism' made in the other
direction. In *Administration Industrielle et Générale* (1916), Fayol
set out his own principles, rather in the *Fürstenspiegel* ('advice to
Princes') tradition exemplified by Bacon and Sir Henry Taylor than
in the sociological and 'scientific' tradition of Le Play (Brodie, 1962,
312). In spite of the title, 'administration' is not for Fayol the all
embracing term; for that he used 'government', in which he
discerned six functions: technical, commercial, financial, security,
accounting, and administration. But, Fayol admitted, 'the managers
of big concerns spend so much of their time on it, that their jobs
seem to consist solely of administration' (Fayol, 1916, 59; 1929, 35;
Urwick, 1943, 16). 'Administration' is then in turn analysed into
five components: foreseeing, organisation, command, co-ordination,
and control—which prefigures the acronym of Gulick for the work
of the chief executive, POSDCORB—Planning, Organising, Staffing, Directing, Co-ordinating, Reporting, Budgeting (Gulick, 1937,
14).

Fayol was first translated into English in 1929, but not apparently
available to the writers of a comparable American scientific-
management style treatise, *The Principles of Organization* (1931,
1939), published by A. C. Reiley and James D. Mooney, a former
President of General Motors. Mooney and Reiley set their account
of the principles of organisation common to government, military,
church, and industrial enterprises in a 'logical frame' or schema of

'principle, process, and effect' (The Co-ordinating Principle, The Scalar Process, The Functional Effect); which produced a certain unity—provided one selected the empirical evidence suitably.

The same burgeoning confidence in the existence of common 'principles of administration' was to be seen in England, in the early 1920s and until the middle 1930s. The ideas of Sir Warren Fisher and Bertrand Russell have been quoted: but perhaps the most notable illustration is the official Report of the Machinery of Government Committee under Lord Haldane (Cd. 9230, 1918), on the first page of which appears:

> We have endeavoured to define in the first place the general principles which should govern the distribution of the responsibilities in question, and in the second place to illustrate the application of these principles in sufficient outline ... Our investigations under the first head have made it evident to us that there is much overlapping and consequent obscurity and confusion in the functions of the Departments of executive Government ... Departments appear to have been rapidly established without preliminary insistence on definition of function and precise assignment of responsibility. Even where Departments are most free from these defects, we find that there are important features in which the organisation falls short of a standard which is becoming progressively recognised as the foundation of efficient action (*Report, paras. 3–4*).

The Committee goes on (after discussing the functions of the Cabinet) to urge the undertaking of more research before the formulation of policy; and then comes a famous passage on 'Allocation of Functions between Departments':

> Upon what principles are the functions of Departments to be determined and allocated? There appear to be only two alternatives, which may be briefly described as distribution according to the persons or classes to be dealt with, and distribution according to the services to be performed (*Report, para. 18*).

As Smellie put it, the Committee, in the 'most thorough examination since Bentham', 'was concerned to solve a problem in administrative science and not to determine a political programme' (Smellie, (1937) 1950, 242).

It was manifestly the same spirit in which the Institute of Public Administration was founded in London in 1922, and which breathes through the first editorial of its journal *Public Administration* in 1923. In the first volume appears an article entitled 'Public Administration: A Science' (Merson, 1923, 220)—without the query-mark which a later generation would expect. 'Rationalisa-tion' was in many ways the English word for 'scientific manage-ment': a World Economic Conference assembled in Geneva by the League of Nations in May, 1927, adopted a resolution:

> that Governments, public institutions, professional and indus-trial organisations, and the general public should influence pro-ducers to direct their efforts [to] diffuse in every quarter a clear understanding of the advantages and obligations involved by Rationalisation and Scientific Management, and of the possi-bilities of their gradual application (*Urwick, 1929, v.*)

and the 'Rationalisation Movement' captured a number (even) of senior civil servants in Britain—notably, perhaps, Sir Henry Bun-bury, long President of the Institute, who contributed an article entitled 'Rationalising the Processes of Administration' to the 1930 volume of the Journal.

By the later 1930s in the United States, however, this European support for the Taylorian gospel and its derivative schools was well known, and as already said, is represented in the *Papers on the Science of Administration* (1937).

The confident assertion of 'general principles' of administration in all fields (Fayol's list was 'commerce, industry, politics, religion, war, philanthropy, and the running of the home'; later Mooney added 'the criminal underworld') persisted even as late as 1956, in the first volume of a new journal, the *Administrative Science Quarterly* (*Litchfield*, 1956, 28; see below, p. 121). But the sap-ping of this confidence in the self-evident truth of the politics/administration dichotomy and the progress of rationalisation had already begun.

Follett, Appleby and Simon

The new science of social psychology had been developing quite separately a set of theories about human behaviour in industrial and other settings whose impact, although its exponents were not interested in the 'general principles' approach or the politics/administration dichotomy as such, had begun to discredit the possi-bility of rational 'will-realizing' processes (Rowntree, 1921; Mayo, 1933). The political philosopher Mary Parker Follett, indeed, had been giving lectures since the early 1920s on, for example, 'The Giving of Orders' and 'Business as an Integrative Unity' (both

1925) not so much attacking as pointing out the fatuity of a strict demarcation between the function of deciding what to do and the function of getting it done (Follett, 1949, 16; Metcalf and Urwick, 1941, 71). Lepawsky, in a chapter entitled 'Administration and Policy', devoted ten pages to expounding the doctrines of the main 'orthodox' writers, Woodrow Wilson, Frank Goodnow, W. F. Willoughby, and John M. Pfiffner (while giving full attention to their reservations); and the succeeding ten to their 'realist' critics, beginning with Howard McBain in 1927 ('The prime function of the President is not executive at all. It is legislative'); Luther Gulick in 1933 ('where there is *discretion*, there is the making of policy', yet discretion is inseparable from administrative decision— Waldo, 1948, 123); E. Pendleton Herring's *Public Administration and the Public Interest* (1936), ('replete with evidence of administrative participation in policy-making'); Marshall Dimock in 1937 ('coordinate rather than exclusive' processes); Carl Friedrich in 1940 (a 'misleading distinction', a 'fetish, a stereotype in the minds of theorists and practitioners alike') (Lepawsky, 1949, 51–6). Not included in this respect by Lepawsky, but of enormous influence on later thinking, was Chester Barnard's *The Functions of the Executive* (1938), another rejection of an *a priori* division between authoritative expression of 'will' and technical expertise of 'putting into effect'.

The scholarly death-blow to the simplistic formulation of the classic dichotomy, and a new classic statement, came in Paul Appleby's *Policy and Administration* (1949). Appleby (1891–1963) occupied high positions in the US federal service throughout the Roosevelt era, and then became an academic; his book is not at all in the 'scientific' style, but rather that of the 'realist' practitioner. He accepts the position that in a modern state 'policy' decisions must be taken 'anywhere along the line', and at all levels; there are too many of them needed, for it to be otherwise. The safeguard is that any matter whatsoever may *become* the subject of higher-level consideration, by being 'called up' from what would have otherwise been its appropriate level of decision:

> Subject to such calling-up, normal administrative or legislative fixing of the order of a particular decision—the level at which it may be made—is done by a subtle process of political evaluation. That evaluation is reached generally through anticipation of popular reaction; as a response to experience, convention, and precedent; under pressure from interests directly concerned; under pressures from other parts of the government;

and in specific cases through popular debate, campaigns, and elections. The order of a particular decision is preliminarily and tentatively determined within the executive branch by political, administrative, procedural, technical or factual and social evaluations ...

The level at which a decision is to be made, therefore, may be shifted downward or upward as evaluations point to more or less controversy, or to more or less 'importance'. Importance within the administrative organization turns in some part in the dimensions and scope of the action—the weight of impact it will have or has had on citizens, and the number of citizens affected; in some part on ideal values, such as are involved for example, in questions of the *kind* of impact on even a single citizen. In very considerable part all this is reaction to diverse political factors (*Appleby, 1949, 12*).

He demonstrates how no progress can be made in a distinction between 'policy' and 'administration' by reference to level or status in a hierarchy, nor by type of issue; a man does not decide policy in the morning and administration in the afternoon, whether he be Congressman, President, head of section or someone much humbler —he must needs deal with whole problems, and labels can be tied on only by observers. The reports he makes and receives are both administrative reports and programme reports of achievements, shortcomings, and difficulties; all decisions have *some* reference to the possibilities of their execution.

In the perspective of each successive level everything decided at that level and above is 'policy', and everything that may be left to a lower level is 'administration'. In the perspective of an outside observer, policy and administration are treated together at every level (*Appleby, 1949, 21*).

Politicians 'administer' on occasions—that is, decide questions which have to do with the carrying out of policy rather than its determination. And officials cannot avoid making policy decisions; but in Government, the representatives of the people have the final say:

Much administration may normally be left to administrators if all administration is part of and subject to the various processes. To this extent, a round, popular separation between policy and administration is valid.

It is not truly a separation, however; it is a kind of tentative delegation of power under which the public says, "We can not and will not bother with such matters as a general rule; we can attend well to only so much. But whenever we are much disturbed about something we are delegating to you, we shall suspend the delegation (*Appleby, 1949, 20*).

I shall argue later that the Appleby formulation cannot be said to be the last word on the 'politics/administration dichotomy', much less the 'policy/administration' one: but certainly, it breathes the air of the 1950s, rather than of the 1880s or even the 1920s.

It was another air of the 1950s (even though the actual dates are all in the late 1940s) which similarly destroyed the confidence of 'scientific management'. Another group of scholars, of which the leading names in this regard are Herbert A. Simon and Robert A. Dahl, had in common a much more rigorous notion of what constitutes scientific method, out of which arose what came to be called the 'behaviouralist' attack on older schools of political science and administrative theory (Charlesworth, 1962; Storing, 1961). Simon's was the first direct onslaught, in an article entitled 'The Proverbs of Administration' (Simon, 1946), published again the next year in his epoch-making *Administrative Behavior* (1947). Simon's earliest work had been concerned with 'The Criterion of Efficiency' in municipal administration particularly (Simon, 1937; Ridley and Simon, 1938); he was then much influenced by Chester Barnard and by the Pragmatism of John Dewey, and reacted against both the vacuousness and inconsistency of the 'classic organisation theorists', as he called those who followed Mooney, Urwick, and Gulick, and the reduction of all organisational behaviour to 'interpersonal relations' which was the tendency of the 'human relations' school which followed Mayo. In dealing with the 'dichotomy', Simon adopts neither the Gulick (1933) approach (policy = discretion) nor the Appleby (1949) approach (policy and administration a seamless web)—except in so far as he says that what one is dealing with is the process of decision-making whatever it be called, policy or administration. But he retains a dichotomy, the logical positivist one, between statements of fact and statements of value: he wants to separate out those aspects of decision-making that are amenable to scientific reasoning, are 'rational', and those which are not. Hence we have a rejection of the scientific pretensions of the older writers not because they were inappropriately scientific, but because they were only pretensions to science. 'Efficiency' was still the essential criterion for Simon; one cannot apply the notion of 'efficiency' to *values*, and so one must first isolate from a decision process those aspects to which one can apply it.

Further criticism came in 1947 from Dahl, in an article called 'The Science of Public Administration: Three Problems' (Dahl,

1947). The first problem was the assumption of the classical theorists that administration was a purely technical matter, value-free, unconnected with ends or purposes. The second attacked the concept of an 'administrative man' who would be purely rational: Dahl concluded that administrative theory must also account for non-rational behaviour and for influences inseparable from the particular environment—democratic, capitalist, industrial, etc. The third problem pointed out the American-centred—or at least Western-centred—nature of classic theory, which is evident even in its claim to 'universal principles'. We will return to Dahl's three problems.

CHAPTER SEVEN

The New
Administrative Science

It is not within the practicable scope of the present book to present more than an outline treatment of the development of thought about administration, management and so on that followed these criticisms in the third quarter of the twentieth century. In America and in Europe the supply of mainly university-based research and writing expanded with almost explosive force in several different directions at once, to meet, and in turn feed, the demand from the tycoons of industry, defence, education, and virtually every other field of endeavour, for guidance in mastering the complexity of the larger enterprises which were seemingly decreed by the historical forces of the period. And the expansion of the universities them-selves provided a small surplus of staff members who became caught up with the purely intellectual description of what was going on, devising new conceptual frameworks to bring a new body of em-pirical observations within the ambit of existing knowledge, developing special and general theories to relate one field to another. In this respect perhaps the most notable single concept was the idea of 'the organisation', which in a very short time enabled many diverse purposes and lines of approach and specific interests to be subsumed under a single new subject heading, 'organisation theory'. But before exploring this, it is necessary to backtrack in time and describe the genesis of an approach merely mentioned so far: the 'human relations' approach.

Human relations

It does both the progenitors of 'scientific management' and Max Weber an injustice, to say that in their theories and recommenda-tions on the running of industrial and other enterprises they 'left the human factor out of account', or 'tended to view organizations as if they existed without people' (Bennis, 1966, 66). The study of individual psychology applied to the industrial setting was well advanced in Britain and America by the first decade of the century. Lillian M. Gilbreth, wife of Frank Bunker Gilbreth the founder of 'motion study', published her *The Psychology of Management* in 1914—not a profound work as psychology, to be sure, but greatly concerned with the reactions of the worker to 'scientific management'. The Reports of the Health of Munitions Workers Committee (1915–18; *Final Report*, Cd. 9065, 1918) are British Official Papers of a significance at least equal to their more celebrated contemporary the 'Haldane Report'. Urwick and Brech (1946) call Robert Owen (1771–1858) 'The Pioneer of Personnel Management', mainly for his own work at New Lanark (housing, canteens, and schools for his workers and their families, in the first decades of the nineteenth century); and B. Seebohm Rowntree (1871–1954), who perhaps has more realistic claim to the title in its modern sense, published *The Human Factor in Business* in 1921. Perhaps what enables such writings to be included in the canon of the 'classical school' is their basic view of the nature of man: 'an economic creature, limited in his pursuit of gain only by his physiological capacities' (Silverman, 1970, 75); or, even more unkindly, the analogy of their assumptions to what is now 'animal psychology'. 'Paint your cowsheds green and play music to your best milkers' is apparently a proven recipe for higher milk yields; and the aim of most of the industrial psychology of the early twentieth century was undoubtedly higher productivity from contented workers, each worker being considered as a unit, independently responding to his individual environment, as is assumed of the cows in the cowshed (Rowntree's profit-sharing was an exception).

The work which ended this way of thinking about workers in industry (amongst the knowledgeable, at least), known as the 'Hawthorne Studies', began from a perfectly orthodox investigation of the effects in a telephone manufacturing plant of variation in standards of illumination on output. These studies, which lasted from 1926 until 1932, were carried out by Elton Mayo and a team from the Harvard University Graduate School of Business Administration at the Hawthorne Works of the Western Electric Company in Chicago: they are too well known to need expounding here (Mayo, 1933; Roethlisberger and Dickson, 1939; Urwick and Brech, 1948; Brown, 1954; Landsberger, 1958; or any general sociology textbook). What emerged was the importance, for the under-standing of the relationship between the individual and his employing organisation, of the intervening social grouping, the small face-to-face work group. Such small groups generate their own codes of acceptable behaviour, social norms, in respect of the work process, the reward system, and authority; and these become an additional set of variables to be taken into account for anyone investigating, or hoping to manipulate, the response of the individual worker to his work environment.

The study of small groups as such, 'group dynamics', took off largely from Hawthorne (Homans, 1950; Klein, 1956). But of possibly more significance even than this was the recognition that work, for the worker, is not merely an economic necessity, but also a psychological one. With emphasis, J. A. C. Brown turns the older view upside down:

> The belief that money is the sole, or even the most important of several, motives for work, is so foolish that anyone who seriously holds this opinion is thereby rendered incapable of understanding either industry or the industrial worker (*Brown, 1954, 188*).

Many later scholars adopted the assumptions of this doctrine of 'psychological needs', which are to be compared with the physiological human needs of food, shelter, and so on, but have to be distinguished from desires or wants. The most quoted treatment of psychological needs is that of A. H. Maslow (1954), who saw a gradation of needs, from the most basic (the physiological) which are always the most pressing, until satisfied; the need for security, including economic security, the assurance of continuing satisfaction of basic needs; then the need for social belonging, integration into a group or community, through which personal security or 'identity' might be assured; and finally, the need for self-esteem, or self-fulfilment, which becomes pressing when the satisfaction of needs of a lower order is assured. From this point of view, the explanation of human behaviour lies in the attempt to satisfy the lowest unsatisfied need. The main question to be asked of the theory as a whole is whether these needs are 'real', and verifiable, or merely postulates. If the latter, then other postulates (a 'scaffolding' to try and get a theory off the ground, so to speak) might make equal or better sense, but the method is legitimate enough. However, explaining a particular behaviour by reference to 'satisfying needs' would require that the existence of needs was 'real', verified in their mode of operation and effects; and that has not yet been done.

Nevertheless, the application of the theory of social and self-actualising needs to the industrial situation has undoubtedly led to a better and wider understanding of human relations in the work situation. It sometimes happens that a solution which is 'good enough' to fit the ordinary run of problem and produce a satisfying outcome in a reasonable proportion of applications is worth applying, even if on a more rigorous appraisal it is fundamentally faulty or 'right for all the wrong reasons'. Certainly at the level of practical recommendation, or industrial consultancy, the social psychology school (of whom the leading American names in the generation following that of Mayo, Whitehead and Roethlisberger are Rensis Likert, Chris Argyris, and Douglas McGregor) have had enormous influence in achieving currency for the idea that authoritarian or disciplinarian attitudes in management and supervision *do not pay off* as well as do attitudes which allow employees to satisfy their needs for social belonging and self-fulfilment at the same time as they work for organisational goals.

Thus, perhaps, was 'evolutionary capitalism' enabled to progress a further stage; and there can be few heads or senior members of other forms of enterprise than the industrial—commercial, welfare, or 'public administration'—who have not absorbed some part of this teaching, through the mass media, even if they have not learned to talk of 'Theory X' and 'Theory Y' (McGregor, 1960). Of course, the post-1945 period is one which has seen considerable increase in popular education, in expectations not only of a rising standard of living but of a greater share in decision, and in the power of trade unions. A theory of employee wants and demands, and of employer response to those, might well make as good sense of what has actually happened in American and British industry since 1945 as would a theory of 'needs'. Perhaps the prime value of the 'human relations' doctrines, in their Hawthorne and post-Hawthorne manifestations, was to enable employers to cope with what was happening anyway, rather than (as has been alleged to be their intention) show them how to change things to their own advantage.

There is a distinction to be made between the 'Hawthorne' group of writers and a number of later writers still broadly in the 'human relations' field, according to whether or not they preach or assume universality in their analyses and recommendations; whether they take into account differences in historical circumstance, or geographical location, or the substantive or technical content of the type of work involved, or any of a number of such environing factors, when considering the relationship between employee and workgroup, and workgroup and organisation. It is one of the touchstones of being 'classical', in this subject, that one assumes the existence of 'principles' that apply to administration or to management, or to supervision, or to the dynamics of groups, *as such*, wherever found. The Hawthorne studies have been criticised by later writers (from hindsight, of course) on a number of such grounds: for instance, that insufficient account was taken of the possible effects of the 'Great Depression' on trade union militancy during the studies; that no allowance was made for the possible effects of the works being in Chicago, an ethnic melting-pot; that the precise effects of the work technology of relay assembly, and so on, were not isolated; and the like. Later researchers then devised other investigations, to explore the effects of whatever variable had taken their interest; and in this way Hawthorne initiated an enormous critical industry, as did the writing of Max Weber, available at about the same time.

Technology and behaviour

One of the lines of development could perhaps have come a bit sooner than it did, given that Karl Marx and Friedrich Engels had described a hundred years earlier the process of degradation of the human dignity of the worker in the new industrial factories, and that Ruskin and Morris, also in England, had used a theory of 'needs', practical and aesthetic, to deplore the degradation of the environment by the mine, the ironworks, and the railway. When the investigatory methods of the new sociology and social psychology came to be applied in the 1940s and 1950s to the study of the relationship between the worker and the factory system, therefore, the results often seemed to be merely documenting or restating in a 'systematic' way much of what was already, for the layman, experiential knowledge, as with Walker and Guest's *The Man on the Assembly Line* (1952). Similarly, much later, the work of Goldthorpe and others among car-workers in England served to refute the inadequate assumptions of earlier sociologists of industry rather than to provide surprises for non-sociologists unaware of what the ruling assumptions were in the first place (Goldthorpe *et al.*, 1968). Hence allegations of 'dressed-up commonsense' which were not always fair.

The results of some studies of the period did, however, go counter to 'commonsense' and received doctrine, and hence can still, decades later, seem persuasive and enlightening to experienced but 'lay' audiences who encounter them for the first time. A pioneering British study of the relationship between group culture and work technology arose out of the puzzlingly small increase in production that had followed the introduction of mechanical coal-cutting machinery into some English coalmines after nationalisation. A team from the Tavistock Institute of Human Relations spent time underground in several pits in Durham and showed that the outcomes noted could be attributed to (i) purely technical effects of the change, mainly the necessity of a three-shift cycle of sequential operations, which meant that time lost on one operation could never be recovered and indeed might escalate in effect; and (ii) the effects of the change on the underground social system, mainly the necessity of a given forty-man group instead of a self-selected eight- or nine-man group over the three shifts at any one workplace, and the necessity of specialisation of task, each man carrying out one task (or 'trade') instead of being multi-skilled. Another change, however, was one which turned out to be reversible; this was in the method of payment—from a single note payment on tonnage produced shared equally among the eight or nine men concerned, to the 'industrial' method of a wage to each individual according to his allotted task. The study (Trist and Bamforth, 1951; Trist et al., 1963) showed how closely the social system of the mine was related not only to the cultural and geographical location of that mine but also to the technical methods and circumstances of coal-getting in that mine; and so suggested an equally close interrelationship of social system and precise technological factors elsewhere, and anywhere: the two sets of factors form one system, the 'socio-technical system'. This theme, that behaviour in the industrial setting is associated with the technological specification of the work process, is taken up, notably, by Sayles (1958) and Blauner (1964).

It will be convenient to note here two other British pioneering studies, which have the technology factor as one of their variables, though the dependent variable is not for them 'human relations' or the social system, but rather the structure of management. The first is a study of one hundred industrial firms in South-East Essex by Joan Woodward (1958; 1965), which began from a desire on her part, as a teacher of management subjects, to provide her students with local illustrative material to support the fairly standard 'classical theory' textbooks of the day, and ended by more or less destroying the validity of the textbooks. Woodward found no clear relationship between business success and 'approved' management structure, until a new set of 'norms' of structure had been constructed: one for 'unit production' firms, which made 'one-off' items to customers' specifications (railway engines, bespoke tailoring); a second for 'mass production' firms (cars, washing machines); and a third for 'process production' firms (chemicals, petrol). Each of these types of industry had its own characteristic management structure, measured in terms of the 'height' of the hierarchy, the 'span of control' of the first line supervisor, and a number of other such dimensions; and its own characteristic decision-structure also, determined by the extent to which research and development decisions, production decisions, and marketing decisions did or did not have to be closely integrated. The characteristics of the 'mass production' successful firms were those most nearly similar to the 'classical' norms; but the lesson clearly is that if, in manufacturing industry, it needs at least three different 'textbooks' to embody the relevant doctrines, the possibility is that each other sector of employment—commerce, transport, hospitals, 'public administration', and so on—needs as many or more: that if there is any such thing as a 'one best way' of organising for management of an enterprise, it is a 'one best way' for enterprises of that precise type only, not a universal.

The other British study to be noted here arose also out of a puzzling failure of a seemingly good idea. In order to stimulate the growth of new—mainly electronic—industry in central Scotland, the authorities had begun a scheme to send promising young engineers and scientists belonging to promising new firms to work with the major Government contractor for electronics work in Scotland, after which these young men would return to their own firms, not only innovation-minded but equipped with relevant research and development skills. But after a few years of operation the experiment was clearly not being successful, for the fruit was simply not appearing. Tom Burns and G. M. Stalker were commissioned to find out why, and the outcome was *The Management of Innovation* (1961), a book whose significance extended almost immediately well outside Scotland and Britain.

Burns and Stalker found that the most important single determining factor of success in incorporating a capacity for innovation, or planned change in the things manufactured and the methods of manufacture, was—surprisingly—not the personalities of individual managers, or 'industrial relations' in the firm, or the specific technology as such, but the management and decision structure of the firm—the way jobs were distributed, the way information was channelled, the way problems were dealt with. Two ideal-types could be constructed, opposite poles of a scale or spectrum: one of them would look very much like a Weberian bureaucracy, or a 'classic' Scientific Management family-tree diagram, each executive having his clearly-defined place in the hierarchy of rank and authority and his equally clearly defined duties and responsibilities, and knowing exactly what to do with any piece of work which did not fall within them, or which raised problems he could not, or was not entitled to, deal with—it must be posted upwards or sideways or downwards to its appropriate home. Only the men at the top could have an overall view of everything; and only a superior, at any level, could co-ordinate the work of lower levels; but if everyone was doing properly the task that had been allotted to him, leaving nothing undone and not duplicating anyone else's work, then in this ideal-type structure, which Burns and Stalker called the 'mechanistic model', no greater efficiency of operation would be conceivable.

The ideal-type at the other end of the scale is much less easy to describe: for it consists fundamentally of the opposite characteristics, and to write them as such seems a mere description of chaos: no clear definition of anyone's place in the hierarchy, no clear allocation of duties, no clear idea of what to do with any piece of work or problem that could not be handled. The man 'at the top' might have no more of an overall view than a man half-way up, and subordinates would be co-ordinating their superiors' work as often as the other way around. There *were* firms approximating to this picture; and it is no wonder that executives in them felt at sea, badgered on all sides, and longing desperately for their 'old' jobs of the safe nine-to-five variety where at least you 'knew where you were'. But it was *these* firms that were the successful ones, by the criteria that Burns and Stalker had been given; so it is clearly necessary to rewrite the ideal-type positively, not merely as the negative of the familiar 'mechanistic' type.

Thus: 'authority', or the ability to get others to do what you see to be necessary, resides not in rank but in functional competence for the problem in hand. If someone half-way up is recognised as 'the man who knows' in a particular situation, he for the time being is the most important man in the firm and wields the authority that goes with it.

Again: each executive's contribution to the total ongoing task of the firm as a whole lies not in his discharge of 'responsibilities', some defined sector of that task, but in his commitment to the whole of the task. Problems are never 'someone else's baby', but his as much as anyone's; only by collective problem-solving and collective implementation can anyone's commitment be discharged.

The result of such an ethos was that a firm in which it was embodied (and there were some firms that, for instance, allowed no executive to have his title on his door, or otherwise indicate the scope of his 'responsibilities') would be guarded against the possibility of 'settling down' into routines, against treating a new problem as necessarily a version of some old problem, against facing not the real world, but some more comfortable world that the firm could handle through existing practices. And the reason that firms so guarded against slipping into comfortable habits were the successful ones was that the world they inhabited, the electronics industry, was one so constantly altering at such an incredible rate—a product being known to be technically obsolete even before it went into scale production—that unless a firm were utterly adaptable, able to change its internal decision structure at will and in almost automatic response to the changing environment, it would not survive.

This ideal-type Burns and Stalker called the 'organic model', and they pointed out that neither model is in itself 'better' than the other, except in certain circumstances. The organic model is, by most ordinary standards, 'expensive' in resources; the money costs of its products are likely to be high in comparison with products that are none the worse for not being 'the latest thing'. There is no point in employing the 'organic' type of internal management structure, therefore, unless having 'the latest thing' is the most important factor in the formula. The organic model is suitable for unstable environments, where mere survival may depend on being able to cope with the latest challenge, at whatever 'cost' in ordinary terms.

The mechanistic model, on the other hand, is the best kind of structure where the environment is highly stable, and therefore predictable. Routinising can reduce unit costs enormously—at the expense of flexibility, of course; but then, in a highly stable environment flexibility of response is unnecessary. In an environment which is partly predictable, partly not, or predictable at one time and less so at another, an enterprise may have to be able to change from being mechanistic all over to being organic in one part, or from being mechanistic in one period to being organic in another. And of course these are not either/or matters, but more/less matters; an enterprise can *tend to* one pole or the other.

Finally, it is not only in manufacturing industry that the models can be used. One football team on the field might be compared with another in the degree of rigidity with which the players stuck to their given roles as defenders or strikers, or appeared to move from one role to the other as the situation required. *Any* group of which it can be said that 'they work as a team', displaying commitment to the goal of the group rather than to some individual sector of it, is showing 'organistic' characteristics in contrast to another group of which it can be said that 'each does to the best of his ability what is required of him' (but he doesn't decide what it is that is required of him).

This is a conceptual tool of great usefulness. It does depend upon the notion of the survival of a system in an environment, and hence has to answer all the objections to 'systems theory' as such, which we will come to in a later section; but there is no doubt of its descriptive value, in situations of many different kinds, which is why 'Burns and Stalker' is by now a household word among organisation theorists.

This might be the point, then, to consider the notion of 'organisations' as such, the concept which enables one to group together such a large heterogeneous body of scholars and number of approaches into a single 'subject', as it might be alongside 'history' or 'political science' in a curriculum.

Organisation theory and theory of organisations

The use of the word in this sense, with the indefinite article, 'an organisation', to designate a human social artifact, is twentieth century. Spencer did not use it this way; he used 'an administration', 'an institution', where we would now naturally say 'an organisation' (see p. 81 above). The OED's quotation from him is equivocal; and the reference of 1894 from the Durham University Journal ('We now have in the University... somewhere about fifty-three different "Organizations", athletic, intellectual, literary, social, and religious') has the crucial word in quotation marks, signifying neologistic usage. When Gulick entitled his paper in *Papers on the Science of Administration* (1937) 'Notes on the Theory of Organization', he was using this word in the sense of 'internal arrangement of parts'; not with the full richness of Spencer's biological metaphor, perhaps, but concerned with the internal organs, not the defining envelope, of an enterprise. Rapoport and Horvath express this distinction by differentiating between 'organization theory' and 'theory of organizations':

> We see organization theory as dealing with general and abstract organizational principles; it applies to any system exhibiting organized complexity. As such, organization theory is seen as an extension of mathematical physics or, even more generally, of mathematics designed to deal with organized systems. The theory of organizations, on the other hand, purports to be a social science. It puts real human organizations at the centre of interest. It may study the social structure of organizations and so can be viewed as a branch of sociology; it can study the behaviour of individuals or groups as members of organizations and so can be viewed as a part of social psychology; it can study power relations and principles of control in organizations and so fits into political science (*Rapoport and Horvath, 1960, 90; quoted in Waldo, 1961, 222*).

There have been many attempts to provide a definitive definition of 'an organization', sometimes elaborate and subtle. In a witty essay entitled 'Organization Theory: An Elephantine Problem', Dwight Waldo quoted E. Wight Bakke:

> A social organization is a continuing system of differentiated and coordinated human activities utilizing, transforming, and welding together a specific set of human, material, capital, ideational, and natural resources into a unique problem-solving whole engaged in satisfying particular human needs in interaction with other systems of human activities and resources in its environment (*Bakke, in Haire, 1959, 37; Waldo, 1961, 219*);

Argyris:

> Organizations are grand strategies individuals create to achieve objectives that require the effort of many (*Argyris, 1960, 24*);

and March and Simon:

> It is easier, and probably more useful, to give examples of formal organizations than to define the term. The United States Steel Corporation is a formal organization; so is the Red Cross, the corner grocery store, the New York Highway Department (*March and Simon, 1958, 1*).

The significance of 'formal' in such definitions is discussed by Blau and Scott (1962, 2) and by Silverman (1970, 8); it connotes an organisation established for a specific purpose and operating to explicit rules, contrasting with a 'social organization', such as is a family, a friendship group, or a community, which has no such instituting goals or rules—a distinction which owes much to Tönnies' (1887) and Durkheim's (1893) distinction between mechanical and organic social bonds. But the concept of 'an organisation' as such is left undefined, which is probably better: it is fairly clear that this use of the term originated in the need for a generic name, an inclusive rather than an exclusive term, to class together perfectly acceptable and intelligible existing terms of less generality, such as firm, army, congregation, department, etc; and for this very reason, it is difficult to use the term as a differentiator, to discriminate between organisations and things that only look like organisations, as it were. After all, if one did find good ways of distinguishing organisations from certain other social institutions, as Silverman suggests (1970, 13), one would then simply have to invent a name for the wider class of things to which they all belonged.

In articles dated 1950 and 1955, Herbert Simon was using 'organisation theory' interchangeably with 'theory of organisation', and both in the sense found in Gulick (1937), Selznick (1948), or Dahl (1947)—theory about organising; although Simon like the others was using the term 'an organisation' and 'organisations' quite freely (Simon, 1950; 1953; 1955). But another article, dated 1952, is entitled 'Comments on the Theory of Organizations', in the plural (Simon, 1952, reprinted in Rubenstein and Haberstroh, 1960, 157). In this article, Simon 'places' the organisation—it is too much to say he defines it—as a level of human grouping somewhere above the primary group (the small face-to-face work or family grouping that is the basic unit of the 'human relations' schools) and somewhere below the entity he calls 'an institution'—of which examples might be 'the steel industry', 'the retail trade', 'public administration'. This may be as much precision as is desirable.

Avoiding a restrictive definition for 'an organisation' does not prevent the devising of typologies of organisations; classifications to show how organisations may differ from one another, and perhaps to explain how they came to be so, or predict some relation within them. Silverman puts it thus:

> Often based on a variable which, to the writer concerned, seems to characterise organisations (e.g. technology, authority structure or specific function), a typology is developed which distinguishes different organisations in terms of their relation to this variable. Implicit in this is the hypothesis that organisations with, for instance, Technology A, Authority Structure B or

Function C will differ (in predictable ways) from those with Technology X, Authority Structure Y or Function Z (*Silverman, 1970, 15*).

Such a hypothesis could then be tested.

As early as 1959, Stanley Udy could say of the following two propositions—

A. The structure of any production organization is determined partly by the characteristics of the technological process which it is carrying on, and partly by the social setting within which it exists.
B. The structure of any reward system is determined partly by the characteristics of the production organization involved, and partly by the social setting, within limits imposed by features of the technological process

—that 'few if any social scientists would take issue with them in the form stated'; and his investigations (incidentally, among non-industrial peoples, not Western societies) were 'to discover the precise conditions under which, and the precise respects in which, each of the alternatives stated in these hypotheses will hold as opposed to another of the alternatives' (Udy, 1959, 125). Stephen Richardson, who carried out a study of 'Organizational contrasts on British and American Ships' in 1949, took for granted in 1956 that 'Variations in organization...can be expected to follow from variations of the cultures from which members of an organization are drawn' (Richardson, 1956, 190). Perhaps the most basic typology, then, would be one which explained organisational variables by reference to a culture variable; but let us deal with that in a later chapter—it is not well developed in theory of organisations as such.

We have already noted two typologies which use the techno-logical-complexity variable (Woodward) and the environmental-stability variable (Burns and Stalker) to predict internal management structure. Silverman in a succinct analysis goes on to describe typologies which use the type of exchange with the environment as the variable: Parsons (1964), and Katz and Kahn (1966), using a functionalist model—organisations are, with respect to their society, satisfying the society's needs for adaptation, goal-attainment, integration, or pattern-maintenance; the 'prime beneficiary' variable (Blau and Scott, 1962)—mutual-benefit associations, business concerns, service organisations, and commonweal associations; and the compliance-structure variable (Etzioni, 1961)—members may have calculative, moral, or alienative involvement with their organisation, and the organisation may have coercive, remunerative, or normative sanctions over them; the types usually found together are coercive-alienative, remunerative-calculative, and normative-moral, which then give to the organisations their particular character—as prisons are different from manufacturing firms and from churches.

An interesting idea which is something short of a typology is Erving Goffman's description of a 'total institution', which is an organisation embracing the whole of its members' lives (no split between work and home, for instance), as in prisons, convents, hospitals, and some universities; the consequent insulation of the value-system from the rest of society has certain consequences for internal structure and behaviour which puts these otherwise very dissimilar kinds of organisation in the same class (Goffman, (1957) 1968).

There are a number of other typologies, and a large number of possible typologies, which need not detain us here. (I would like to return to the question of typologies for 'public administration' in the final chapter.)

Decision theory

A major element in the new approaches to the study of administration in the 1950s does not fall happily under 'organisation theory' (or 'theory of organisations')—except in the work of Herbert A. Simon, whose main contribution it was to introduce the concept of the organisation as a decision-making environment. His book, *Administrative Behaviour*, published in 1947, is sub-titled 'A Study of Decision-Making Processes in Administrative Organization'. Summing up the development of theory of organisations to date, in the first textbook on *Organizations* (1958), March and Simon set out formally what Simon had said less succinctly in earlier writings (Simon, 1947, chap. 1; 1955, 30):

> Propositions about organizational behavior can be grouped in three broad classes, on the basis of their assumptions:
>   1. Propositions assuming that organization members, and particularly employees, are primarily *passive instruments*, capable of performing work and accepting directions, but not initiating action, or exerting influence in any significant way.

This would apply to most 'classical' theory, to all economic theories of 'labour', and to the studies of fatigue and work-place conditions that antedated Hawthorne.

2. Propositions assuming that members bring to their organizations *attitudes, values,* and *goals*; that they have to be motivated or induced to participate in the system of organization behavior; that there is incomplete parallelism between their personal goals and organization goals; and that actual or potential goal conflicts make power phenomena, attitudes and morale centrally important in the explanation of organizational behavior.

In this class would fall not only all the 'human relations' approaches, but also all views of organisations as instruments of goal-seeking members, and studies of the 'politics of organisations'.

3. Propositions assuming that organization members are *decision-makers and problem solvers*, and that perception and thought processes are central to the explanation of behavior in organizations (*March and Simon, 1958, 6*).

The third class included a great deal of micro-economics, some theory of the firm, theory of choice individual and collective; the growing body of work on 'planning' and 'operational research'; and the study of information theory, communication, and control as technical rather than social problems.

There might be overlapping between these classes of proposition; but on the whole the classes were separate because each was the characteristic province of different academic disciplines, each kind of scholar tending to see behaviour in organisations through only his own kind of spectacles; and Simon was reacting to what he saw as a contemporary excessive reliance on one approach:

We are in danger, through our renewed interest in power struggles and human attitudes, of neglecting one central truth that was known to the older administrative theory. Behavior in organizations is neither completely emotive nor completely aimless. Organizations are formed with the intention and design of accomplishing goals; and the people who work in organizations believe, at least part of the time, that they are striving towards these same goals. We must not lose sight of the fact that, however far organizations may depart from the traditional description of neutral instruments of governmental policy, nevertheless most behavior in organizations is *intendedly rational behavior* (*Simon, 1955, 30*).

'Rationality' was as central to Simon as it ever was to the scientific management 'efficiency experts'. But he begins in *Administrative Behavior,* and continues in successive works, from the proposition that it is futile for a theory of organisational behaviour to base itself on the kind of abstraction from human reality that had served the economists so well—'economic man', who always knows all he needs to know, and always knows what he prefers, and how much, when faced with a choice. 'Administrative man', if an abstraction were required, was a man who had to take decisions in imperfect conditions—and for two quite different sorts of reason. One was mere time and circumstantial pressure: there was seldom the opportunity to devote as much time and attention to searching for the *perfect* solution to a problem as it would require; rather was one obliged to accept the first satisfactory solution, to let not the best become the enemy of the good—and then move to the next pressing problem. Simon called this the 'satisficing' solution (1957, 204). This word is puzzling if it is meant to contrast with the usual economist's word 'optimise', for 'satisficing' can be seen as a trade-off of one satisfaction against another, or against several, in the ordinary way; the use of the term tends to suppress appreciation of what these other satisfactions are, that inhibit search. It is an expressive term nevertheless, and immediately acceptable to administrators as descriptive of their situation (Vickers, 1965, 42n).

The other reason for less-than-perfect decision making is more fundamental. A perfect decision would be one that selected, out of all the possible courses of action open, that one which had the maximum of desired consequences and the minimum of undesired consequences. But a real man in a real decision situation *cannot* know all the options that are open (only that sub-set about which he is aware), *cannot* foretell future consequences accurately, and *cannot* put appropriate values now on events that have not yet occurred, except approximately. So *all* decision-making is grossly imperfect, or as Simon puts it, subject to these limits on rationality.

A decision-maker in an organisation, taking decisions for the organisation, can however be put in a slightly easier position. He may be *given* the options between which to choose; he may be told what consequences are to be taken into account 'officially', and what can be ignored; he may be given also an approved method of calculating or estimating consequences; and he can be assured, that, if the values he uses are appropriate (if he decides 'properly' now), he will be protected against any change in 'official' values in the future. Thus the organisational decision maker chooses within 'an environment of *givens*', and the decision he makes has a higher probability of 'organisational rationality'. The task of the remainder of the organisation in relation to each individual decision maker within it is to channel to him the information he needs for his decisions to be 'organisationally rational'.

The philosophical implications of this model, and of Simon's avowed positivism in wishing to separate out the factual and the value elements in the statements that constitute the decision maker's 'raw material', have been heavily criticised (see, for instance, Storing, 1962). But this is not the place to go into it: the importance of Simon in the development of administrative science rests less on the details of his formulations than on his rehabilitation of 'intended rationality' in the face of the wave of social psychological attacks (or apparent attacks).

Simon's interest in the limits of 'rationality' took him into the realms of psychology, and the process of 'thinking'; and thence, via information theory and cybernetics, to the programming of a computer to play chess (Newell, Shaw and Simon, 1958a, 1958b; see Welsch and Cyert, 1970; Miller, Galanter and Pribram, 1960). But the mainstream of decision making theory since the 1950s has not run that course—how humans make choices—but rather what choices they ought to be making; how to make better decisions. The battery of 'aids' now available for the improvement of 'corporate decision making' is extensive, and can only be indicated here.

Using the three elements of the Simon decision model as pegs, let me suggest that aids fall into three classes: those that are good for widening the range of options considered; those that are good for predicting and presenting logical and empirical consequences; and those that are good for ranking and marshalling outcomes for evaluation. It seems to me, then, that the group of techniques and methods that goes under the general name of 'operational research' has its most striking successes in encouraging fresh and clear-eyed approaches to a problem, and generating surprising options, that often lie quite outside the range that would have been considered by the organisational decision makers (see Beer, 1966, 1967; Lawrence, 1966; Bane, 1968; etc.).   Secondly, the prime value of the increasingly sophisticated 'projection' techniques that are based on 'systems analysis' or 'network analysis', from the relatively simple Critical Path Analysis to the latest form of output budgeting and programme planning, is their ability to 'foresee the future' with greater reliability than the unaided human brain. The difficulty was never the guessing what was likely to happen (other things being equal) if one did x rather than y, but the intractability of things that would not stay equal; one could work out in one's head (or even on paper) what effect a likely change in a would have on the probable range of values of b consequent upon a stated variation in the size of c, only to a limited number of variables, if one

worked at it for a year. Networking, or in general, 'planning' techniques, and the 'estimating' (as distinct from the control) side of
budgeting, with the aid of machines and computers, enormously
increase the human capacity to look ahead (see Lockyer, 1969;
Stewart, 1969; Argenti, 1969; etc.)

Thirdly; there are nevertheless times when the choice that has
to be made is perfectly plain, and the consequences of each option
predictable within small degrees of error, and yet the decision is a
difficult one because we cannot easily tell which outcome we prefer;
or perhaps, we prefer some bits of one outcome and some bits of
another, but do not know how to weigh them against one another.
Where much hangs on such decisions—for instance, large-scale and
long-term capital investment—it is obviously better that *all* the
consequences, desirable and undesirable, are brought into consideration, since the absolute size of a small error of omission might be
quite large in the future; and this is not only a matter of calculating
probabilities in stochastic networks, but of finding bases for weigh-
ing one outcome against another, and of envisaging surprising outcomes. This is the realm of the body of economics techniques known
generally as 'rescource allocation', for which 'cost/benefit analysis'
is the best-known name. Of course, cost/benefit analysts will use
'networking' techniques and Operational Research teams will employ cost/effectiveness techniques, and so on, if they seem fruitful
for the work in hand. My distinction between the three classes of
decision aid is a device of presentation (see Feldstein, 1964; Arrow
and Scitovsky, 1969; Walsh and Williams, 1969; Mishan, 1971;
Keeling, 1972; etc.).

Theories of the administrative process

Another stream of administrative theory aimed at an explanation
of the 'administrative process' in organisations, purporting to
describe the stages or elements of decision making and implementing
the decisions afterwards. We will look at some of them: those of
Gulick, Litchfield, March and Simon, Lindblom, Downs, and
Vickers.

Luther Gulick's celebrated mnemonic for 'the work of the chief
executive', POSDCORB, was derived from Fayol, and appeared in
'Notes on the Theory of Organization' (Gulick, 1937, 13). The word
is made up of initial letters:

Planning, that is, working out in broad outlines the things that need to be done and the methods for doing them to accomplish the purpose set for the enterprise;

Organizing, that is, the establishment of the formal structure of authority through which work subdivisions are arranged, defined and co-ordinated for the defined objective;

Staffing, that is, the whole personnel function of bringing in and training the staff and maintaining favourable conditions of work;

Directing, that is, the continuous task of making decisions and embodying them in specific and general orders and instructions and serving as the leader of the enterprise;

Co-ordinating, that is, the all-important duty of inter-relating the various parts of the work;

Reporting, that is, keeping those to whom the executive is responsible informed as to what is going on, which thus includes keeping himself and his subordinates informed through records, research, and inspection;

Budgeting, with all that goes with budgeting in the form of fiscal planning, accounting, and control.

In a complex enterprise founded on sub-division of work among specialised units, Gulick says, co-ordination is essential. Experience shows, however, that co-ordination may be achieved in two primary ways:

1. By organization, that is, by inter-relating the subdivisions of work by allotting them to men who are placed in a structure of authority, so that the work may be co-ordinated by orders of superiors to subordinates, reaching from the top to the bottom of the entire enterprise.

2. By the dominance of an idea, that is, the development of intelligent singleness of purpose in the minds and wills of those who are working together as a group, so that each worker will of his own accord fit his task into the whole with skill and enthusiasm.

These two principles of co-ordination are not mutually exclusive, in fact no enterprise is really effective without the extensive utilization of both (*Gulick, 1937, 6*).

Here Gulick is shown prescient: the 'Notes' move towards the idea that

the more important and the more difficult part of co-ordination is to be sought not through systems of authority, but through ideas and persuasion, and ... the absurdities of the hierarchical system are made sweet and reasonable through unity of purpose (*Gulick, 1937, 39*).

But it was the first of these two methods of 'co-ordination' that represented the 'commonsense' assumption about implementation of decisions in organisations: orders were given at the top, and filtered down through the hierarchy to those at the bottom who actually did the work.

Litchfield (1956) began from what, in historical perspective, might seem a rather odd judgement:

> ... so far are we from broad generalizations about administration that we appear to maintain that there is not a generic administrative process but only a series of isolated types of administration. We seem to be saying that there is business administration and hospital administration, hotel administration, and school administration. But there is no administration (*1956, 7*).

What he is saying in 1956 is what Simon was saying in 1955, that reaction from the 'universal principles' school of the 1920s and 1930s has gone too far; the baby has gone out with the bathwater.

> That circumstances modify administrative activity we concede, but we must go further and affirm our view that administration is not only a constant and universal in some respects but is also a variable in an equation of action; that one of its fundamental characteristics is its relationship to the other variables in that equation. Beyond this we must articulate those other variables so that we may understand their interrelationship (*Litchfield, 1956, 9*).

Moreover, thoughts should be 'set forth in straightforward propositions which we may then establish, modify, or destroy as research or more careful analysis may dictate' (1956, 10). There was urgent need for codifying existing knowledge, as a guide to further research, and as a measure of practical performance in administration. But what Litchfield was able to put forward is not itself a 'general theory of administration', merely a series of working hypotheses or propositions, major and minor, some of which ran as follows (the supporting descriptive paragraphs are omitted):

> *First Major Proposition.* The administrative process is a cycle of action which includes the following specific activities: A. Decision making. B. Programming. C. Communicating. D. Controlling. E. Reappraising. (Followed by A again.)
> *Minor Propositions.* Decision making may be rational, deliberative, discretionary, purposive, or it may be irrational, habitual, obligatory, random, or any combination thereof. In its rational,

deliberative, discretionary, and purposive form, it is performed by means of the following subactivities: a. Definition of the issue. b. Analysis of the existing situation. c. Calculation and delineation of alternatives. d. Deliberation. e. Choice.
—Decisions become guides to action after they have been interpreted in the form of specific programs.
—The effectiveness of a programmed decision will vary with the extent to which it is communicated to those of whom action is required ...
Second Major Proposition. The administrative process functions in the areas of: A. Policy. B. Resources. C. Execution.
Minor Proposition. Action in each functional area is accomplished by means of the action cycle previously described ...
Third Major Proposition. The administrative process is carried on in the context of a larger action system, the dimensions of which are: A. The administrative process. B. The individual performing the administrative process. C. The total enterprise within which the individual performs the process. D. The ecology within which the individual and the enterprise function.
Minor Propositions. While constant in basic structure, the administrative process will vary in important aspects, depending i. upon the personality of the person performing it; ii. upon the character of the total enterprise within which it is performed; iii. upon the environment in which the individual and total enterprise function ...
Fourth Major Proposition. Administration is the performance of the administrative process by an individual or a group in the context of an enterprise functioning in its environment.
Minor Propositions. Administration as totality has definable attributes. They are: a. It seeks to perpetuate itself. b. It seeks to preserve its internal well-being. c. It seeks to preserve itself vis-a-vis others. d. It seeks growth ...
Fifth Major Proposition. Administration and the administrative process occur in substantially the same generalized form in industrial, commercial, civil, educational, military, and hospital organizations (*Litchfield, 1956*).

Litchfield's debt to Parsons is clear and acknowledged: this is a 'systems model', using the three levels of individual, enterprise, and environment in conscious parallel to Parson's personal, social, and cultural levels of action (Parsons and Shils, 1951). But its mixture of structural elements (the 'cycle' of the administrative process, the subactivities of the decision process, the 'areas' of operation of the administrative process, 'function' being there used in a non-Parsonian sense) with purely empirical, or normative, generalisations that are no part of the model as such (habitual, random, etc.

decisions, enforcement of standards of performance, the self-per-petuating drives, and so on) helps to obscure the model and gets sadly in the way of Litchfield's purpose. At any rate, this attempt at the outlines of a 'general theory' did not arouse enthusiasm in the profession, and there were few direct imitators.

March and Simon (1958) also were concerned to express their thoughts in testable hypotheses, and used an elaborate apparatus to assist this; but their understanding of the process we are inter-ested in must be pieced together.

A decision maker always exercises choice within a limited, approximate, simplified 'model' of the real situation (1958, 139). Presented situations evoke responses that can be of a routinised kind, a simple stimulus triggering off a possibly quite elaborate 'programme' of performed activities that have been previously learned as being appropriate to that situation; or else the response can be one of search, aimed at discovering action options or their consequences, or solving problems (140). Most human decision making, whether individual or organisational, is concerned with the discovery and selection of satisfactory alternatives; only in excep-tional cases is it concerned with the discovery and selection of optimal alternatives (141). But more than that: situations in which a relatively simple stimulus sets off an elaborate programme of activity without any apparent interval of search, problem-solving, or choice, are not rare; they account for a very large part of the behaviour of persons in relatively routine positions. Most behaviour in organisations is governed by such 'performance programmes' (142). The whole pattern of programmed activity in an organisation is a complicated mosaic of programme executions, each initiated by its appropriate programme-evoking step (149). Any organisation possesses a repertory of programmes that, collectively, can deal in a goal-oriented way with a range of situations. New situations are usually coped with by a recombination of lower-level programmes already in existence (150). Higher-level action of this kind involves a complex interweaving of affective and cognitive processes: what a person wants and likes influences what he sees, what he sees in-fluences what he wants and likes (151).

Information is necessarily filtered and selected in many ways, and knowledge may be 'stipulated fact'—the 'official version'—or so summarised that the uncertainties present in the raw data are removed and what are really interpretations are treated as 'facts' (155). One particular form of summarisation is classification; this can be combined with repertories of performance programme, so that once a situation has been assigned to a particular class, the appropriate action programme can be applied to it. Such repertories of performance programmes, and the requisite habits and skills for their use, appear to make up the largest part of professional and vocational training (155). Organisation structure consists simply of those aspects of the pattern of behaviour in the organisation that are relatively stable and that change only slowly (170).

There is a great deal more that is relevant, concerning the processes of search and innovation in decision making, communication, and the 'division of work' problem in organisation structure. But perhaps enough has been quoted to show the nature of the March and Simon approach. More is owed to the Watson-Skinner school of behavioural psychology than to any school of sociology (nothing to Parsons—we are in a rival camp); and although the elements of Litchfield's cycle can be detected, they do not form a cycle and the 'process' has no separable existence. The emphasis is upon the ongoing pattern of routine performance programmes, which can be modified and recombined to meet change in the external situation, as perceived by the actors, each operating in his own network of influences, understandings and channels of filtered information.

Charles Lindblom's contribution, originally made in papers in economics journals in 1958, but achieving wider circulation in an article entitled 'The Science of Muddling Through' (1959), and developed in later books (1963; 1965; 1968), was to question both the realism and the desirability of the ideal-type of decision-making suggested by Simon and used by many who followed, including Litchfield—even when modified in the direction of 'limited rationality'. The argument is succinctly put in a paper by Hirschman and Lindblom (1962):

> Lindblom's point of departure is a denial of the general validity of two assumptions implicit in most of the literature on policy making. The first is that public policy problems can best be solved by attempting to understand them; the second is that there exists sufficient agreement to provide adequate criteria for choosing among possible alternative policies. Although the first is widely accepted—in many circles almost treated as a self-evident truth—it is often false. The second is more often questioned in contemporary social science; yet many of the most common prescriptions for rational problem solving follow only if it is true.
>
> Conventional descriptions of rational decision making identify the following aspects: (a) clarification of objectives or values,

(b) survey of alternative means of reaching objectives, (c) identification of consequences, including side-effects of by-products, of each alternative means, and (d) evaluation of each set of consequences in the light of the objectives (*Hirschman and Lindblom, 1962, 215*).

Such a form of decision-making Lindblom regards as only one type, and he calls it *synoptic*. He then follows Simon in pointing out how impossible a process it is; necessary information being either unobtainable, unreliable, or inordinately expensive; the complexity of the variables to be held in the mind or of the calculations to be made, rapidly outrunning human capacity even when machine-aided; and stressing perhaps more than Simon how often clarification even of simple and proximate goals founders on social conflict. Synoptic decision making might, nevertheless, be held as a sort of ideal to be always approached as closely as feasible (this might be Simon's reaction); but Lindblom points out that this not only does not follow of logical necessity, but is not the strategy of decision making most often found in practice. The kinds of thing that are most often done, he suggests, are these:

1. Attempts at understanding are limited to policies that differ only incrementally from existing policy.
2. Instead of simply adjusting means to ends, ends are chosen that are appropriate to available or nearly available means.
3. A relatively small number of means (alternative possible policies) is considered, as follows from 1.
4. Instead of comparing alternative means or policies in the light of postulated ends or objectives, alternative ends or objectives are also compared in the light of postulated means or policies and their consequences.
5. Ends and means are chosen simultaneously: the choice of means does not follow the choice of ends.
6. Ends are indefinitely explored, reconsidered, discovered, rather than relatively fixed.
7. At any given analytical point ('point' refers to any one individual, group, agency, or institution), analysis and policy making are serial or successive; that is, problems are not 'solved' but are repeatedly attacked.
8. Analysis and policy making are remedial—they move away from ills rather than toward known objectives.
9. At any one analytical point, the analysis of consequences is quite incomplete.
10. Analysis and policy making are socially fragmented; they go on at a very large number of separate points simultaneously (*Hirschman and Lindblom, 1962, 215*).

This type of decision making Lindblom called 'disjointed incrementalism'. It should not be thought that Simon would necessarily take issue with Lindblom on all, or indeed any, of these matters, as empirical descriptions of administrative decision making; parallel statements can be found in Simon's own writing (see particularly, Simon, 1957, 196–206). The main difference between them is that Simon sees men in organisations as 'intendedly rational', whereas Lindblom is concerned to argue that this incremental method is 'safer', and in a democratic society, better in the long run than synoptic 'ideals' which in practice lead to attempts at centralised planning, with its world-wide record of disastrous and costly failure, never mind the effect upon 'freedom':

> ... through various specific types of partisan mutual adjust-ment among the large number of individuals and groups among which analysis and policy making is fragmented, what is ignored at one point in policy making becomes central at another point. Hence, it will often be possible to find a tolerable level of rationality in decision making when the process is viewed as a whole in its social or political context, even if at each individual policy-making point or centre analysis remains incomplete. Similarly, errors that would attend over-ambitious attempts at comprehensive understanding are often avoided by the reme-dial and incremental character of problem solving. And those not avoided can be mopped up or attended to as they appear, because analysis and policy making are serial or successive (*Hirschman and Lindblom, 1962, 216*).

Lindblom is throughout concerned with policy making aspects, to the virtual exclusion of implementation or execution aspects, of administrative organisation. The influence of classical economic theory of the market can be plainly seen in his ideas of 'partisan mutual adjustment', or accommodations among decision makers each pursuing his own interests. It was another economist, equally interested in decision theory, who said that according to Lindblom 'we do stagger through history like a drunk putting one disjointed incremental foot after another' (Boulding, 1964, 931; quoted in Etzioni, 1967).

Amitai Etzioni, comparing the Simon and Lindblom approaches, sees them complementary rather than alternative. He suggests using incrementalist approaches to the preparation of important decisions, synoptic methods for the decisions themselves, and incrementalism again for implementation and adjustment of detail (Etzioni, 1967). I have myself likened the two approaches to the difference between the use of a panoramic wide-angle lens, and a telephoto or long-focal-length lens, to take a picture of the same scene with the same camera from the same spot. With the first, you can place an object in its setting, and get it in perspective, but you cannot show great detail and landscapes are liable to be distorted; with the second, a small area of the scene can be examined in considerable detail, but the context is lost, and there is foreshortening of distances fore and aft. Switching from one to the other provides Etzioni's 'mixed scanning', and may well be a better analogue of actual administrative decision making than either the unreal 'synoptic' or the overcomfortable 'incremental' approaches.

Gordon Tullock (1965) and Anthony Downs (1967) are two other American economists who have provided accounts of the administrative process inside 'bureaucracies' (not quite synonymous with 'organizations', but not restricted to a Weberian definition either, or to Government Departments). As theories, they can be said to be amalgams of the March and Simon model of the process of internal communication and information processing, with Lindblom incrementalism added. Both books, however, are polemic rather than strictly academic, being consciously directed against the further growth of American federal agencies, by highlighting the Mertonian 'dysfunctions' (Merton, 1949) that accompany growth in size. Neither book shows any deep familiarity with organisation theory literature as it had developed by then; the writers make their own comparisons of the 'classic' theory with 'reality', and on many points write somewhat as 'primitive' painters paint. But Downs' analysis of the hierarchical goal structure that a single decision maker brings to any problem, his concept of 'free information' (that is, as it were, 'in the air' and absorbed by the decision maker from radio and TV, from conversation with friends, and in the comings and goings of their daily work, apart from 'official channels') that provides a minimum of constant, involuntary 'search', and his spelling out of the 'translation' function in implementation of orders, are among his real contributions to the theory of the administrative process.

As noted earlier (p. 10 above), Sir Henry Taylor had in 1836 sketched a fairly complete theory of the 'feedback' process, by which 'crude' information collected at operative levels has to be refined 'by a system of filtration', and move stage by stage upwards, 'more and more digested and generalised in its progress', until it is in a form that can initiate a change in policy. March and Simon noted that this process involved 'uncertainty absorption'. What Downs (to some extent following Tullock) shows is that the process in the opposite direction, the transmission of orders downwards from top to lower levels, involves a sort of 'uncertainty injection' (although he does not use any such term). We assume a hierarchy of officials, arranged in seven levels, with A at the top and typical officials B, C, D, E, F, and G at successively lower levels:

> ...the orders of top-level officials to their subordinates are almost always relatively broad in nature...[A gives an order]
>
> When B receives this order, he begins translating it into more specific directions for lower-level officials. But B also has limited time for this task; hence he too must delegate the details to his C-level subordinates, and so on down the hierarchy. Finally, the general policy issued by A becomes transformed into specific actions performed by G-level personnel.
>
> In this process, orders from the top must be expanded and made more specific as they move downward. There are a number of different ways in which these orders can be made more specific at each level, and each official has some lee-way in selecting the one he will follow. Even if his superior has merely ordered him to propose a set of alternatives, an official exercises discretion in designing the choices he will present.
>
> The result is that the policies of any organization are defined at all levels, not just at the top, as Chester Barnard has pointed out. At every level, there is a certain discretionary gap between the orders an official receives and those he issues downwards, and every official is forced to exercise discretion in interpreting his superior's orders. These orders are a form of information flowing downward through the hierarchy, just as reports are a form of information flowing upward. In passing information upward, intermediary officials must translate data received into more general and more condensed form. In passing orders downward, they must translate commands received into more specific and expanded form. This symmetry occurs simply because there are many more people at the bottom than at the top (*Downs, 1967, 133–4*).

I would not myself say that is the 'simple' reason for the 'symmetry'; rather is it a matter of the 'level of consideration', of the successively broader 'width of view' that is required as one moves upward, necessitating the bringing together of different kinds of information and hence the reduction in bulk of each kind so as not to overload the higher level. (My own view is that, on the way downward, the interpretation, or expansion of an order is done more by the lower level after an order has been transmitted, than on an upper level before it is phrased for 'passing downwards'; these points are elaborated in a forthcoming book on the execution process.)

There is, of course, much room for both genuine misunderstanding and wilful distortion in a process like this; and Downs has earlier shown how distortions can occur on the upward passage (Downs, 1967, 116). Now he goes on to demonstrate mathematically that if at each level in the B to G chain there is a 'transmission error' (from whatever cause) of only 10 per cent, then of all the work done by G-level employees, only 53 per cent will be even *aimed at* accomplishing the policy goals set for the organisation by A (Downs, 1967, 134; Tullock, 1965, 140).

Sir Geoffrey Vickers (1965) has written an enormously stimulating book on decision-making which acknowledges freely his debt to H. A. Simon and yet is a contribution in its own right. Vickers is concerned, however, with the policy making aspects primarily ('appreciation', in his term), rather than the execution or 'instrumental' aspects, and he says comparatively little about the 'administrative process' as a whole. But he adds a vitally important insight to this question of the relationship between superior and subordinate, in the translation of policy into instructions. Vickers' basic model is a cybernetic one, and policy making is for him a matter of regulating, optimising, and balancing: 'every decision-making body is to be regarded as a regulator of the dynamic system of which it forms part' (Vickers, 1965, 25), though 'regulation' at social level is a very complex matter, and 'policy making and execution... describe phases in the regulative cycle, rather than different kinds of decision or decision maker' (Vickers, 1965, 41). Then there follows one of the pregnant analogies in which the book is rich:

> In human regulators the two phases are notably interlocked; for the development of the power of appreciation makes it possible for executive action to be tried out hypothetically before it is submitted to the test of actual experience, and such hypothetical appreciation provides in fact by far the most abundant and cogent body of feedback to which such regulators respond. Each solution proposed by executive judgement is appraised, not merely as a solution to the problem which evoked it, but also for its impact on other problems which it may make easier or harder of solution. Thus the criteria by which one solution is preferred to another cannot be derived merely from the problem set. The 'executive' even at the simplest level is never wholly relieved of the problem of 'optimizing-balancing' which is the hall-mark of policy making (*Vickers, 1965, 42*).

The cybernetic framework, where the ever-present metaphor is that of the steersman being given and holding the ship on a course by means of stars or compass, provides a crucial distinction between the setting of goals and the setting of standards:

> I have described policy making as the setting of governing relations or norms, rather than in the more usual terms as the setting of goals, objectives or ends. The difference is not merely verbal; I regard it as fundamental. I believe that great confusion results from the common assumption that all course-holding can be reduced to the pursuit of an endless succession of goals . . . goal-setting is a distinct form of regulation, with its own specific mechanisms; a form less important, in my view, than norm-setting . . .' (*Vickers, 1965, 31–2*).

The ship's 'goal' is perhaps getting to a particular port; getting it there safely, etc., is the *standard* by which the captain will be judged. But the helmsman, indispensable though he may be to the captain's purposes, is not judged by them, but by standards applicable to him; he may have a goal (continued employment, perhaps promotion), but he is judged by how reliably he keeps a course and so on. Performance is not measured against a goal, but against a standard—which, in some cases, might be 'expected degree of achievement of given goal'—and this is both more difficult to set, and more important, than the setting of the goal.

Vickers' book is now recognised in Britain as one of the bases for a new departure in political science, known as 'policy analysis' or 'public policy making'—which, although in some quarters it is subsumed under Public Administration, takes us into a different field from that of the present section (Braybrooke and Lindblom, 1963; Dror, 1967, 1968, 1971; Lyden *et. al.*, 1968; Ranney, 1968; Sharkansky, 1970a, 1970b; in Britain, Barnett, 1969; Chapman, 1969; Richardson, 1969; Rose, 1969; Self, 1972. For a review of 'policy analysis', Heclo, 1972). The best recent British treatment on a general level is R. G. S. Brown's excellent text *The Administrative Process in Britain* (1970)—the title, however, being used to cover a much wider field than is intended by the title of the present section.

Science, knowledge, and understanding

The new 'administrative science' of the 1950s and early 1960s embraced the post-Hawthorne 'human relations' work, the theory of organisations, decision theory, and post-Weberian bureaucracy theory (to which we will return in another context). A good impression of the scope can be got from the contents pages of the first few issues of the journal *Administrative Science Quarterly*, begun in 1956:

'Notes on a General Theory of Administration' (Litchfield)
'Contributions to Administration by Alfred P. Sloan Jr. and GM' (Dale)
'Suggestions for a Sociological Approach to the Theory of Organizations' (Parsons)
'A Problem in Soviet Business Administration' (Berliner)
'On Building an Administrative Science' (Thompson)
'Small Groups and Administrative Organizations' (Demarath and Thibaut)
'Perspectives on Administration in Psychiatric Hospitals' (Caudill)
'A Critical Appraisal of the Study of Administration' (Millett)
'Organizational Contrasts on British and American Ships' (Richardson)
'Position Conflict and Professional Orientation in a Research Organization' (McEwen)
'Dysfunctional Consequences of Performance Measurements' (Ridgway)

The third issue was given over to problems of Research Administration; the final number of the first volume was more typical:

'Community Decision Making' (Rossi)
'Hospital Administration—One of a Species' (Lentz)
'Administration of Manufacturer-Dealer Systems' (Ridgway)
'Organizational Size' (Caplow)
'Executives and Supervisors: Contrasting Definitions of Career Success' (Pellegrin and Coates)

Volume 2 contained many now-celebrated articles:

'The Individual and Organization: Some Problems of Mutual Adjustment' (Argyris)
'Power and Union-Management Relations' (Dublin)
'Traditional and Behavioral Research in American Political Science' (Easton)
'Cosmopolitans and Locals: Toward an Analysis of Latent Social Roles' (Gouldner)
'A Communication Model for Administration' (Dorsey)
'Technology, Organization, and Administration' (Thompson and Bates).

The 'ASQ' attempted to straddle the intellectual divide referred to in Easton's article, the sometimes bitter controversy between the 'traditionalists' and the 'behavioralists', which we ought to notice here (albeit reluctantly) not so much for its own sake as because it was antecedent to a continuing debate that is relevant to the next chapter. Any attempt to simplify this controversy will misrepresent it, usually in the direction of saying what, if its protagonists had been clear-headed enough, it ought to have been about.

'Behaviorism'—without the 'al'—is a doctrine in psychology associated with the names of Watson, Pavlov, and Skinner, which eschews all speculation about what may go on in the 'thought processes' of an organism and sticks to observation of what a subject actually does—what can be observed by an outside observer; hence the investigation of animal learning processes by means of salivating dogs, rats in mazes, and pigeons in a laboratory. The theoretical basis is a correlation of response with stimulus, as mediated by the experience of the organism—so-called $S \rightarrow O \rightarrow R$ Theory. In March and Simon's book *Organizations* (1958), the foundation in stimulus organism-response theory is explicit (p. 9). But most of the writers who might have accepted the label 'behavioralist' did not take things quite so literally; they borrowed what they saw as an outlook, a mental set or attitude towards evidence and 'proof', a language which rejected mumbo-jumbo—in which they were clearly descendants of the eighteenth century 'Enlightenment', of Benthamite 'utilitarianism', and of the more recent approaches exemplified in A. F. Bentley's scorn for 'soul-stuff' in political analysis, and A. J. Ayer's philosophical positivism. Over-correction, however, appeared in the uncritical adulation of 'scientific method' as, it was thought, was applied in the 'exact sciences', physics and chemistry—in an idealised form (Gunnell, 1969, 148); and the rejection of 'metaphysics'. Dwight Waldo described 'behavioralism' as 'an attempt to move from the philosophical to the positive, the empirical, the existentialist' (Waldo, 1964, 7); David Easton adds (in 'The Current Meaning of "Behavioralism" in Political Science') the assertion that 'behavioralism' looks not only for empirical rigour but for a *unity* in the whole of the social sciences, a single conceptual framework, a stable unit or coin of discourse which would transcend subject frontiers (Charlesworth, 1962, 7). One such coin was found, perhaps: the concept of 'system'. But it is hardly an observable or scientifically detectable entity. We will discuss the problems associated with its use in the next chapter.

The 'traditionalists', in so far as they form a coherent school at all, linked by more than a shared scepticism about the possibility of 'a social science' and scorn at the gap between their opponents' precepts and their example (Storing, for instance, taunted Simon with preferring logic to magic, though any grounds for doing so could not be 'behavioral' (Storing, 1962)), were inclined to see the necessity for 'deeper' explanations of the conduct of men in historical situations than could be inferred from merely external observation of events. What a man does in a specific situation depends upon how he sees that situation; that is to say, he is *selecting* what is to be his 'stimulus', and his response cannot be understood, or used as a 'fact' in an appreciation of his role as an actor amongst other actors, unless an observer can somehow arrive at an understanding of his subjective state of mind, the meanings he gives to his perceptions. This is the normal outlook of the historian, seeking to 'get inside the skin' of his actors ('Namierism', the meticulous assembly of verifiable facts about, for instance, an eighteenth-century House of Commons, is history's 'behaviouralism'); but this traditional method was given a measure of rigour (and perhaps 'respectability') by the careful attention of some sociologists, particularly Max Weber. The German word *Verstehen*, meaning simply 'understanding', has come to stand in methodological literature for this method of imputing meaning into an event, using whatever knowledge of comparative and historical circumstance is available, in order to generate a hypothesis which, in suitable conditions, may then be tested against 'the concrete course of events', or where these conditions do not obtain, by an 'imaginary experiment'—which, however, Weber himself called a 'dangerous and uncertain procedure' (Weber, 1947, 97; Fletcher, 1971, II, 428, 434). Thus, although it perhaps over-clarifies (and certainly reduces) the conflict, the difference between the behaviouralists and the traditionalists in political and administrative science can be seen as an epistemological one, with the traditionalists (no doubt to their surprise) lining up with Weber, Parsons, and the sociologists of their school—at least temporarily (Charlesworth, 1962; Ranney, 1962; Storing, 1962; Eulau, 1963; Dahl, 1961).

CHAPTER EIGHT

The Rise of
Comparative Administration

If the 'behaviouralist' controversy can be seen as a storm in a Common Room teacup, the same cannot be said of another intellectual development of the 1950s, the equivalent in scholarship of the ending of 'isolationism' in foreign policy; and indeed, to no small degree brought about by the outgoing generosity of American aid and technical assistance programmes, first to Europe and Asia, and then to virtually all parts of the world.

There is a (by now) standard account of the 'rise of Comparative Administration' (Riggs, 1962; Waldo, 1964; Heady, 1966; Henderson, 1966; etc.), in which the three major turning points are seen as (i) Woodrow Wilson's essay 'The Study of Administration' in 1887, (ii) Robert Dahl's article 'The Science of Public Administration: Three Problems' in 1947, and (iii) the symposium *Toward the Comparative Study of Public Administration* edited by W. J. Siffin in 1957, which contained Fred Riggs' essay 'Agraria and Industria'.

The spirit of Wilson's essay (from which a key passage has already been quoted—see p. 88 above) was epitomised in the title of Dorman B. Eaton's influential book, *Civil Service in Great Britain: a History of Abuses and Reforms and Their Bearing Upon American Politics* (1880). Comparisons with other countries could yield suggestions for improvement in one's own, because the process was seen as relatively constant, though the setting and the purpose be entirely different. Even if this assumption were mistaken, the outcomes were relatively harmless at that time, because of the degree of adaptation that accompanied the empirical borrowing. Addition of the 'scientific management' assumptions produced the development of universalist principles into 'administrative techniques' which, by contrast, were transferable as they stood, like principles of engineering. In the years between Goodnow's *Politics and Administration* in 1900 and the first programmes of technical assistance to developing countries in the 'Third World', the 'principles' approach had had time to become thoroughly orthodox; the logical gap between descriptive theory and prescriptive blueprint, between regularity and regulation, had been so well bridged as to have all but disappeared.

There had been scholarly dissent, as far back as John Gaus' contribution to the Gaus, White and Dimock collection *The Frontiers of Public Administration* in 1936, entitled 'American Society and Public Administration'; but it took explicit shape in a volley of publications in 1947; another Gaus lecture (Gaus, 1947), on 'The Ecology of Government'; a seminal sentence or two in Waldo's trail-blazing book *The Administrative State* (1948, 189); but above all, Dahl's article, wherein the 'third problem' is that 'we cannot afford to ignore the relationship between public administration and its social setting':

> There should be no reason for supposing, then, that a principle of public administration has equal validity in every nation-state, or that successful public administration practices in one country will necessarily prove successful in a different social, economic, and political environment. A particular nation-state embodies the results of many historical episodes, traumas, failures, and successes, which have in turn created peculiar habits, mores, institutionalized patterns of behaviour, *Weltanschauungen*, and even 'national psychologies'. One cannot assume that public administration can escape the effects of this conditioning; or that it is somehow independent of and isolated from the culture or social setting in which it develops . . .
>
> These conclusions suggest themselves:
>
> 1. Generalizations derived from the operations of public administration in the environment of one nation-state cannot be universalized and applied to public administration in a different environment . . .
>
> 2. There can be no truly universal generalizations about public administration without a profound study of varying national and social characteristics impinging on public administration, to determine what aspects of public administration, if any, are truly independent of the national and social setting. Are there discoverable principles of *universal* validity, or are all principles valid only in terms of a special environment?
>
> 3. It follows that the study of public administration inevitably must become a much more broadly based discipline, resting not on a narrowly defined knowledge of techniques and processes, but rather extending to the varying historical, sociological, economic, and other conditioning factors that give public administration its peculiar stamp in each country. (*Dahl, 1947, 11*).

It was in 1948 (December) that the United Nations General Assembly passed a resolution that recognised the need in the less developed countries for training in public administration, and programmes were begun in 1950. In 1951 the Public Administration Division of the Technical Assistance Administration was established, and its programme included not only training of officials but 'advice and assistance to governments in the improvement of public administration'. The Public Administration Division of the United States Technical Cooperation Administration (later the Foreign Operations Administration, the International Cooperation Administration, and the Agency for International Development) was founded in 1955. The first of several contracts made directly between American universities and overseas countries was made by the University of Michigan with the Philippines in 1952. Paul Appleby's consultancy in India in 1951 was among several supported by the Ford Foundation. One way and another, then, scores of American professors of political science and Public Administration were sent abroad in the years 1950–60; and even if some of them were aware of Dahl's article, they found themselves with nothing to replace the 'tried and tested' principles of good administrative practice in which they had been brought up. Weidner (1964) produces instance after instance of intellectual bankruptcy, and worse. But the experience was traumatic: scores of American professors became personally aware of a whole universe of ways in which the 'universal principles' did not fit, indeed were almost totally useless.

The search was on for some scheme, some framework to render manageable the mass of new information coming from the developing countries. The search merged with another, starting from dissatisfaction amongst teachers of comparative politics with the old syllabuses which, typically, consisted of serial studies of Britain (for US students; USA for British students), France, Germany, Italy, and Soviet Russia, built up from the work of scholars specialising in these countries, and related in a general fashion to the constitution and politics of the base country by the use of categories such as Single Chamber and Two Chamber Legislatures, Parliamentary and Presidential Executives, Two-party and Multi-party Systems, and so on. Teachers found that these methods offered little help in understanding such events as the collapse of the Weimar Republic and the rise of the European dictatorships, and no help at all in even describing the virulent politics of the colonial and post-colonial countries. *Sui generis* accounts of each country, on the other hand, would not offer a basis for comparisons. What was wanted, therefore, was a better scheme for the recognition of types, or 'polities' (Aristotle's word came back into vogue), hopefully one that would meet the stringent requirements of 'science'—a thing to compare, in two specimens, while something else is held constant:

> to compare political institutions and functions in the sense that a common denominator for diversified phenomena is found and deviations from the standard pattern are explained (*Loewenstein, 1944, 542*).

The signs of breakthrough came with Riggs' 'Agraria and Industria' (1957), and what would be generally accepted as the key work in the new comparative politics, Almond and Coleman's *The Politics of the Developing Areas* (1960).

Systems, structures, and functions

The way forward was this. Using the basic concepts of the sociologists Talcott Parsons and Marion Levy, the new wave of comparative politics scholars began to study not political institutions but societies or 'cultures'—wholes made up of parts kept together by mutually beneficial interaction. Certain aspects of such interactions can then be distinguished, so that, conceptually, a society cannot sustain itself unless they are present; these are the 'functional requisites' of *any* society, that can provide a constant, or common denominator. There can also be distinguished in any particular society certain enduring or recurrent patterns of discrete behaviours (routines, customs, 'institutions' in the sociologist's sense) that can be called 'structures', which are typical of that society and different from those of another. It can then be shown that structures which may look alike in two different societies actually perform different societal functions, and structures which may look very different are found to perform essentially the same function. A function may be discharged by a single structure in one culture, by a complex of many structures in another. Although the logic of it is not impeccable, it is a powerful conceptual tool.

Some 'functional requisites' of a society can be grouped together in 'systems'—the economic system, the political system, the social system, and so on. The 'political system' is recognised by noting the structures which incorporate the society's mechanisms for (amongst other things) controlling the use of violence. Adapting then an input/output model pioneered by David Easton for the description of the American political system (Easton, 1953, 1965), Almond isolated seven essential political functions: four requisites for system creation and support (inputs: political socialisation and recruitment, interest articulation, interest aggregation, and political communication), and three expressive of the system's action upon its environment, the society (outputs: rule-making, rule-application, and rule adjudication).

Riggs, in the comparative administration movement, had trod the same path. Most of the flavour of Riggs' evocative and inventive writing—and it is exceedingly voluminous—is lost in boiling down; but his best-known contribution is a scale or spectrum on which whole cultures (not 'political systems') can be ranked, and the teasing out of the implications for administrative behaviour that he can then demonstrate.

Starting from F. X. Sutton rather than from Parsons, Riggs employed a version of structure/function analysis, along with some communication theory, as did the comparative politics scholars. In a tradition of sociology that goes back to Spencer, he pointed out that some kinds of society (the 'traditional', mainly unindustrialised) betrayed characteristic structure/function relationships: there are comparatively few social roles or institutions, each (in Western eyes) performing a great many social functions. As a father even in a Western family is 'everything' in his family circle by turns or indistinguishably—breadwinner, teacher, playmate, rule-maker, rule-applier, rule adjudicator, and several more; so in the traditional society this family-like relationship is found in larger social groupings, and in government of 'the State' as a whole. 'Officials' draw their authority from being known to be of the household of the king or chief; they expect and receive deference, and form a powerful class in themselves. Their governing is the compound of shrewd self-preservation, manipulation, whim and mercy that is associated with royal 'despotism'.

Advanced industrialised Western societies are, by contrast, highly differentiated and specialised, with a great profusion of separate structures each performing a single function or small aspect of a function, and a phobia against 'overlapping' of these jurisdictions. Relationships are articulated, specific, and highly rule-governed. Achievement rather than status is respected, and government officials receive no deference and rank somewhat lower than successful businessmen.

Contrasts between the traditional and the modern societies (which in Riggs bear remarkable resemblances to Thailand and the United

States of America respectively) extend to their ways of knowing things, their ideas of truth, their concepts of reality, their language *rules*, and so on. If one sums all this up in the contrast between ritual and 'rational' modes, one misses the impact of Riggs' fascinating extended *obiter dicta*—the following, perhaps, on training for officials in 'Agraria' and 'Industria', his earliest ideal-types of the traditional and the modern society:

> Since the bureaucracy in Industria is segmented into occupational classes, each class has its corresponding 'pre-entry' training in which its own specialised jargon and knowledge is imparted. Thus Industrians entering public service will not be trained to be 'humane', 'cultivated' or 'superior' men. Rather, they will be lawyers, foresters, engineers, budgetary technicians, and accountants, representing the diverse fields into which Industrian knowledge is divided.

But in Agraria, we will

> expect that everyone preparing for administrative élite roles will obtain a roughly equivalent education.

Knowledge will concern correct conduct or behaviour more largely than truth or facts:

> ... religion and ethics, codes of etiquette, of 'chivalry' or 'bushido', the qualities of 'nobility', 'humanism' or 'urbanity' ... history will be taught chiefly for its moral lessons and its 'inspiration'. The content of knowledge in Industria, by contrast, will largely concern propositions for which tangible 'proof' is offered, and the learning of demonstrable techniques and methods whereby accepted goals can be implemented. (*Siffin ed.*, *1957*, *57*).

It may be seen that Britain (the world's first industrial country) is (according to Riggs' theory) emerging but slowly from a traditional into a modern mode in the training of élite civil servants.

Of greatest interest to Riggs is the 'developing' society which is at neither end of this scale. By a grossly ill-fitting analogy with the prism which is interposed between 'fused' white light and the 'diffracted' rainbow of all the colours, he named the intermediate society 'prismatic'—halfway between fused or undifferentiated societies and diffracted or modern societies with high internal specialisation. In prismatic societies, people hold two ideals at once, switching from the traditional set of behaviours to the modern without apparent embarrassment or confusion. Conflict between the two is not often articulated, but is recognised by the acceptance of an endemic gap between formal expectations and actual behaviour.

In a sub-model Riggs brings together the implications for the ambience of bureaucratic decision making, which in general is the 'bureau', but for which he suggests three types in respectively the traditional, the prismatic, and the modern societies: the 'office' in modern parlance, the 'chamber' in traditional, and in the prismatic society the 'sala'—a word much in use in Latin countries to designate 'public rooms', whether in private dwellings or government buildings.

Riggs uses bureau and bureaucratic to include any hierarchic structure of officials, not in any precise Weberian or Crozierian sense. One needs to remember in reading Riggs, then, that although called bureaucrats, officials in traditional bureaucracies do not make rules; decisions in the fused society are particularistic choices, not universalistic policies. Officials choose for themselves whatever norms they think fit; the main concern of the king their superior is his own security and that of his realm, and so long as they remain loyal to him, they may run their own domains as they please. Petty officials under the high officials may have to pay tribute, and otherwise beware the wrath of the mighty (whether superior or 'client'); but they too are unhampered by detailed rules laid down by the centre.

The logical consequences of being a 'sala' rather than a 'chamber' of the above type are explored by Riggs in considerable detail, showing the steps by which institutionalised corruption, nepotism, and general prodigality with public funds can be seen to be implicit in the situation—or at least, in the model. The hypothesis amounts to this: the official in a traditional society is relatively well controlled by, on the one hand, the fear of the immense sanctions in the hands of his superiors, and on the other, the restriction of his social importance in a family-oriented non-industrial society. The bureaucrat in a modern society is relatively well controlled by, on the one hand, the ease by which his departures from rule-governed conduct can be detected by his bureaucratic superiors, and on the other, the specificity and clarity of what is expected of him by the political organs and clientele alike; so that even though the potential power and capacity to affect ordinary living given to the modern official are incalculably greater than those given to the traditional official, so are the capacities of the control organs.

The sala official has ostensibly 'universalistic' policies and goals laid down for him by modernising political organs, but they represent aspirations rather than realistic, achievable standards. From such aims, decision rules can be derived, and an apparatus capable of extensive intervention in economic and social life in imitation of modern bureaucracies can be erected. But where public expectations are ambivalent, where the place of the official is halfway between being 'of the household of the king' and being the servant of the electorate, where political organs are given over to power struggles rather than to control (see Wilson, 1887 (1941), 488; Riggs, 1965, 70; Weidner, 1964, 235), then any rule that is made is as liable as not to become (like the franchise or jurisdiction of the traditional official) the property of the sala official in whose domain it falls, to be applied or not as he sees fit, or as it is made worth his while. The more the apparatus of modern bureaucracy is limited, with internal audit and budgeting and personnel programmes and so on, the more opportunities for conversion are created. The making of rules, the very essence of upright, incorrupt, bureaucratic organisation in the Weberian canon and as we are using it in the present analysis, presents itself in the prismatic society as an insult to traditional mores, and so 'fair game' to half-traditional officials. The traditional sanctions governing the relations between superior and subordinate and between official and client are laid aside as unbefitting a society moving towards the modern; the modern sanctions are still weak and easily shrugged off.

Some features of this model have by now gained almost the status of 'common sense', so immediately enlightening and explanatory are they. There is a large body of empirical work in what has come to be known as 'development administration'; studies of country after country in the Middle East, the Indian sub-continent, South East Asia, Africa, and Latin America, each study self-consciously theoretical and carefully comparative in some particular. Not all scholars in this field are structure/functionalists, or follow 'prismatic' models; some are post-Weberian, some use economic models, one or two begin from organisation and decision theory approaches. But all would accept the 'ecological' assumptions, the only 'universal' being that there are no universals. There is no real sign yet of a swing back from that. (In a voluminous literature, see Riggs, 1961, 1964, 1971; La Palombara, 1963; Swerdlow, 1963; Weidner, 1964, 1970; Montgomery and Siffin, 1966; Braibanti, 1969; Leys, 1969; Waldo, 1970.)

Trends in comparative public administration

In a paper of 1962, Riggs noted three trends in the comparative study of public administration. The first was the trend from normative to empirical approaches. Under normative he described the 'mirror for Americans' style epitomised by Wilson and Eaton, the 'mirror for others' style of the early UN and US bilateral aid 'public administration experts', and an emerging 'mirror for all' style, exemplified by the UN *Handbook of Public Administration* (1961) where, Riggs said, the author tried to synthesise from the 'good' features of several national systems those which might be recommended for general use. (Weidner found this to be a characteristic of UN programme planning; it 'reflects a little bowing in the direction of each of the several major administrative systems of the world' (Weidner, 1964, 29).) Under empirical, Riggs distinguished between two approaches which make the second trend: the shift from idiographic towards nomothetic approaches:

> ... any approach which concentrates on the unique case—
> the historical episode or 'case study', the single agency or
> country, the biography or the 'culture area'—is basically *idio-
> graphic*. By contrast, an approach which seeks generalizations,
> 'laws', hypotheses that assert regularities of behavior, correla-
> tions between variables, may be called *nomothetic* (*Riggs,
> 1962, 11*).

There is an intermediate approach which although idiographic rather than nomothetic is nevertheless comparative: Riggs names it the 'classified data' approach, and instances the work of Finer and Friedrich, and Brian Chapman's *The Profession of Government* (1959). These works, he says, are 'homological': they find similarities and differences of structure for constant function. Others might be 'analogical', and would be concerned with functional variables rather than structural. Some notable modern comparative studies are thus homological idiographic; for instance, Bertram Gross's *Action Under Planning* (1967), A. H. Hanson's studies of public enterprise (1959), Rowat's work on the Ombudsman (1965), and so on. The International Institute of Administrative Sciences has produced some unexciting studies of how the countries of the world deal in statute and regulation and executive process with certain closely-defined problems, such as ascertaining entitlement to compensation for an industrial injury, the prevention of cattle diseases with special reference to foot-and-mouth disease, and the control of river pollution by industry (Spielmeyer, 1965; Heilbronner, 1965; Litwin, 1965). Even to the modern 'lay' reader, let alone the student of comparative public administration, these accounts have an air of superficiality, of truths that are so formal as to be really not truths. It is clear that there are values being glibly assumed to be held constant (so that variations in method can be compared), which are not at all constant over the countries being compared. A proceeding under one country's judicial forms would not be thought to be 'judicial' in another. What is acceptably 'administrative' in one country, where perhaps officials are notably impartial and neutral, would not be tolerated if done by administrators in another. At the extreme of this line of reasoning lies the implications of Professor Vile's remark

> men could be condemned to death, and in some countries are, by an administrative procedure (*Vile, 1967, 347*);

and discussion of the nature of executive values in a totalitarian system, which is matter for another book.

Riggs' own work he characterises as nomothetic and analogical; but his third trend is the shift from all such approaches to the *ecological* approach, which he said in 1962 was as yet 'barely discernible'.

Ferrel Heady, in *Public Administration: A Comparative Perspective* (1966), sought to compare higher civil bureaucracies in a variety of existing political systems, asking the following questions:

1. What are the dominant internal operating characteristics of the bureaucracy reflecting its composition, hierarchical arrangements, pattern of specialization, and behavioral tendencies?
2. To what extent is the bureaucracy multifunctional, participating in the making of major public policy decisions as well as in their execution?
3. What are the principal means for exerting control over the bureaucracy from sources outside it, and how effective are these external controls? (*Heady, 1966, 22*).

He concluded at the end of his book that, although there were still great gaps in the empirical data, we were best prepared to respond on the third question. The dominant interest of recent scholars in comparative public administration has been the political role of civil servants in development, and the relationship of bureaucracies to political organs. On the second question, he thought there was by then fair consensus among scholars as to the relationship between modernity and specificity of bureaucratic function, and bureaucracies in developing countries were apt to be concerned with the Almond input categories as well as all three of the output categories. We are least ready, said Heady,

> to compare the internal operating characteristics of national bureaucracies. Aside from a few Western civil service systems, which have been studied in depth, and a scattering of non-Western systems, the workings of which have been reported much less thoroughly, we have only impressionistic and usually incidental comments to go on. We know little about internal behavioral patterns in individual bureaucracies, or about degrees of consistency or variation among them. This is an area that urgently calls for systematic attention (*Heady, 1966, 106*).

The picture has not changed markedly since 1966 (Marx, 1969; Mackenzie, (1970) 1971).

'*National character*' in administration

One of the Western civil service systems that has been studied in depth is the French, in a book that already ranks as a classic, *The Bureaucratic Phenomenon* by Michel Crozier (1964). Crozier's empirical base was a study of two public organisations, the 'Clerical Agency' and the 'Industrial Monopoly'. The first was in Paris, the work was mainly the processing of application forms in great numbers, and the staff were mainly young girls. (From internal and other evidence, although it is not stated in the book, it is clear that the locale was an office of the Giro, or State money transfer service.) The second was one of a number of identical factories all remote from Paris, each with a work-force divisible into three main groups: machine operators, maintenance engineers, and directing staff. (This was a tobacco manufacturing plant, which in France belongs to a State monopoly.) Crozier's principal method was the free interview.

From the first study, Crozier noted that this force of some 4,500 women had extremely little social interaction in groups other than their formal work-groups; the general atmosphere was dispiriting, the work was routine and of no intrinsic interest, with little scope for any specialisation, and there was virtually no promotion for the girls to work for. So it was a case of the girls' arranging to make life in the Agency tolerable, doing a respectable day's work for one's money but with no sense of commitment to the organisation or one's employers or superiors. Higher authority, in fact, had to be kept in its place; and the means employed were two: an earthy solidarity, without conspicuous comradeship, among work-teams (groups of four); and the arriving at formally-sanctioned conventions, understandings, and rules governing virtually every exchange between superior and subordinate. The latter was assisted by the 'technological' fact that work-flow was influenced mainly by the rate of incoming applications rather than by 'output' requirements, and allocation among teams was fixed by geography; so that supervisors were not (save in crisis) involved much in production control, their main prerogative in other situations. The making of rules, here, was far from being a symbol of the bosses' domination of the workers; rather was it a device employed by the workers for their own protection from 'face-to-face relationships and situations of personal dependency whose authoritarian tone they cannot bear' (Crozier, 1964, 54). And to remove 'authority' from the scene even further, all disciplinary sanctions were in the hands not of the immediate superior, who was seen daily and with whom one 'had to live', but of the rank above that, 'two up', whom one seldom saw and who could safely be the target of displaced hostility. (This applied at all levels up to the Ministerial.)

The main interest of the 'Industrial Monopoly' study lies in its meticulous and subtle analysis of the internal power politics game that was played between the three groups of actors—machinists, technical engineers, and directing staff—and between the managers themselves. Crozier's hypothesis is that a man has power over another if the second's behaviour is more predictable by the first than the first's behaviour is predictable by the second. All the actors are seen as striving to create or preserve an area of discretion within which they can act freely, however small and circumscribed it be. Workers

> restricted by scientific work organisation to a completely stereotyped task use every available means to regain enough unpredictability in their behaviour to enhance their low bargaining power (*Crozier, 1964, 162*)

including the universal device of working at high speed when they feel like it to pile up a stock for when they do not—but not too high a stock, or too frequently, lest it reach the ears of the rate-fixers. Maintenance men would allow no one else to use a tool to a machine, and burned all the official instruction manuals, so as to preserve their secrets (their 'mystery') and their indispensability.

The Director of the plant had no more freedom of action than anyone else, so standardised and rationalised were the factories and their processes; all production targets and prices were decided in Paris, hiring and firing and discipline were according to service-wide rules, and of the two-edged variety found in the Clerical Agency so that he was denied the discretion involved in condoning or permitting breaches of rule. Some space for manoeuvre could be created by his role as arbitrator between groups in the factory, but he had few sanctions or rewards to use as bargaining counters, other than his smiles and frowns. Only in periods of plant construction or large-scale reorganisation could he wield real power, and make real decisions. The Director's strategy, therefore, was to fight for change—if not large-scale, then small-scale—although his background and community role would make him a natural conservative; for change enhanced his own power and devalued that of the technical engineers. The technical engineers, on the other hand, who politically and otherwise might be expected to play an innovatory and progressive part, resisted change, as an attack on their corner in technical know-how (Crozier, 1964, 155–6).

In the theoretical half of the book, Crozier builds on the contributions of Merton, Gouldner and Selznick to the discussion of bureaucratic 'dysfunctions'—those 'other sides of the coin' by which the same attributes that give bureaucratic methods their advantage over non-bureacratic methods also produce undesired effects that the latter are free from. Crozier isolates and documents from his case-studies four such: 1. the extent of the development of impersonal rules; 2. the centralisation of decisions; 3. staff 'grade' separation; 4. job specification and control of performance; showing how in each case a 'vicious circle' develops. If a gap is found in the working of a rule, the reaction is to plug it with a new rule; each new rule created further reduces the flexibility of the organisation, its adaptability in a changing world. Every piece of evidence that peripheral offices are unable to handle peculiar local circumstances because of the rules made centrally is treated as evidence that they are not to be trusted with local discretion. The more that vertical hierarchical pressure is applied, the greater is the horizontal group pressure against 'authority'. The more predictable an employee's work is designed to be, the harder he strives (against the aims of the organisation) to create an area of uncertainty, and the more vital internal power struggles become. In each instance, any attempt to apply more of the standard bureaucratic remedy only makes the situation worse. Crozier offers some explanations as to why the situation seldom gets completely out of hand; but nevertheless he ends up holding that *all* bureaucratic behaviour is dysfunctional. In unequivocally cybernetic terms he contrasts the bureaucracy with the 'normal' organisation, where

> a constant feedback of information ... permits and even obliges the organization to take account of its errors and to correct them. We shall describe as a 'bureaucratic system of organization' any system of organization where the feedback process, error-information-correction, does not function well, and where consequently there cannot be any quick readjustment of the programmes of action in view of the errors committed (*Crozier, 1964, 186*).

What Crozier is assuming here is that the slow registration in large-scale organisations of changes in the environment that require changes in their response to it, brought about by what might be called 'official vision' or organisational perception, is a property not of large-scale organisation as such, but a (presumably avoidable) consequence of individual or collective behaviour choices, which he sums up as a 'will to escape from reality'. He implies that an equally large and complex 'normal' organisation, which differed from a 'bureaucracy' only in that its members were willing to face reality, could adjust speedily. In the light of the work of Burns and Stalker, we would probably prefer to say that the structure of the rapidly adjusting organisation would have to be of 'organic' form—which is more than a matter of willingness to face reality.

The more significant part of Crozier's book for the development of the present chapter is the last section, where he poses the question whether the four 'vicious circles' he found in the French bureaucratic organisations he studied might not be more 'French' than they were 'bureaucratic'; that they were due to personality traits embedded in the culture and so might not be found in another culture, or not in the same form. Grasping boldly the methodological nettle of 'national character', he shows satisfactorily enough that impersonal rules, isolation of groups, flight from face-to-face relationships with authority, and the tendency to withdraw into whatever 'private freedom' can be won, are indeed common findings of most students of French culture and community life generally.

> To compromise, to make deals, to adjust to other people's claims is frowned upon; it is considered better to restrict oneself and to remain free within the narrower limits one has fixed or even those one has had to accept. This insistence upon

personal autonomy and this pattern of restriction are old in France (*Crozier, 1964, 223*).

'Bureaucratic behaviour', as defined by Crozier, is found to be endemic in French society. Crozier concludes that it is not the work-situation, the hierarchic or the governmental nature of the two agencies that creates the bureaucratic tendencies—or at least not that only; for French citizens bring these tendencies with them into the organisations they join. Accordingly, one should not read off from Crozier's definition of

> a bureaucratic organisation... an organization that cannot correct its behaviour by learning from its errors (*Crozier, 1964, 187*)

any conclusions of immediate application to other cultures: which is undeniably a pity, because it is a very elegant definition.

Crozier then looks at American and Russian organisational behaviour (with an occasional glance at British) to see whether they betray their own styles of flight from reality, and finds that they do, even if the conditions are diametric opposites of French conditions. In American municipalities, for instance, instead of high centralisation, there are multiple decision centres, great functional specialisation and fragmentation of legal authority. 'The American system', he says, 'may also be viewed as a system that cannot correct its errors easily' (Crozier, 1964, 236)—and hence, by definition, is a bureaucratic system. Thus far does he depart from the Weberian connotations of the term, which if not perverse is at least confusing of him.

System thinking

The difference between 'national character' studies and 'cross cultural comparisons' (Almond and Verba, 1963; Banks and Textor, 1963; Russett, 1964; Lyden, 1968; etc.) is as marked as one wishes to make it. The study of 'national character' went under a cloud for a whole generation of scholars because of where it apparently led, in the hands of Gobineau and Chamberlain, the theorists of the 'master-race' (Hertz, (1944) 1957), and it has not yet quite emerged. It has its illustrious ancients in Aristotle and Hippocrates, Montesquieu and de Tocqueville; among moderns, Graham Wallas, Salvador de Madariaga, George Orwell, Geoffrey

Gorer, George Mikes, and many more. If this seems a curious company (not all of them usually seen as serious scholars) in which to put Crozier, it is done because all share a method which, by and large, is literary rather than scientific, judgemental rather than mathematical, synthesising rather than analytical, summatory (I will not say holist) rather than reductionist. They aim to understand and explain behaviour by intuiting that a certain group of people will react in a certain 'typical' way in a given situation, just as do scholars who find different cultural responses to certain basic 'functional requisites'; but the mode of explanation is different— it is not the needs of societal survival that influence the response of the individual, but the common experiences of the members of the group, their history of exposure to the same ways of seeing the world and possession of the same habits and traditions of what is done in a given situation.

Crozier did not use a 'structure/function' analysis and his use of the word 'system' is not loaded with operational meaning as it is in Almond and Coleman, for instance. At the risk again of over-simplifying, let me distinguish between two usages, calling them those of the engineer and of the biologist. For both, a 'system' is a whole made up of parts, connected by some principle of relationship that defines the system they are talking about and marks it off from other systems and its environment. Thus a hot water system in a house is a system marked off from the cold water system, except at one point of transfer, and the water pipe system is quite distinct from the gas pipe system that it may run alongside. The nervous system in an organism is a system, distinct from the blood-circulation system and the digestive system, except where there are trans-fer-points from one system to another. The solar system is a system; and so, indeed, is any part of the real world which we might care to identify as a focus of our interest for the time being (Porter, 1965, 7)—the system is in the eye of the beholder. But an organic, or bio-logical, system is more than just a physical manifestation of a rela-tionship; for the whole and the parts are not separable without destroying the nature of the system, the link between them is one which is one-way and irreversible—they grew together, and the whole is not just the sum of the parts because they were not 'sum-med'. By contrast, the engineer's system is a more modest affair; wholes are sums. 'Systems analysis', which is what is done pre-paratory to programming a computer, for example, is 'engineering' only, not organic, whatever mystic language may occasionally be used. (For the concepts of General Systems Theory, see Beer, 1966;

Kast, 1968; Litterer, 1969; Emery, 1969—but note the footnote on p. 7: 'Throughout the volume we have kept to the strand of thought that runs from theorising about biological systems in general to social systems. We have practically ignored the strand that arises from the design of complex engineering systems.')

Crozier's use of 'system', then, is that of the engineer. Again: in so far as he obtains his evidence for the nature of the peculiarly French approach to authority and power from putting together what a number of researchers and writers have reported in particular instances and places, rather than from consideration of what would be necessary for the survival of France as a nation, or of the French small town in an industrialising society, or the like, he lines himself up with those sociologists who adopt what has come to be called the 'action' approach, with its roots in Weberian *Verstehen.*

So those political scientists who, as we saw in the previous chapter, once divided themselves from 'behavioralists' on the question of the imputing of motives of action, had now to be divided again: into those who were willing to use the notions of 'ideal-type' or the 'typical actor', and to impute characteristic patterns of belief and action (but not to speak of 'cultural response', or of patterns of activity as 'meeting societal needs', or of collective actions as having 'survival value')—and those who query the notion of 'type' but are happy enough with needs and functions.

Silverman (1970) prefers to contrast organisation theorists who adopt an 'action frame of reference' with those who use the 'systems approach'. But in 'the systems approach' he includes three assumptions: 'that organisations are composed of a set of interdependent parts; organisations have needs for survival; and organisations, as systems, behave and take actions' (Silverman, 1970, 27). We can, however, distinguish between these three assumptions. No use of the term 'system' can reasonably avoid the first. But it is not inevitable that a systems theorist adopt the assumptions of 'survival in an environment', or that the concept of survival in an environment is necessarily a 'systems' one. And if the theorist is using the 'engineering' or purely relational concept of 'system', several constant features of a system may be deduced, but one of them is not that 'systems have needs for survival'.

The third assumption is also disposable, as being not only a reification from the abstract system to a real organisation, but further, a personification; both of which errors can surely be avoided by a careful systems theorist whether a biologist or an engineer.

It is thus at least logically possible to be a systems theorist of

organisations without being at the same time a structural/
functionalist—though Silverman is no doubt justified in noting
that in social science the two go together more often than not. It
is also logically possible to be a functionalist, using the concepts of
'role' and 'needs', without reifying; but it is certainly an ever-
present danger, that one may slip from a postulated 'assumed role'
or 'felt need' (concepts not incompatible with an 'action approach'),
being a construct in the attempt to explain an observed behaviour,
into regarding the existence of roles or needs as facts, external to
the perception of the actor, real phenomena.

In such ways and with due care to avoid the cardinal sin of reification, it is perhaps barely possible to be *at once* a systems theorist, a
structural/functionalist, and a devotee of the action frame of
reference. Weber himself (see e.g. Fletcher, 1971, II, 399), and
Talcott Parsons also, would claim to be so. The truth surely is that
any form of explanation of human social action (or behaviour) walks
a tight-rope, strictly comparable with the tightrope that historians
of ideas walk, according to Mary Mack:

> It is as easy to plunge down one side, by reading more recent
> developments into a distant past, as it is down the other, by
> treating historical figures as merely a product of their pre-
> decessors (*Mack, 1962, 19*).

For the social scientist, whether for the behaviouralist, the
functionalist, or the action theorist, the one side is the reading into
the data the ordering principles of the observer; the other, the
treating of actors as either less free agents than they are or less
governed by external forces than they are.

The choice of an 'action' or a 'functional' model may depend
upon what point of view the observer takes up: principally, whether
he is willing to stay outside the system he is trying to observe, or
needs for his purposes to know what it is like to be inside. An
observer outside the system can detect regularities in the exchanges
that the system has with its environment, and from them he may or
may not be able to infer what might be going on inside the system;
but if there are alternative possible models each or all of which
are consonant with the observations, he cannot choose between them.
A 'functional' model, which tries to explain what appears to be the
pattern of the relationships between the system and its environment
whatever is going on inside, by a teleological postulate about what
it is apparently all 'for', is making as much use of the observations
as is possible—short of getting inside, or 'taking the lid off the
black box', in cybernetic jargon.

An observer who wants to 'explain' the observed exchanges between the system and its environment directly, by reference to what is going on in there, has either to get inside, or try to imagine what is going on in there by, as it were, thinking through what would make *him* act in the pattern that he observes. He may feel he can get very close to the truth, or he may not be able to 'understand' the pattern at all; if the latter, there is nothing more he is able to do with the data. He cannot work with a 'whatever is going on inside' condition, because that is precisely what alone he is interested in.

It is perhaps clear that, given the trauma of the 1950s, the consultant/scholars of comparative public administration adopted a functionalist approach because it did not depend upon empathising, or getting inside the skin of the stranger; they had a way of getting to know his system, whatever really 'made him tick'. On the other hand, as 'change agents' they were not tremendously successful (see below, p. 208); perhaps because it is difficult to foster change from the outside.

CHAPTER NINE

Administrative Science and Popular Understanding

However valid it may have been to say of Appleby's book in 1949 that it dealt the scholarly death-blow to the 'policy/administration dichotomy', the dichotomy is apparently alive and well and living in England, as the Committee on Management of Local Government found in 1966–7. It is the formula that most people, outside the small world of the academic students of administration, still use to express a dividing-line they need to draw, between what it is proper for a politician to do, and what for an official. The Committee (under Sir John Maud, later Lord Redcliffe-Maud and chairman of the Royal Commission), came to believe that the root cause of English local government's internal malaise was a misconception about what democratic government entails:

> ... the word democracy has come to have ... a special meaning: it is thought to imply that, unless the members determine how the smallest things are to be done, they are failing in their duties. To allow any but the most trivial discretion to an officer is thought to be undemocratic...
>
> We believe that the lack of clear recognition of what can and should be done by officers, and of what should be reserved for decision by members, lies at the root of the difficulties in the internal organisation of local authorities. Until members are prepared to change their attitudes towards their own functions and those of the officers, there is little prospect of any improvement in the effectiveness and efficiency of the organisation (*Maud, 1967, paras. 72, 101*).

In what would be tiresome repetition if it were not so clearly intentional, the Committee came back to the point time after time—as, indeed, did their witnesses, usually expressing the necessity

> to distinguish between policy and administration; this is a constantly recurring theme in the written evidence. ... if only

153

policy could be separated from administration, the former to be exercised by members and the latter by officers, this would be a solution to problems and a step towards reform (*Maud, 1967, para. 109*).

But the Committee, which contained among its members one of Britain's leading teachers of public administration, rejected any such distinction:

> We refer in paragraph 109 to the often expressed view that the function of members is to decide 'policy' and of officers to 'execute' or 'administer' it. We argue that 'policy' cannot be defined and indeed that it should not be defined. Some issues are, to reasonable men, so important that they can safely be termed 'policy issues'. But what may seem to be a routine matter may be charged with political significance to the extent that it becomes a matter of policy. Other routine matters may lead by practice and experience to the creation of a principle or a policy; an isolated case may itself be a precedent for a line of similar cases. In advising on major issues officers are clearly contributing to the formulation of policy, but in shaping administrative decisions officers may also, even if less obviously, be formulating a policy. 'Policy' and 'administration' will not serve to distinguish between the responsibilities of members and of officers. How they can be distinguished is set out in the following paragraphs (*Maud, 1967, para. 143*).

What is set out in the paragraphs that follow is summed up at the end thus:

> We recommend that local authorities consider a division of functions and responsibilities between members and officers as follows:
> (a) Ultimate direction and control of the affairs of the authority to lie with the members.
> (b) The members to take the key decisions on the objectives of the authority and on the plans to attain them.
> (c) The members to review, periodically, progress and the performance of the services.
> (d) The officers to provide the necessary staff work and advice so that members may set the objectives and take decisions on the means of attaining them.
> (e) The officers to be responsible for day-to-day administration of services, decisions on case-work, and routine inspection and control.
> (f) The officers to be responsible for identifying and isolating the particular problem or case which in their view, and from their understanding of the minds of the members, has such implications that the members must consider and decide on it (*Maud, 1967, para. 151*).

It is noticeable both in the evidence and in the Report that those who find 'policy' too slippery a concept to use do not appear to have any such difficulty about 'administration'.

Policy and political

'Policy', in the dictionary, has even more senses than has 'administration'; and it would be a thankless task to embark on the same kind of elucidation as we have attempted for 'administration'. Yet something has to be said about this side of the dichotomy too. The Oxford English Dictionary begins with the obsolete senses, where 'policy' equates with 'polity' and 'political science'; then comes a group of senses conveying 'prudence, skill, or consideration of expediency in the conduct of affairs; statecraft; diplomacy; in bad sense, political cunning; prudent or politic course of action; a stratagem;' and so on. Number 5 is given as 'The chief living sense':

> A course of action adopted and pursued by a government, party, ruler, statesman, etc.; any course of action adopted as advantageous or expedient.

(Other senses deal with 'park around a gentleman's house'; insurance policies; a kind of gambling; and so on.) (*OED*, (1933) 1961, 1071).

Webster gives much the same, but is more specific in its Fifth Sense:

> I. 5a: a definite course or method of action selected (as by a government, institution, group, or individual) from among alternatives and in the light of given conditions to guide and usually determine present and future decisions (*Webster's Third New International Dictionary, 1961*).

Let me identify two 'dictionary' senses of 'policy' that may be relevant to the dichotomy, calling them for reference the Third and Fifth Senses:

Third Sense: expediency in the conduct of affairs.
Fifth Sense: a course of action, a decision intended to shape future decisions.

In Appleby's book, the word 'policy' occurs perhaps a thousand times, but is nowhere explicitly defined; when he comes closest to explication, it is always in terms similar to the usage of Gulick noticed earlier: 'policy-making is... the exercise of discretion' (Appleby, 1949, 15); 'value-judgement, hence policy-making' (1949, 17); and

> At every level, the answer to the question 'What is my judgement about this which I have to decide, or about this on which I need to have a judgement?' is a policy question (*Appleby*, *1949, 21*).

One cannot replace 'policy' there by the 'course of action' meaning without either failing to make sense, or enormously extending the import beyond the plain sense of the context; the 'expediency' meaning, on the other hand, works satisfactorily. Appleby, however, certainly uses the Fifth Sense meaning *passim*, in phrases like 'foreign policy', or 'government policies' towards this or that problem; but always with the 'expediency' sense included. The point Appleby wished to ram home, using shock tactics to do it, was that the administrative function is wholly part of 'politics'—he called it the 'eighth political process', the other seven being the Presidential nominating process, the general nominating process, the electoral process, the legislative process, the judicial process, the party maintenance process, and the agitational process (Appleby, 1949, 27–8). 'Politics', to be sure, is defined as coextensive with government, and includes administration by definition: but Appleby thinks also of a 'scale of politicality':

> An official, an action, a function or an agency of government is viewed as 'more political' or 'less political' according to degree of involvement in the various processes characteristic of government, degree of subjection to popular control through elected officials and representatives, and degree of exposure to citizens. An official or agency in acting on behalf of the government is by that token political, but officials and agencies vary in the extent to which they partake of the whole governmental scene and its processes (*Appleby, 1949, 26*).

All administration is political, but some is more political than other. Some administration is also more of a 'policy-making' kind than is other administration; but the relationship between 'political' and 'policy-making' is another that is left to be assumed—and the assumption must be that they are thought to be equivalent:

> Thus, the long attempts to make sharp and real the separation of powers, the separation of policy-making and administration and politics and administration, have been undergoing abandonment (*Appleby, 1949, 16*).

If all policy-making is political, the dichotomy is certainly dissolved;

but what about policy-making that is minimally political, on the scale of politicality, compared with policy-making that is maximally political? Is there a point, or zone, on this scale beyond which policy-making is pre-eminently the work of elected persons and not of appointed person; and if so, how does one name the distinction, having denied oneself the use of the terms 'policy', and 'political', and 'administration'? This is the formula the Maud Committee tried to find.

One may deduce from the several stated equivalents of the term 'policy' something of what witnesses before the Maud Committee understood by it: it is

'a matter of great significance'
'not administrative detail'
'important issues'
'issues involving significant political or social reaction'
'issues involving political significance beyond a certain extent'
'the determination of a general guide to action arising out of particular problems'
'a principle'
'a precedent for a line of similar cases'.

The last three are visibly different from the others, and in fact are taken from the research reports written by the Committee's staff; they are consonant with the Fifth Sense meaning, the others are not. It is, surely, only in this sense that 'a policy' can emerge or be induced from a set of past decisions, even when these decisions were taken independently of one another—a point is reached where a similarity in these past reactions to what can then be recognised as a recurring situation is transformed into a species of regulation for the future; and one might, if one looked, surely find such 'policies' at a very trivial level indeed. Indeed, a 'routine' is just such a determinant of future action.

The first five equivalents for 'policy' listed will, by and large, fit the Third Sense; but they lead to some absurdities. It would certainly be only by an exercise of prudence, statecraft or political cunning that one could distinguish between an issue involving significant political or social reaction and one involving political or social reaction at an insignificant level; between an issue involving political significance beyond a certain extent and one involving political significance up to that extent. So, in order to establish whether a matter may be dealt with on a non-policy (or non-political?) level, one must take a political decision about it. These witnesses before Maud were followers of Appleby in spite of themselves. So was the Committee itself, in recommending that it should be for officers to decide which matters were to be brought before members—clearly a 'political' decision in itself—although the Maud Committee would have been grievously misunderstood and misrepresented if it had said so.

The ambiguity over 'policy' is finally demonstrated by noting that the making of a (Fifth Sense) policy may be a (Third Sense) policy issue or not, according to its degree of political significance. Vickers avoids ambiguity by sticking to one meaning for 'policy':

> Thus the activity of the local authority consists in maintaining through time a complex pattern of relationships in accordance with standards or within limits which have somehow come to be set as governing relations. Its regulative function consists partly in maintaining the actual course of affairs in line with these governing relations ... and partly in modifying these governing relations ... That element of the regulative function which consists in maintaining the course of affairs in line with the current governing relations I regard as the executive element. That element which consists in modifying the governing relations I regard as the policy-making element (*Vickers, 1965, 27*).

But that distinction will not do to separate the work of members and officers. It would certainly be allowed by Maud, and by common sense, that making sure that the actual course of affairs is maintained in line with current governing relations is legitimate work for members: and if *all* modification of governing relations is work for members only, we come up against the trivial/important measure again.

Officials and politicians

Common sense, or the plain man's point of view, says that there must be *some* dividing-line, if only to make it sensible that some people in government are elected and others are appointed. To say that that is a matter of 'democracy' or 'popular control' gets us nowhere, as Maud pointed out—it depends upon what 'democracy' entails, and that debate is an old and perennial one; moreover, it has a second dividing-line to be considered—the relationship between elected representatives and their electors (Pulzer, 1967; Pateman, 1970). Again: should we try to alter local government practices to suit the kind of people the electors elect, or should we try to alter the kind of people that get elected (Stanyer, 1971;

Self, 1971b)? Leaving aside the radical end of the 'participation' argument (which would, after Rousseau, deny validity to any representative institution whatsoever), and stressing the 'control' or 'accountability' element only, a model of the local government situation may be drawn thus: we, the masses, need a category of people in public office who will be on 'short term' tenure, so that the quality of their stewardship of office can be frequently assessed, and innovation made possible; a class of person who can be got rid of without violence to our consciences or theirs. But we need also a category of public officer on 'long term' tenure, so that there can be assurance of the development of skills and expertise, experience and specialisation; and in respect of these persons it is better that we should never be put in the position of wishing to get rid of them. So it is clear that this 'long term' tenure class must be inhibited from taking sides in matters on which we are likely to be divided amongst ourselves, and that on such a matter, sides should be taken only by the 'short term' people.

Thus far, the model is fairly unambiguous. Ambiguity sets in when we try to describe the content of 'matters on which we are likely to be divided amongst ourselves': not only criteria like 'policy-making' and 'political issues', but also 'determination of values', 'modification of governing relations', and even 'priorities in the use of public resources', 'amount and incidence of taxation', or 'distribution of public benefits', are all susceptible to the trivial/important measurement, and to the dilemma that, if they were applied strictly, there might have to be as many 'short term' persons as there were 'long term', or perhaps considerably more, if as at present the 'short term' people were also part-time, while the 'long-term' people are also full-time. If a trivial/important measurement *is* applied, and the measuring done by long-term people because in practice they being full-time are alone in the position to do so, then the fear exists that a wish to get rid of them may follow, whereas the machinery makes no simple provision for it and many provisions against it.

The Maud formula attempts to cut this knot by making the trivial/important measurement by officers dependent upon 'their understanding of the minds of the members', a notion similar to Friedrich's 'rule of anticipated reactions' (Friedrich, 1937, 16; Simon, 1947, 129). This however, raises issues of a social and psychological nature; firstly, whether officers, as such, can be expected to understand the minds of members, as such; and secondly, how the institutional 'defended frontier' mentality, which attempts to use the 'policy/administration dichotomy' as a weapon, can be overcome.

Officials are commonly of a higher educational calibre, and in the case of senior men, commonly of a higher social standing, than many of the elected members. Senior officials may have wider horizons, move on the national stage of their profession, be called upon by Ministers for advice, be more cosmopolitan in all ways, than the average of the elected members in their own authority. The official's training and experience, and career development, gives him a longer time-perspective, and places him altogether in a more cause-and-effect universe, where one can recognise the reasons for success and failure and devise corrective measures for error; in contrast, the world inhabited by the politician may seem to the official arbitrary, random, dependent upon swings and wheels of fortune, where because of the perpetually myopic scale of vision good men and good work are ill-rewarded. If there is a fear of 'bureaucracy' among members in the name of 'democracy', there is certainly an equal fear of 'democracy' on the part of many officers in the name of 'good government'—even, 'the public interest'. It is perhaps inevitable that 'understanding of the minds of the members' may be replaced by 'understanding of what ought to be the minds of the members', or what they might 'legitimately' be; or if it is not inevitable, it may yet be suspected of being so.

On the second point: the Appleby doctrine that 'all things are political' in administration, along with the doctrine of 'anticipated reactions', produces an asymmetry in the member/officer relationship that many officers, since the first appearance of the dichotomy, have been unwilling to accept. That is, that whereas there are some matters about which the elected member can say to the officer, 'This is not for you', there is nothing about which, in principle, the official can say the same in return. Hence a search for a countervailing asymmetry, for 'technical processes' or the like, from which politics and politicians could be excluded. There were comments to Maud about members 'always breathing down your neck', 'keeping you away from your job', and so on, which can be 'explained' simply by the fact of full-time propinquity of officials, which may lead to a sense of proprietorship over the organisation, a commitment to one another which is (perhaps subliminally) outraged by the intrusion of people whose loyalties appear to be centred elsewhere. Amongst senior officers, there is likely to be a 'professional pride' which (quite properly) may lead to an insistence that the employer take the professional advice that is given, or find another adviser; and in this sense, 'technical processes' mark off an officer not only from the members but also from fellow officers of other professions. A legal officer does not expect to be instructed how to draw up a conveyance except by another legal officer. Although a civil engineer may admit that there is room for argument as to just what diameter of main stormwater drain is the minimum for what area of paved roadway in what weather conditions, he would expect to argue this only with another civil engineer. In any matter which can be called a 'professional' one in this sense, an exercise of judgement is ordinarily questionable only within the professional community—a body which extends outside the official's employing organisation, and to which he claims a right of appeal against his employer in such a matter.

The frontier here is set by what is and what is not a 'professional' matter. If civil engineers are arguing about technical specifications, the possibility is that they are balancing performance against cost, or speed, or availability of materials, or the like. That is, the argument can be presented in the form of a choice between equally-effective means to one end; and where this is so, the choice must be made by reference to a different sort of end; and choice between or among ends is not the same sort of thing as 'technical' choice of means. Yet this is only another measurement that is subject to the trivial/important scale.

Amongst the comments from officers to Maud about the behaviour of members, however, was another scornful complaint: that members in committee would spend hours debating, for instance, the placing of a bus-stop or the colour of school curtains, while letting through 'on the nod' decisions involving expenditure of £100,000 and upwards. That is to say in the terms of the present discussion, that it appeared to them that there were *two* thresholds in the trivial/important scale: one below which members were not interested, and one above which members were apparently incapable of taking a view.

The problem might disappear if we stated the 'trivial/important' scale properly—it is clear that the units are not amounts of money. But it might remain true that there are issues which in importance on almost any scale that might be devised are undoubtedly for members, but which are too complicated or difficult to be grasped by lay members without considerable assistance from the officers in presenting, and clarifying, the questions that are for decision. So because of the officer's permanence, his full-time presence, his expertise, and his control of information and its communication, he can again derive great influence from his ability to present for decision only those matters, or aspects of matters, which he chooses to present. This is indeed a countervailing asymmetry, although it is one of power, not authority.

Such a situation fairly teems with occasions for mistrust and suspicion. Understanding the complexities of a problem is not deciding the question, but it is a prerequisite; the man who does not quite grasp a matter may feel he is being presented by one who does with a *fait accompli*. Selection of the most relevant information for presentation, or the most important choices for decision, where the whole cannot be presented within reasonable limits of time, paper, etc., may be seen as the 'concealment' of the rest. A decision on one part of a question may have implications for later choices that are not immediately apparent, resulting in allegations of 'being led up the garden path'. And so on. It looks like power without responsibility, simply because, by definition, those who are aware that they carry the responsibility are unable to wield the power that expertise, permanence, and information bestows.

In such a situation, technique of presentation is crucial. If an officer has conducted the analysis of the problem, and the other preparatory stages, by 'rational' methods—that is to say (for the present) by methods other than mere habit, or tradition, or hunch—then it is likely that he can briefly take a committee through the process he has gone through, enabling members to 'ratify' or question the process stage by stage. (If his own 'staff work' is shoddy, he will be unable to do this, save by skill in 'rationalising', which is an officer's version of myopic vision.) The battery of 'decison aids' now available (Operational Research, cost/benefit analysis, and so on) cannot, in principle, *make* the choice for the decision maker; they can only go to make it clearer than it might be without such aid. It will often be the case that the professional chief officer in local government, for example (and senior departmental heads in other walks of life), is not himself equipped to carry out analyses of this sort, so that in respect of the 'management services' experts who are, he is in a position only marginally different from the elected member. Where both principal officer and elected members can be seen to be in the same boat, the 'defended frontier' shifts to a less sensitive area: it is up to the chief officer to satisfy himself that *he* is not being presented with a *fait accompli*, or being led up the garden path, or whatever; and having done so, he will be in a good position to satisfy a committee likewise.

The fact is, of course, that in questions not involving the use of these 'sophisticàted' aids, but only more conventional methods, the principal officer is very often in precisely the same position, *vis-à-vis* his specialist subordinates. But it is seldom in his interest to admit this, and in preserving his own professional status he reinforces the conventional placing of the 'dividing line' in local government between committee and chief officer, in contrast with the civil service, where the line between Minister and Permanent Secretary is seen in terms much less stark.

But however much we might be able to 'analyse away' the justification of a 'defended frontier' mentality, there is a basic difference of outlook between members and officers, in some cases though by no means all, that remains a problem for those who would like to generalise (by formalising) that amicability of division of function that undoubtedly exists in British local government most of the time, in most of the places, among most of the people concerned. This is, that clarification of choice, by any technique, is not inevitably welcomed by elected members, whose own decision environment may require a 'fudging' rather than a sharpening of focus on the ends to be served (and so the ends *not* to be served). In Wildavsky's words, for elected members as such

> ... the political problem is always basic and prior to the others ... This means that any suggested course of action must be evaluated first by its effects on the political structure. A course of action which corrects economic or social deficiencies but increases political difficulties must be rejected, while an action which contributes to political improvement is desirable even if it is not entirely sound from an economic or social standpoint (*Wildavsky, 1966, 288*).

The 'political calculus' embodies a rationality with a different base from that of the 'management services' tools; and such a difference of base is a recipe for conflict, often of a bitter, frustrated and non-communicating kind. That this element appears from time to time in the member/official relationship can hardly be denied: sometimes the use of the dichotomy (the 'politics/administration' one rather than the 'policy/administration' one) is a rationalisation of this conflict.

It is not only officers who find 'politics' sometimes exasperating. At various periods in human history, those who depend upon the favour of the people rather than upon the supposed light of pure reason have come in for obloquy from philosophers, scientists, soldiers, and even other 'statesmen'—Charles de Gaulle's views on the party politicians of France being perhaps the most recent notable example. For many, the activities of political parties and of politicians are seen as a costly squabble between rival groups of power-seekers, with eyes set never on anything higher than the next election and their return to another period of meaningless power, in which they will legislate for so much of an ideological programme as will keep their followers lined up behind them for the election after that. This disreputable activity is then sometimes contrasted with an alternative where 'real' experts in social and other sciences would give unbiased and independent advice based solely on the evidence of 'fact' instead of ideology and opinion— the utopian vision of Saint Simon, and many before him and since. At least since Hume (1740) it has been possible to expose the logical fallacy in such ideas (you cannot derive what ought to be the case in the future from consideration of what has been the case in the past); but that, as periodical waves of letters to newspaper editors calling for a coalition government of the 'best minds from all parties' make clear, does not destroy the attraction of such a 'rational alternative to politics', in the making of collective decisions.

The positive defence of 'politics', in this sense of competition for power, was in nineteenth-century thinking expressed in terms of 'freedom' or 'representative government'; the alternative to this being seen as 'caesarism', or 'dictatorship' as we should now say. But after the work of Arthur Bentley (1908), 'politics' in this sense could be identified with 'democracy' directly. If 'freedom' required that anyone with an opinion might mobilise a majority for it if he could, and 'representation' required that any opinion, even a minority one, had the chance of being taken into account, 'democracy' was seen as the form of government that enabled governmental decisions to be the resultant of the free interplay of such opinion-forming and opinion-expressing agencies, whether or not the 'opinions' were altruistic ones with the good of the community at heart, or blatantly self-interested ones—provided only that the ground of play, the arena wherein such pressures were equilibrated, was in the public domain, open to view. A recent defender of 'politics' put the case thus:

> For politics represents at least some tolerance of differing truths, some recognition that government is possible, indeed best conducted, amid the open canvassing of rival interests. Politics are the public actions of free men. Freedom is the privacy of men from public actions (*Crick, 1962, 14*).

In the work of Downs (1957) and Buchanan and Tullock (1962) the idea of a 'political calculus', a more-or-less precise estimation of gains and losses of votes, has been developed into the equation of 'politics' with the 'market' of the liberal economists; and Lind-blom (with Dahl, 1953; Lindblom, 1965) was then able to contrast this preferred model of 'partisan mutual adjustment' with another (whose claim to being 'democratic' he was disposed to question), based upon so-called 'rational' modes of decision for a society, which in his opinion led to centralised planning and another form of 'caesarism'—known as 'bureaucracy'.

In some circles, the contrast that is most clearly seen is that between a 'centralised' and 'bureaucratic' State or 'public sector', and a 'free enterprise' market-dominated 'private sector', some-times between the helpless citizen and the powerful customer. Let us see what this argument amounts to, and what it means for the relationship between politician and official.

CHAPTER TEN

Public Administration and 'Private Administration'

Let me first draw attention to two senses of the term 'public'. The noun has different connotations according to which article is used: 'the public' or 'a public'. 'The public' is often used loosely to mean 'everybody'; more often, 'everybody other than us', 'people in general' as compared to our group, whoever 'we' are. Thus to bus crews 'the public' are the fare-paying passengers; to television producers 'the public' are the viewers; to the Transport Users Consultative Committee 'members of the public' at a hearing are people who have not entered an objection in writing beforehand (CTUCC *Handbook*, 1963, 10). On the other hand, 'a public' is a much smaller body: the following of a pop-star or actor is 'his public', there is 'a public' for advice on collecting antiques. As an economist will speak of there being 'a market for' some product or service, so a political scientist may speak of there being 'a public for' some policy or outlook. A political scientist will usually interpret 'public opinion' not as 'the opinion of all' or 'the general opinion' (a concept whose reality he will probably be disposed to question), but as the common opinion of a particular public, whatever be its size or proportion of the population.

It is mainly in the adjectival usage of 'public', however, that ambiguity seriously arises. 'Public' can mean not only 'belonging to all' in ownership, the property of the community or collectivity, as applied to things, but also, as applied to actions, 'open to all', patent, not hidden. 'Private' has the same duality of application; not owned by the community, but by a definable one or a few, and on the other hand, secluded, secret, not in the open. So what is done 'in public' can be contrasted with what is done 'in private', without connotation of ownership or property rights, unless remotely. A phrase such as 'public policy' can then bring the two applications together, ambiguously.

There are two corresponding senses of 'political', also: the one referring simply to the affairs of the *polis* or State, having to do with Government; the other referring to a method of collective decision-making by openly competing interests (as in Crick, 1962). (*Res publica*, after all, is Latin for *politeia*.)

'Public administration', therefore, can mean simply the collective noun for the complex of Government Departments, local authorities, independent State corporations, and so on, in the way that was coming into use in the time of Mill and Bagehot; but 'public administration' can also have an overtone, that it is administration which is public, and hence ought to be different from administration in the 'private sector'. And then, to fail to hold clearly in mind the two different applications of 'public' as an adjective is to land in a confusion. If one carelessly assumes that 'private' implies 'not open to public scrutiny' *because* of not being publicly-owned, that one sense of 'private' entails the other, then one may also suppose that being publicly-owned entails being open to the public scrutiny. To be publicly-owned, in the public domain, and yet to be shielded from public gaze, with operations performed in secret (which of course is the condition of most activity in British Government Departments, and not only in the Defence or semi-commercial fields) appears as a simple contradiction in terms and therefore a flagrant scandal. It is a different thing, to hold the opinion that public administration ought to be conducted in a more open fashion than it is, not only 'above-board' but with all cards face up; and to advocate more 'publicity' of documents, for instance, as in Sweden (Hurwitz, 1958, 50). All I am saying is that one would be naïve to argue one's case on the basis of what the word 'public' means or implies, by running together the two ideas for which we use the word.

Representative and responsible government

A process which is in the public domain and yet takes place behind closed doors cannot easily be justified on a theory of direct or popular democracy, and only with difficulty on a theory of representative democracy; yet it may be quite easily justified on a theory of responsible democracy. The difference in the respective ideal types is quite marked. *Direct* democracy allows of no representatives, executives or powers separate from the powers of the assembly of all the people. An ideal-type *representative* system would have to have an assembly which although considerably smaller than the total population, was a microcosm of it, a sample along as many dimensions as were politically significant—economic status and ideological commitment, certainly, but also, perhaps, occupation, age, sex, religious affiliation in some places, race or ethnic grouping, regional and local loyalties and interests, and whatever else (unimaginable now) may turn out to be politically significant in other times and places. Some mechanism for renewing the representativeness of the sample would be needed; but not for changing the Executive as such, for the Executive in such a system would be the mere arm of the Assembly, acting in nothing save as instructed by, and hence authorised in advance by, the sample of the people. Nor would the assembly be held to account by the people: one does not hold a sample accountable for what it is or does, if it *is* a sample its behaviour is identical with the behaviour of the people from which it is drawn.

An ideal-type *responsible* system, on the other hand, would have no need of an assembly at all: someone acting on behalf of the sovereign (monarch or people, given appropriate mechanisms) might go to a street corner and appoint the first sixteen persons he met as 'The Government', giving them the control of the legislative power, the taxing power, the civil service and the machinery of government, the army and the police, and so on—to do with as they thought fit: with one proviso, that at the expiry of a certain (or uncertain) period of time, their actions would be reviewed by the sovereign, and if found unacceptable, they would each undoubtedly suffer grievously and in person.

Fairly clearly, it is on a theory of responsible government, rather than on one of representative government, that the British Parliamentary and Cabinet system must rest any claim it has to being called democratic at all. By and large, the Government does act as it thinks fit, without prior authorisation in detail, subject mainly to *ex post facto* accountability. So the system can accommodate a high degree of secrecy, or lack of publicity, without logical self-contradiction. By this logic, it is as much beside the point to criticise Cabinet Government for the secrecy of its operation as it is to criticise it for not being representative of the whole of the people. But *total* secrecy, the keeping of the doors closed against all but the agents of Government, *is* a self-contradiction—of that 'one proviso' which requires review by the sovereign of what has been done. Accountability presupposes a measure of openness, the amount decided (in anything that is going to have the least title to being called a responsible system) by the sovereign. In the language of control theory, keeping a responsible government system responsible depends upon the ability of the sovereign to match the 'variety' disposed of by the Executive, and that ability depends upon the flow of requisite information and the presence of sufficiently powerful generators of countervailing variety.

It is a commonplace that a difference between public administration and 'private administration' (a coinage to balance the conventional term, indicating the institutions of the private sector of the economy) lies in the extent to which the internal processes, as well as the substantive outputs, of public Departments are subject to monitoring by representatives of the people; public administration is not allowed merely to 'get results', it must stay within the law, achieve fairness or equity, conduct its affairs with utter financial and moral probity, behave correctly at all times and in all circumstances. From the private body, by contrast, the client or customer tends to look for preferential treatment rather than equity, and to strike his own bargain if he can. The shareholder is interested in the overall profit-and-loss performance of the company as judged by the Stock Market, rather than the internal procedures of the firm. Requiring only a crude measure of success or accountability for failure, the private business client or shareholder needs comparatively little information to arrive at his conclusions; and, in the simple market model from which this contrast is derived, he has a comparatively simple sanction to wield—he 'votes with his feet', or 'takes his custom elsewhere'. The public administration client and 'shareholder' or citizen has no such direct sanction to wield, and those available to him require judgements of a more complex kind, so that he needs as much information as he can get. 'Procedural monitoring', the constant watch (or threat of a watch) on internal processes, can be seen as an attempt to increase the flow of information, to generate variety of response to match variety of Executive action.

However, the simple public/private dichotomy of this model is not a good predictor of the real world. For many public services, there are 'customers' and clients whose interests are very similar to the interests of the private business customer. The private business shareholder, as represented by the jobbers and brokers of the actual marketplace, must compare an actual profit-and-loss figure with whatever he thinks it 'ought' to have been; and in any case, judges less on actual profit-and-loss figures than on a species of public opinion about what these are likely to be in the prevailing economic climate, state of the world, etc. (the Stock Exchange calls it 'sentiment'). And for either of these operations, the private business sovereign is liable to make use of any information that comes to hand as 'variety generators', often making mountains out of molehills in the same way as is done with an official fall from grace; including information about internal processes and about the legality, propriety, and equity of procedures.

The smallest firms, particularly family firms, have sometimes chosen to pay deliberate attention to what one might call 'procedural goals' such as these, for philanthropic or merely idiosyncratic reasons; and it is another commonplace today that the operations of the largest 'private' businesses are so politically significant for national welfare that the criteria applicable to them come more and more to be the same as for government. If we turn to non-business private bodies—for instance, professional association, churches, clubs, voluntary social welfare societies—it is apparent that the degree of interest in their procedural matters is often just as high as for public administration. Indeed, we would soon begin to find classification into 'public' and 'private' very dubious; bodies such as St John Ambulance and the Royal National Lifeboat Institution have wholly 'public' functions but are 'privately owned'. Nor, if we were able to construct a scale running from 'high substantive' to 'high procedural' interest, would it be likely to dichotomise between public and private bodies even where we could satisfactorily classify these; a continuity between public and private, or even a random distribution, is much more likely.

Resource tests and policy tests

A recent commentator on these matters, Peter Self (1971a), contrasts 'public administration' with 'business administration', and considers the question of what tests of efficiency can be applied to each:

> An imperative requirement of business efficiency—some would say its first rule—is market *innovation*. New products must be developed which consumers want sufficiently to yield a profit. But in government the problem is more one of market

compression. Administrative controllers must somehow weed out the surplus of political demands for expenditure as best they may. It is true that governments often and increasingly need to innovate, but innovation is guided by political not by market tests and must make its way against a sluggish head-stream of numerous existing commitments (*Self, 1971a, 6*).

An example, comparing a social security agency with a large insurance company, makes it plain that it is expansion of share of market that is being contrasted with market compression, thus preserving logic; but the true contrast is perhaps not even that. A page or so earlier, Self had said:

> The closest analogy to market competition for resources among business firms is political competition for resources among public agencies (*Self, 1971a, 4*)

and given an account of budget infighting, which makes expansion of share of market a goal equally of a public agency as of a business one. But Self's main point is that, whereas in the business world it is (?should be) 'the market' itself which determines, by a decision-less process of equilibration among thousands of individual choices, what goes to what competitor, in public administration these allocations are (?should be) matters of decision by overall controllers. Thus although an individual agency may in this respect behave like any competitive business firm, the system in which it behaves is not a market. The true contrast is not between individual business firm and individual public agency, but between 'business' as a whole and 'public administration': the former allocating resources by an 'outcome', the latter by an 'output'. As my parenthetical inter-jections may suggest, Self may here be committed to a 'Powellite' norm or a classical economics ideal-type of 'the market', and at the same time a 'Stalinist' norm or a synoptic-planning ideal-type of the public sector—which is not necessarily a self-contradiction, but a fairly conventional distinction between 'market forces' and 'politics' which tends to fail rather easily in empirical analysis.

Tests of efficiency, however, must be applied to individual units of business or public administration, not to the systems as wholes; and Self considers that, whereas that can be done for business, it cannot satisfactorily be done in public administration:

> Business management is guided by specific but socially narrow tests of resource efficiency, which can be confined to the firm in question. The equivalent tests for government must refer ultimately to the welfare of the whole society, as politically

articulated. Tests of resource efficiency therefore dissolve into a seamless web of the interacting benefits and costs of the whole set of public policies and the internal costs of any programme must theoretically be weighed against its net social benefits (*Self, 1971a, 8*).

What for the individual public agency in these circumstances takes the place of tests of resource efficiency (understood as the ratio between resource inputs and product outputs) are tests of 'goal effectiveness'. Self makes clear that this does not allow public agencies to abandon all economy in the pursuit of substantive goals; but resource efficiency operates primarily as a constraint upon goal achievement rather than as a determining test—whereas in business, substantive goals are subordinate to (or incorporated in) tests of resource efficiency. This is akin to the simple comparison of governmental and personal finance: whereas I count my money and decide what I can buy with it, government decides what it must buy and then raises the money. There are, of course, political constraints on tax-levying which modify this; but Self's point is that they are constraints on, not prime determinants of, goals. Self refers to the two kinds of test as 'policy tests' and 'resource tests'—tests of goal effectiveness, and tests of efficiency in use of resources.

For some public agencies, resource tests are indeed the appropriate ones: for instance, the public corporations operating nationalised industries. But for other public corporations, though resource tests may be applied, the dominant tests are policy ones—for instance a New Town Development Corporation:

> This body is lent capital by the Treasury which it must repay together with interest; it is assisted by certain housing subsidies and initial financial concessions. The new town corporation is also handed certain policy objectives, which typically include the development of an economically balanced town (i.e., one with employment roughly proportional to the resident population); the provision of housing for all social classes and of adequate social facilities; and a contribution to the relief of congestion in some large city through drawing off industries and through rehousing lower-income workers.
> Thus the new town corporation is subject to both goal and resource tests of efficiency. There seems little doubt, however, that the success of the new town will primarily be judged by its social achievements rather than by the state of its accounts. The resource tests will work essentially as constraints (more or less vexatious) upon its policy objectives, rather than as an end in themselves (*Self, 1971a, 11*).

This policy test/resources test mix thus provides for Self a tool for categorising different public agencies; the Treasury, the Foreign Office, the Department of Social Services, the Stationery Office, the Forestry Commission, the Independent Broadcasting Authority, the National Coal Board, British Rail, and so on, can be ranked according to the balance of policy test and resource test that seems appropriate to each.

This leaves unanswered the question of what a 'policy test' is, what its scales and units of measurement are; Self admits that 'ultimate judgements remain crudely qualitative' (Self, 1971a, 12). Perhaps, then, this is what one has 'short term' people for—to make these 'crudely qualitative' judgements, and take the responsibility for the consequences. Perhaps we have learned enough by now not to dichotomise; to pretend that all qualitative judgements can be made by elected persons, or that career officials never in practice make qualitative judgements: but a restatement of the old 'policy/administration dichotomy' in terms of a 'policy test/resources test spectrum' may be as close as we can get to an acceptable formulation, in the following way. Let us postulate that 'policy test' implies a qualitative judgement not only about the goal to be pursued (or the order of priority among goals), and about the scales along which achievement is to be measured, but also about the actual placing in each particular case; and that 'resources test' implies the adoption of generally accepted or 'universal' goals or (better) criteria (e.g. greater output for less consumption of resources is always good), along with generally accepted or 'rational' scales of measurement, and that the judgement involved is limited to the application of such rules to the particular case, the taking of the 'reading' in a specific situation. Thus we would recognise that there is judgement involved in both tests—qualitative judgement; but that in the 'resources test' it is considerably circumscribed. We can easily conceive of circumstances in which it could be virtually nil, others in which it could be very significant; and then, we may think of circumstances in which the scales of measurement of a resource test were not 'given', but were themselves problematic, requiring a degree of qualitative judgement; finally, a situation where it was somewhat difficult to decide which of two or more criteria to adopt in a resource test—so that the difference between a 'policy test' and a 'resource test' begins to crumble. We have converted the dichotomy into a single-variable scale running from nought to infinity—degree, scope, or weight of qualitative judgement involved —of which the units may be no easier to determine, much less quantify, than a 'policy test', but which avoids qualitative dichotomy.

Now it is clear that the setting of goals to be pursued in a 'private' business—the determination of which market to enter, what product to manufacture, and so on—is a definition of 'entrepreneurship', and that 'policy tests' applicable to business entrepreneurship will (*pace* Self) often be not at all subordinate to or incorporated in 'resource tests', but prior and fundamental. But I do not wish to pursue this question; the main interest is in the public sector.

Politicians and officials again

If we wish, we can now seek for some point on the scale of 'degree of qualitative judgement involved' which will serve to separate the kind of decision made by elected members from the kind of decision made by career officials. Even if there is a continuity, a marked bunching seems bound to be found on each side of a middle zone of overlapping; and then we can move to the final stage, from description to prescription, designating the thresholds beyond which either group of decision-maker shall be held to be trespassing. So we can meet the apparent need for a division of labour that can be made into a frontier between jurisdictions, into codes of acceptable behaviour, so long as a difference between the two groups is seen to exist.

It is my belief that something like this is what in fact takes place now, say in English local government, the locale of the current British argument on these matters. A scale is in practice found which is a scale of the right sort (nought to infinity, not a dichotomy), though it may be a different scale not only for each different local council, and perhaps not only for each different committee and department of a council, but for each different mind which is brought to bear on the matter. A scale is in practice adopted even if it is not made conscious or articulated. The smaller the group concerned, the greater the need to communicate and the greater the frequency of communication, the more likely is a consensus to emerge about what the applicable scale is, even if entirely unspoken and only 'felt'; and by the same process the point on the scale at which a particular behaviour becomes unacceptable for the group is arrived at—partly by precedent in the group's own experience, partly by comparison with other groups, partly by prediction or experience of results, partly perhaps on 'ideological' or other unexamined premises; but essentially particular to the group itself in its own peculiar setting, and not always transferable even to similar groups in the same local authority. It is self-evident that the actual members and officers of the several hundred local authorities of relevant size have, over a century or so, evolved a *modus vivendi*, a way of accommodating themselves to their perceived roles, of arriving at the necessary consensus, severally—including their several *de facto* solutions to the problem the 'politics/ administration dichotomy' was intended to deal with; even while their verbalisations of what they were doing, and of the problems they were solving, were grossly inadequate as descriptions, easily demolished in logic. The difficulty, in other words, has not been one of finding an acceptable division of labour between elected members and career officials, relevant to their different terms and modes of appointment; but one of generalising it, normalising it, turning it into a prescriptive formula which might then be transferable and applicable in all times and circumstances. This, perhaps, is the will-o'-the-wisp that the Maud Committee pursued, and which many 'laymen' would cheerfully still pursue (see The Bains Report, 1972).

Take your stance at another point, and the distinction between elected member and career official disappears entirely: both, from the ratepayers' point of view perhaps, become 'they'; or, as seen from the extreme Left, dedicated upholders of the existing order. But the same is true of the 'public/private' distinction from which we began: all such distinctions belong to their own frame of reference, and are meaningless in another.

Structural adaptation tests

Parker and Subramaniam (1964) made a similar point to Self's: 'public administration' (as opposed to private administration), they concluded, refers to

> ... these organisations in a society which have been differentiated from other sub-systems so as to specialise in integrative and resource-allocation functions for the whole society; and

secondarily [to] organisations with productive or service functions which are directly sponsored by and integrated with Governmental organisations.

The societal functions of Government, that is, are integration, and resource-allocation for the *whole* society. Mackenzie commenting on this article said:

> They go on to emphasise that in a modern state a tremendous effort is made to integrate government organisations with one another; so that government in a sense is 'one enormous quasi-organisation'. This is of great practical importance, because this effort to integrate, and not simply to live (like the business world) in 'particularistic interdependence', is one thing that stamps the institutions of public administration, their atmosphere, their procedure. It is no less important that there is a general norm or myth in the society that government administration is or ought to be integrated, that private administration need not be (*Mackenzie, 1967, 275*).

In the ideal-type business field, integration, co-ordination, control, and planning is acceptably decision-less, an outcome of the interplay of market forces. If a unit sub-system of such a system should fail, no effort need be made to maintain the system whole; one simply accepts the new situation, and redefines the system as one with one part fewer. In public administration, on the other hand, this is not acceptable; it is expected that nothing happens save by intent and decision, that all contingencies are prepared for, and that the system is maintained against failure of any part. These are chimerical expectations, of course; standards impossible to meet. The failure of 'public administration' to come up to public expectations is guaranteed, almost by definition.

Whether this, or any other, distinction between 'public' and 'private' administration can be made truly operational or not, the existence of an assumption that it is so leads, as Simon, Smithburg and Thompson carefully noted (1950, 8–12), to a set of expectations about public administration, and a range of likelihoods of these expectations being fulfilled. Another such expectation by 'the public' is that they will be wooed by 'private' administration, and coerced by public administration. The intrinsic regulation of 'the market' by no-one in particular, by the 'hidden hand' or 'impersonal market forces', may be called 'economic coercion' or 'rationing by the purse' by its enemies, but it is liable to be accepted, and even equated with 'freedom', by citizens who are conscious of an apparent absence of hierarchical authority and central decision-making. Where 'the State' operates in the same fashion, by manipulation of prices, subsidies, grants and the like, this also 'preserves freedom'. Other kinds of State action fulfil the expectation, and can be opposed in the name of 'the liberty of the individual'. In a mixed economy, large 'private' businesses occasionally find themselves in the same camp as the rabid individualist, in protest against regulation by 'the State'; but perhaps more often the bigger they are, find themselves in the same camp as Government, because of their preference for a relatively stable political situation, for 'law and order'.

In the mixed economy too, the social functions of Government or public administration cannot but be plural, and at times self-contradictory. Where responsibility for the creation of a large part of the Gross National Product is in 'private' hands, but the remainder in the hands of 'the public sector', the setting of goals for the public sector which are dominated by 'policy tests' rather than 'resource tests', in Self's terminology, can only be at a sacrifice of GNP, even if overt calculations are carefully avoided; yet because this is 'State action', the Western liberal democratic tradition decrees a structure of 'safeguards of freedom', whose cost is assumed to be unavoidable. Again, let us assume that the 'integrative' function of Government is not limited to the integration of Governmental activities, the public sector alone, but refers to integration 'for the whole society', in Parker and Subramaniam's words—the harmonisation of all the goals that the whole society wishes to pursue (given some acceptable method of recognising and registering such wishes). 'Resource allocation' has as its goal, surely, maximisation of general welfare. But this is but one of society's goals; and 'the State' cannot wholeheartedly pursue its resource-allocation function and its integration function at the same time. Failure to come up to expectations is again 'built-in'.

We may be able to bring all these considerations together into a single model, adding to the terminology used earlier in this chapter, a third test of performance: structural adaptation. (The other two are substantive success, and procedural correctness.) A test of structural adaptation is 'survival value' (which in certain conditions is seen as 'growth'). A system survives in its environment if it is able to adapt its structure to changes in the environment. If survival is in question, then all other performance tests are laid aside until survival is assured; consequently, tests of substantive success ('policy goals' in Self's terminology), or of procedural correctness (our own earlier characteristic of 'public' administration), are applicable only where survival is not in question. 'Resource tests', clearly, are of the structural adaptation kind; poor performance in those would, others things being equal, indicate low survival value.

Now the survival of ideal-type business firms is always in question, by definition: in a competitive environment, structual adaptation tests ('resource tests') naturally take precedence over other kinds of test. But for ideal-type public administration agencies, survival is not in question (Gulick, 1937, 43); the State protects them against a hostile environment by the use of the taxing power and other coercions, for the sake of the job they were set up to do. Consequently resource tests, while not wholly irrelevant, are not dominant, and one or other of the two sorts of test is more appropriate. If the job is of the resource allocation kind, with a goal of maximisation of welfare, then the test that is most relevant, however difficult to devise and apply, is the one of substantive success, a 'policy test' of achievement of goal. If the job is one of integration, this may indeed involve the maintenance of the current system, and hence survival: but it is the survival of the State, not the agency, that is at stake. To maintain the *status quo*, the State (or its ruling powers) will support the integrating agency ever more surely, and keep it going even if there is no way of testing its substantive success; then, the only tests that can be applied are those of procedural correctness. Here is another possible tool for classifying public agencies along a common scale with private ones; but again, it will not happily dichotomise between 'public' and 'private', and it pays more attention to discriminating between different kinds of public agency. ('Survival', above, does not entail the full organic analogy: it is short for 'maintenance of the governing relations', in Vickers' phrase.)

It will be argued later that more and better tools for classifying the kinds of public agency are needed (see Chapter 12). Griffith (1966) has pointed out that British Government Departments adopt a 'style' towards central-local relations that is consonant with the main job they have to do; something of the same can be seen in the field of Government-industry relations, and no doubt it would have been difficult, in the old days before their merger, to apply identical tests to the Foreign Office and the Commonwealth Relations office. Not all nationalised industries are equally close to 'private business', and some, as Self pointed out, are more regulatory than others. Inside one agency, differences may be found: the Home Office, it is well known, is a congeries of purposes and traditions and styles; like Social Services, it contains branches with distinctly 'professional' outlook on the making and implementing of social policy, and others which are in the mainstream of the 'bureaucratic' orientation (Blau's distinction: Blau and Scott, 1962).

In short, it may be wiser to take the view that any character that one gives to 'public administration as such' is likely to apply only where it applies, even in the broad perspective in which it is being compared and contrasted with 'private' or 'business' administration. Look at public administration just a little more closely, and internal distinctions that seem much more significant than these contrasts stand out clearly. On the other hand, step back a pace and look at both public and business administration in the West together, in contrast to another culture—as do the comparative administration theorists in one way, and the domestic New Left or 'dissident youth culture' in another—and they are seen as intertwined parts of the same system, inseparable from one another, the values of the one dependent upon the values of the other.

CHAPTER ELEVEN

Centralisation
and Specialisation

Administrative values are increasingly liable to be seen, from the viewpoint of the developing country or of dissident youth in particular, to be either 'capitalistic' or 'bureaucratic' or both, each term in more or less rigorous definition. This is a mine-strewn field we enter, one in which scholastic pedantry often accompanies high emotional commitment; I can but apologise to its denizens in advance for rushing in, on the excuse that it is not possible to write about administration in this epoch without at least noting the arguments of those for whom the revolution to come is one not so much for control of the executive organs of State as against the very existence of such organs.

Sjoberg (in Riggs, 1971, 277) suggested that not only did the Western advisers who accompanied aid to developing countries in the 1950s and 1960s take with them 'principles of administration' that were culture-specific to a degree few of them suspected, they also took a preference for 'developmental' change—evolutionary or gradual change, an orderly and controlled transition from the present to a future state—which, often unconsciously, rested on their experience of successful change in their own countries but not on any evaluation of the experience and need of the developing country. They were 'anti-revolutionary' on a purely technical level, as well perhaps as on the level they more clearly perceived, where they were opposed to an overturning of existing authority structures in other countries precisely because they feared its spread into their own. In many development situations, Sjoberg noted, only 'revolutionary fervour' can hope to break the existing mould and exact the sacrifices necessary to rapid industrialisation; only a 'revolutionary bureaucracy' (one which stands the Weberian ideal-type on its head, having high ideological commitment to the régime in the upper echelons and relative neutrality at the lower levels) can provide the necessary flexibility of rule application and the means of rapid socialisation of the population.

As already noted, the study of bureaucratisation provided the main focus for many of the 'development administration' scholars. The central unresolved dilemma is of the chicken-and-egg kind: development, however lavishly aided, will not occur unless there is a civil service sufficiently 'Weberian' to cope with the problems, so perhaps one should begin by 'developing the administration' (Riggs, 1956); but to try to impose a Weberian bureaucracy on a political system that cannot support it is to make the archetypal error everyone now knows about, and the form of each polity is an expression of its social ecology, which one tinkers with at one's peril. So an optimistic 'social engineering' approach is opposed by a somewhat pessimistic 'social organism' view, and common ground is found by describing what development entails once it has begun, without being able to say much about how it begins. Thus Riggs (in Weidner, 1970) notes that development means an increase in the number of things a society can make decisions about, instead of take as immutable; for Landau in the same volume, development means an increased reliance on rationality in decision making. Perhaps the first is equivalent to a move along Riggs' own earlier scale away from the 'fused' society and towards the 'diffracted' society, an increase in specialisation. Perhaps the second is equivalent to an increase in the collecting of information together in order to enable a rational choice, and the collecting of authority together in order that decisions can be taken where the information is, which is an increase in centralisation. If it is permissible to strip the Weberian definition of 'bureaucracy' down to these essentials—a certain degree of specialisation of task and function and a certain degree of centralisation of information and authority ('legal-rational' authority), then certainly development appears to mean an increase in bureaucratisation; but we are still ignorant of which comes first, if either. Nevertheless, if the argument holds, the relationship would obtain whether the initial movement of development were evolutionary or revolutionary, capitalistic or socialistic.

Reactions to bureaucracy

Scholars of bureaucracy from the beginning have elaborated what Merton (late in the line, but an early post-Weberian) called the 'dysfunctions', or 'social pathology' of the form in the real world, that accompanied the advantages claimed by Weber ('its purely technical superiority over any other form of organization', comparing with other forms 'exactly as does the machine with the non-mechanical modes of productions'—Weber, in Gerth and Mills (1946) 1961, 214). Merton suggested that these dysfunctions were of two main types:

> The first type, which may be called *over-organization*, involves an excessive development of those bureaucratic routines which, kept within limits, are functionally necessary to the operation of a large administrative apparatus. For example, documentary records are to a certain point indispensable to large-scale organization, but when these are so valued for their own sake as to be needlessly multiplied and elaborated, they involve a degree of over-organization that gets in the way of discharging the functions of the bureaucracy. The second type is *under-organization*. This includes those bureaucratic ills, as instanced by nepotism, favouritism, graft, corruption, and the like, which, upon analysis, are found to represent failure to live up to the requirements of bureaucratic structure. Some critics, adopting an attitude of *anti-organization*, do not confine themselves to these pathologies, but oppose bureaucratic structure in principle. This attitude is commonly based on the values of a more simply organized society in which much of life's business could be conducted within a parochial sphere characterized by personal ties rather than by structures of impersonal relations (*Merton et al, 1952, 396*).

This last observation should serve to remind us that anarchic reactions to bureaucracy have a history that goes back beyond 1968. But the main concept that may be derived from that passage is the attractive idea of an 'amount of organization' in a bureaucratic structure that would be 'just right', not over, not under—in contrast to, say, Crozier's understanding of 'bureaucracy' as the pathology itself.

These two reactions to bureaucracy can be designated the 'remedial' and the 'radical'. The assumption of most Weberian scholarship (see Diamant, 1962) is that the undoubted technical benefits of an organisational structure emphasising specialisation of task and authoritative co-ordination can be obtained at acceptable cost, by making modifications to the structure and mitigating the dysfunctional effects. The second and more pessimistic reaction tends to the belief that the unwanted aspects of bureaucracy are inseparable from the positively-valued aspects, and that above a certain size, at least, the unwanted aspects inevitably predominate, so that the costs of bureaucratic structure *as such* outweigh the benefits, and the only cure is the radical one of 'root out and start over'.

It was the second view that was first taken in nineteenth-century English discussion; 'bureaucracy' was a disease the continentals had, but Parliamentary Government and 'local self-government' (whether in the Gneist or the Toulmin Smith sense) could keep it at bay in England. By the beginning of the twentieth century, however, the unreality of this myth was apparent, and the inevitability of 'bureaucratisation' began to be accepted, however reluctantly; naturally, attention then turned to a remedial approach, devising means of keeping its excesses under control and preventing it spreading (Muir, 1910; Hewart, 1929; etc.). English Guild Socialism in the early decades of this century was in effect a denial of the inevitability of the trend towards increasing 'bigness' and centralisation; but official Labour Party policy became committed to 'nationalisation'—bigger units still, more and more centralised, on the grounds that the basic defect in the way Britain was run was not the structure of capitalism but the profit motive. The 'big machine' was acceptable as long as it was a socialist machine, controlled by 'the people' (see Cole, 1948; Pelling, 1961; Miliband, 1961; etc.).

Nowhere are the mines more thickly strewn for the non-expert than in the field of the history of the Russian Revolution and its aftermath. To pursue the present theme in a few paragraphs is virtually to ensure misconception and misunderstanding; and of all the available techniques, out-of-context quotation from V. I. Lenin is probably the most foolhardy of all, especially if one proceeds by contrasting a pre-1918 passage with a post-1918 one. Let me nevertheless do just that, because it is the positions held that are interesting, irrespective of who held them at what time. The Party, for instance, had its own version of the choice between *collegium* and *Einheitssystem*: between control of a factory by a workers' council, and centralised control through a manager appointed by the Party. Lenin held both positions, at different times (Bell, (1960) 1962, 375), according to what he thought would best serve the interests of the Bolsheviks. But his conversion to single-headed management appeared whole-hearted, and based on a belief in what might now be called 'technological imperatives', as enshrined in Taylorian 'Scientific Management'. Lenin was in no doubt that 'large scale machine industry' was 'the material productive source and foundation of socialism', and that such a manufacturing system called for 'strict unity of will', ensured by 'thousands subordinating their will to the will of one'. 'The possibility of socialism', he said in 1919,

> will be determined by our success in combining Soviet rule and Soviet organization or management with the latest progressive measures of capitalism. We must introduce in Russia the study and teaching of the Taylor system and its systematic trial and adoption (*Lenin*, Collected Works, *VII; 'Scientific Management and the Dictatorship of the Proletariat'; quoted in Bell, (1960) 1962, 261*).

In *State and Revolution*, written in August 1917, he advanced a theory that socialism could simply adopt and adapt the structures of capitalism, even *fulfil* them:

> Capitalist culture has created large-scale production, factories, railways, the postal services, telephones, etc., and on this basis the great majority of functions of the 'old state power' have become so simplified and can be reduced to such simple operations of registration, filing and checking that they will be quite within the reach of every literate person, and it will be possible to perform them for 'workingmen's wages', which circumstances can (and must) strip these functions of every shadow of privilege, of every appearance of 'official grandeur'.... Such a beginning, on the basis of large-scale production, of itself leads to the gradual 'withering away' of all bureaucracy, to the gradual creation of a new order, an order without question marks, an order which has nothing to do with wage slavery, an order in which the more and more simplified functions of control and accounting will be performed by each in turn, will then become a habit, and will finally die out as special functions of a special stratum of the population (*Lenin*, Collected Works *XXI, 184–9; quoted in Bell, (1960 (1962, 372; and see Megill, 1970, 106*).

One is reminded of President Andrew Jackson's first annual message to Congress in 1829:

> The duties of all public officers are, or at least admit of being made, so plain and simple that men of intelligence may readily qualify themselves for their performance (*quoted in White, (1926) 1948, 316*);

and of the early Marx and Engels in *The German Ideology*, going to extraordinary lengths to demonstrate that 'special functions' will not be as necessary in a communist society as they are in the capitalist one:

For as soon as labour is distributed, each man has a particular, exclusive sphere of activity which is forced upon him and from which he cannot escape. He is a hunter, a fisherman, a shepherd, or a critical critic, and must remain so if he does not want to lose his means of livelihood, while in communist society, where nobody has one exclusive sphere of activity but each can become accomplished in any branch he wishes, society regulates the general production and thus makes it possible for me to do one thing today and another tomorrow, to hunt in the morning, fish in the afternoon, rear cattle in the evening, criticise after dinner, just as I have a mind, without ever becoming hunter, fisherman, shepherd or critic (*Marx and Engels, (1846) 1969, 295*).

(This is so vivid a sketch of the life of a tweed-clad English country landowner as to be ironic—it surely cannot have been intended that way.)

Capitalism for Lenin in 1917, then, as for Marx and Engels, and indeed for the British Labour Party, was a matter of the ownership and control of the means of production; and Lenin was ready to separate that from the large-scale nature of the production machine. In the terms of the present chapter, he was not a 'radical' over bureaucracy; in *State and Revolution*, he held that it would 'wither' of its own accord, for although there would be centralisation, there would be no need for specialisation, in governmental administration. It was a curious piece of unrealistic optimism (akin perhaps to some similar hopes for computerised administration a generation later), and was retracted in an oft-quoted speech to the Miners' Congress in 1920:

> Can every worker know how to administer the State? Practical people know this is a fairy tale... The trade unions are a school of communism and administration. When they have spent these years at school, they will learn, but it progresses slowly... (*quoted in Bell, (1960) 1962, 382; Harris, 1968, 166*).

In the West, the debate over bureaucracy, now a century old, continued; opposition to it bolstered by Michels' 'iron law of oligarchy' (increase of size in organisations ensures a growing gap between leaders and followers, between the self preservation aims of the administrative staff and the ostensive *raison d'etre* of the organisation); its defence put on a new footing by the reception of Weber's demonstration of its technical superiority, its 'rationality'. But the specifically English strain of opposition, which had been to centralisation above all, spread and deepened. Huxley's *Brave*

New World (1932) and Orwell's *1984* (1949), though apparently directed against what were being called 'totalitarian societies', as were the 'mass society' and 'fear of freedom' theses of Mannheim (1940) and Fromm (1942), were warnings about perceived trends in the non-totalitarian West. In Burnham (1941) and Berle (1954), the analyses are clearly directed against the *industrialised* nature of Western society; and the first of the new wave of radical attacks on capitalism in America arrived in 1956 in C. Wright Mills' *The Power Elite*—a critique not only of 'big business' but of 'big government' as well, and of the 'sham democracy' of the political processes of control over the 'military-industrial complex'. Then, by the 1960s, it was not only bigness and power that came under attack, but once again, complexity: specialisation of function, even expertise—'the technocracy':

> In the technocracy, nothing is any longer small or simple or readily apparent to the non-technical man. Instead, the scale and intricacy of all human activities—political, economic, cultural—transcends the competence of the amateurish citizen and inexorably demands the attention of specially trained experts. Further, around this central core of experts who deal with large-scale public necessities, there grows up a circle of subsidiary experts who, battening on the general social prestige of technical skill in the technocracy, assume authoritative influence over even the most seemingly personal aspects of life: sexual behavior, child-rearing, mental health, recreation, etc. In the technocracy everything aspires to become purely technical, the subject of professional attention. The technocracy is therefore the regime of experts—or of those who can employ the experts. ... For our purposes here it will be enough to define the technocracy as that society in which those who govern justify themselves by appeal to technical experts who, in turn, justify themselves by appeal to scientific forms of knowledge. And beyond the authority of science there is no appeal (*Roszak*, (*1968*)*1970, 6, 7*).

Amongst the critics of the existing order in the West, and amongst those of them who concentrate on the problem of 'bureaucracy' or 'technocracy', there can now be seen an old division: not between centralisers and decentralisers, for all are more or less agreed on decentralism; but between the 'remedial' and the 'radical' views on the other of bureaucracy's main features: specialisation. The contemporary radical view was enshrined in the *Manifesto of the Enragés de Caen*, in the French student uprisings of 1968, quoted by the Cohn-Bendits in *Obsolete Communism, The Left-Wing Alterna-*

tive; among the principles proclaimed there, 'principles that are valid for all industrial societies, and for all the oppressed of our time', were 'To destroy all hierarchies' and 'To put an end to the division of labour and of knowledge.' For many of the students, as for a strain of philosophical dissent that runs (to go back no further) from Rousseau through Bakunin and Kropotkin to the Marx and Engels of *The German Ideology* and the Lenin of *State and Revolution*, it is not only hierarchy and authoritarianism and centralisation that is objectionable in 'bureaucracy', but also specialisation, expertise, division of labour. Thus the dividing line in modern critics lies between those who reject hierarchy and centralisation but not specialisation and 'technique', and those who reject both.

Marcuse, for instance, in *One-Dimensional Man* avoids attacking technique, expertise, and rationality, and finds conditions in which centralisation of control is acceptable:

> The goal of authentic self-determination by individuals depends upon effective social control over the production and distribution of the necessities (in terms of the achieved level of culture, material and intellectual).
>
> Here, technological rationality, stripped of its exploitative features, is the sole standard and guide in planning and developing the available resources for all. Self-determination in the production and distribution of vital goods and services would be wasteful. The job is a technical one, and as a truly technical job, it makes for the reduction of physical and mental toil. In this realm, centralized control is rational if it establishes the preconditions for meaningful self-determination. The latter can then become effective in its own realm—in the decisions which involve the production and distribution of the economic surplus, and in the individual existence (*Marcuse, 1964; reproduced in Oglesby, 1969, 36*).

The question turns into this: whether the evils to be abolished are the result of capitalism only, or of industrialism itself. The students in the Sorbonne in 1968 were clear that it was a whole way of life that must go; the French car workers were not so sure that they wanted to return to a pre-industrial state. It is not all that long ago since 'mechanisation' was being equated with progress toward plenty, and since the breaking down of tasks into specialisms ('rationalisation', it was called) was promising such abundance of social wealth that men would forget their bickering over its division.

The nineteenth-century critique of the machine age took two

main forms: the one, led most notably by Ruskin and Morris, concerned with the accompanying degradation of the environment and the growing mismatch between the uniform products of industry and the variety of human needs practical and aesthetic; the other, led by Marx and Engels, concerned with the degradation of the human dignity of the worker and the growing mismatch between the rewards of labour and of capital. Ruskin and Morris had in mind the mines, the railways, and the 'black Satanic mills' of manufacturing industry, and might gladly have abandoned 'progress' in those fields, to return to the technology of the horse-carriage and the craftsman (though perhaps less happily to medieval medicine and sanitation): but they were not much listened to except by other romantics, for the attractiveness of replacing manual labour by mechanical aids was overwhelming to most people, and often seen as 'God's plan' for mankind. Marx and Engels saw as clearly as had Fourier that monotony of task is soul-destroying, and looked for methods of what is now called 'job enlargement'; but they in no way wished to turn back the clock of discovery and innovation, or the movement towards mechanisation—on the contrary, they expected that the removal of the capitalist incubus would release the creativity of the workers themselves, and enable diversion of the wealth that industrialisation was capable of creating, into greater, leisure rather than greater profits.

What has happened since then, to make 'deindustrialisation' almost as attractive an idea, is by now a commonplace of discussion even amongst the 'men in the street'. Technology has got more and more complicated, and units of management have got bigger and bigger, and there appears to be no way of halting the trend: what Galbraith called the 'imperatives of technology and organisation' seem to have taken over (Galbraith, 1967).

But what are these imperatives, and precisely what is the mechanism that is out of control? In order to prevent the discussion getting mixed up with 'capitalism' again, let us talk not of manufacturing industry, rather of an experience widely shared but not basically industrial—moving from primary school to secondary school in England.

Imperatives of organisation

It is a good principle of town planning that primary school children should be able to walk to school, without crossing main traffic arteries; so new housing estates are, as much as anything, built around the primary school, and an easily-understood set of principles can determine what number of dwellings will supply the children needed to comfortably fill a school of a given size—the school's 'catchment area'. But a secondary school is always bigger, and the average secondary school child's 'journey-to-work' is longer, and the question is why this should be so.

The main difference a school child finds on moving from primary to secondary school is that he is no longer taught by the same teacher all day; the class goes to different teachers for different subjects. This is the key factor in the larger size of the school. Whereas in a primary school six teachers, each taking one year-group class of thirty children for five school days a week, would have their time filled by 180 children, a specialist teacher of French, say, giving a typical average of three hours a week of French to six secondary school classes of thirty children would be busy for only 18 hours, or three days out of the five. If he or she is to have a full week's work there must be ten classes of thirty children to teach. But a 'French Department' of only one teacher would not allow of much development of specialism *within* the subject—say, into beginners' and advanced teaching, or into language as such and literature, drama, etc. To give both kinds of expertise scope, you need a minimum Department of four teachers; and hence a school of forty classes of thirty pupils, or 1,200 instead of 180—assuming all took French among their subjects. The actual figures and details are not significant, of course; it is the principle which holds, and which is one of the reasons why the size of, and consequently the catchment area of, a secondary school is so much larger—by an 'order of magnitude'—than that of a primary school.

Of course, it is not *necessary* that every teacher of French should have a full working week; that is a matter of economy, or cost in resources. A father who was rich enough might provide all the services of a school for one pupil if he was so minded, each teacher having a tiny work-load. The relationship between degree of specialisation and size of organisation is mediated by unit cost: one can have high specialisation in a small organisation at high unit cost, but if cost is not to rise with increase of specialisation, organisation size must be permitted to increase.

However, increase in size allows of a second kind of division of labour, or rather of task. In the primary school, the teacher is not only teacher of all subjects, he or she is also nursemaid, collector of savings, meals supervisor, and so on; because of the small number of children, it is not 'economic' to employ separate persons for those tasks—even though such persons might be paid considerably smaller salaries than teachers. So professional labour is used for non-professional tasks because of the tiny throughput, or work-load, in each of these tasks. In a larger school, however, the work-load may well be large enough to permit breakdown of job into higher-paid and lower-paid elements; so that size of itself, in terms of work-load and throughput, brings possibilities of economies. Given the enlargement by 'an order of magnitude' necessary for the employment of subject specialists, a relatively small further increase—say a doubling—may allow a disproportionately great saving in staff costs, by enabling the 'full working week' threshold to be crossed for a nurse, secretary, non-teaching lab assistant, and so on, allowing professional teachers to spend more of their time on purely academic tasks, or inseparable community activities such as sports and the school play.

The appearance on the market of specialised equipment of various sorts may engage the interest of educationists, giving promise of enabling teachers to demonstrate things they simply could not otherwise—raising the quality of their teaching. The advantages of devoting bits of school space to specialised uses will occur, again in order to improve the quality of the teaching as well as save time and bother. But each of these improvements probably has a threshold of 'utilisation' below which it is 'uneconomic', and utilisation is again a matter of throughput and size. Some of these specialised devices or space uses might require an increase of another 'order of magnitude' if costs were not to escalate unacceptably, others might need only a further doubling, say. Then further 'breakdown of task' economies might come in sight; by centralising control over several schools, some 'real savings' might be made on staff costs, by some form of mechanisation of routine tasks perhaps.

It may be apparent that there are two kinds of driving force behind increase in size of school: one, the attempt to make use of specialised teachers, equipment, rooms, etc., in order to maximise the quality of the education provided; the other, the attempt to match grade of work and grade of worker, or machine, or accommodation, in order to avoid waste and minimise the cost of whatever quality of education is provided. The second is perhaps well enough known as the drive for 'economies of scale': a large enough total throughput enables, first, a 'vertical' division of task into programmable and non-programmable elements, maintaining full work-loads of each; then, further breakdown of programmed elements into a number of routinisable segments, perhaps (if through-put increases sufficiently) several work-loads in each segment; then, mechanisation. There are other possible savings, from bulk-buying of materials, economies in accommodation and domestic services, and so on.

It is less often recognised, I think, that it may be the first of these two drives—advance in specialisation—that has the higher gearing, that produces tenfold increases in size as against doublings. An advance in technology is seldom indeed associated with a simplification of work processes; more commonly, it means that several persons are engaged each on only a part of a task that one man did before by himself—perhaps indirectly, through the manufacture of machines which make it *look* as if one man can now do much more work than before. It is another illusion that new methods are more economical of space or capital: they usually are not if manufacturing space and capital are included. Yet it is true that it is commonly a much higher quality of product or service that is the result.

There are hundreds of other possible illustrations. The introduction of mechanical coal-cutting into British mines has been well documented; the necessary size of workgroup at a single coal face (a much larger face) typically increased from nine to around forty, the different tasks performed by one man fell from twelve or more to one or two (Trist and Bamforth, 1951; Trist, 1963). The change from tar-and-chip macadamising methods of road repairing to 'black top' laid by a Barber-Greene machine similarly creates some new specialised skills, the machine itself (unlike the barrows and lorries employed in some parts of the lower technology operation) cannot be used for any other job whatsoever, the size of the necessary gang is increased tenfold. Many members of the larger higher-technology gangs are working to more exacting specifications and closer tolerances than were their low technology counterparts (hence the higher quality of the product or service); so they must become specialists in their segment of the total task, and to that extent are not interchangeable. Hence, with advance in technology, organisation size increases *and* internal differentiation increases too.

Output capacity is increased at the same time, of course; not by as large a factor as increase in personnel or capital employed, since working to finer tolerances and so on mops up some of it; but if whatever extra capacity is created is not fully utilised, if specialists are employed on non-specialist tasks or left idle, the cost of each unit of production or service will go up by even more than would be warranted by the higher quality. Consequently, to absorb increased capacity, 'demand' must be found or created.

In certain circumstances, where demand is linked to some version of catchment area, the extra demand required can be created by enlarging the catchment area. The effect is one of 'centralisation'. A rural district which maintained its own roads *could* change to a Barber-Greene, and achieve full utilisation by sending it round the roads of the district continuously, so that each mile of road was resurfaced every year or so. The ratepayers of that district would enjoy roads of a silkiness unmatched anywhere in the world, a standard of service which would be reflected in their local rates. If the rate bill were to be reduced to an acceptable level, an acceptable standard of repair would have to be fixed, and the machine's capacity utilised by finding more miles of road, extending its 'catchment area', until the factors balance again. That, of course, is why Barber-Greenes are operated by county councils and not districts. Perhaps it is why R.D.C.s no longer have highway powers. But from the viewpoint of the district councillor or ratepayer, the decisions about its road maintenance have, on the introduction of the higher technology methods, been 'centralised' to county level. A local demand which in the lower technology could be absorbed by local productive or service capacity, and the decisions about it taken locally, has now to be 'fed into' a single centre in order to utilise its greater capacity. The quality of product or service is, by definition, higher; it is a quality that could not have been obtained from the low technology local provider; but to the local (now peripheral) observer, centralisation may be the more obvious effect.

The other drive, for economies of scale, also produces the centralisation effect. Work-loads are being pushed up so as to concentrate in one place enough work of a single category to allow of its routinisation. If a threshold is being approached but not quite reached, the temptation is to widen the category a little so as to capture enough work, or to reduce the number of categories into which incoming work is sorted so as to maximise the flow through each. The result is that pieces of work are treated as conforming to standard patterns when they do not; pieces get their awkward edges knocked off, as it were; variety is reduced by simply ignoring it; tolerances of fit, instead of being closer than under other methods, are looser than ever. This amounts to a tendency to *reduce* quality of product or service; and this is what is likely to be noticed by the observer, though it is true that costs are also considerably lower. Again, examples are legion. It is the difference between the

Rolls-Royce and the mass-produced car; it is the effect that exasperates the person with the 'difficult' foot size, who has to look long and hard for a shop that stocks a shoe that will nearly fit, or order specially at extra cost. Where the work consists of the problems of human clients, reduction of variety from 'person' to 'case' appears as 'dehumanization', and the other 'bureaucratic dysfunctions'. It cannot be claimed, as with the other driving force, that quality of product or service is higher; but the *costs* of the centralised operation are likely to be lower than those of the decentralised operation possibly by an order of magnitude.

It is not at all necessary, in order to explain centralisation or dehumanisation, to postulate either a 'desire for power' or a particularly nasty disposition among the decision-makers involved. On the contrary, the phenomena are sufficiently explained by postulating only praiseworthy motives—the desire to make the highest possible quality of service available at acceptable cost, the desire to avoid waste and ensure equity. The effects are not those of motivation: they are caused by 'the imperatives of technology and organisation'.

It may be, of course, that those who propose increase in size mistake the wishes of the people, and are wrong in assuming that if a choice were to be given between higher quality of service and local self-government, the people would always opt for higher quality; or if a choice were given between personalised attention and a tenfold increase in taxation, they would always opt for lower taxes. But certainly, the people cannot have higher quality, local self-government, personal attention, and lower taxes, all at once.

The two drives analytically distinguished here are unlikely to be found separately in the real world, as 'pure types'. Rather will any situation of organisational change probably show both of them operating together, one against the other: the drive to keep down costs by reducing quality inhibiting the drive to utilise specialisation and increase quality. But both drives operate together to increase organisation size and internal differentiation.

The Sorcerer's Apprentice

Amongst biologists, increase of differentiation of parts in an embryo, from the unspecialised egg to the specialised organs, as the foetus grows to full term, is a process which is called 'organisation'.

Spencer, we saw, used the analogy at social level, contrasting un-developed societies precisely by the greater specialisation, the higher organisation, of the latter (Spencer, 1876, I, 582; see p. 80 above). Riggs noted that

> Only the more advanced countries create 'organizations' in the sense that this term is used in the sociological literature

and suggested that

> the less developed a social system, the more difficult it is for that system to create organizations; the fewer the organizations in a society, the more difficult it is for that society to develop. Perhaps above a certain minimum level or critical threshold ... a society finds it relatively easy to produce new organizations, and therefore relatively easy to accelerate its rate of develop-ment as a fruit of organized activity ... (*Riggs, 1971, 87*).

If it is permissible to put these two analogies together, then both are saying that a developing society is like an early embryo, its cells relatively undifferentiated, and that development of the society, as of the embryo, *means* the creation of organs with specialised functions (we do not specify the cause of the development); finally, Riggs suggests that when a certain degree of organisation has been completed, the society is ready to be 'born' into the world of developed societies, growth thereafter proceeding more or less in-dependently to 'maturity'.

The analogy, of course, breaks down there, at least: maturity, or adulthood, in the organism has a precise reference, the point when the potentiality of the genetic material is exhausted; whereas there is no such reference in the organisation or the society. But: what if there were some such point of full organisational development for the organisation and the society, that we have not yet recognised? Are the troubles that some organisations, and some societies, are undoubtedly experiencing, due to their having unwittingly passed that point, become 'over-organised', entered an 'unnatural' stage of development for which there is no parallel in the organism? Is technocratic society a society that has gone beyond its blueprint, gone on differentiating, centralising and dehumanising until the whole thing has outrun human scale?

It is only poetry, of course; but others have played with the notion of a society 'out of control'. Lewis Mumford introduced in *The Pentagon of Power* (as in several of his earlier books) what he called the 'great paradox of automation', put once and for all in Goethe's fable of the Sorcerer's Apprentice:

Our civilisation has cleverly found a magic formula for setting both industrial and academic brooms and pails of water to work by themselves, in ever-increasing quantities at an ever-increasing speed. But we have lost the Master Magician's spell for altering the tempo of this process, or halting it when it ceases to serve human functions and purposes, though this formula (foresight and feedback) is written plainly on every organic process.

As a result we are already, like the apprentice, beginning to drown in the flood. The moral should be plain: unless one has the power to stop an automatic process—and if necessary reverse it—one had better not start it. To spare ourselves humiliation over our failure to control automation, many of us now pretend that the process conforms exactly to our purposes and alone meets all our needs—or, to speak more accurately, we cast away those qualifying human traits that would impede the process (*Mumford*, (*1964*) *1971*, *180*).

Not automation only, perhaps, but 'industrial society': according to a report of the Zeno Philosophical Symposium held in Cyprus in late 1971, there was general agreement among the world's leading philosophers that

society is moving into a post-industrial stage in which either the cumulative horrors of the last 150 years will be generalised to complete the destruction of human values or society will have to be transformed into something quite other than it is today . . . For them, for the Yugoslavs no less than the British and Americans, the organisation of the means of production and distribution, although important, is secondary to the problems now presented by the nature of industrial society itself (*Peter Jenkins*, '*The Guardian*', *13 September 1971*).

The radical Left, feeling in their bones as Marcuse put it once that

this society is getting increasingly repressive, destructive, of the human and natural capabilities to be free, to shape one's own life without exploiting others (*Marcuse, in Teodori*, (*1969*) *1970*, *469*)

tend to lay the blame at the door of capitalism—or sometimes, accepting Weber's and Tawney's theses about the conditions of the growth of capitalism, at the door of the Protestant ethic. Perhaps the blame should be laid farther back still; to that dawn where societal differentiation into non-State, non-Church organisations was rendered possible. Wherever the blame must lie, there is clear consensus about impending disaster unless the process can be reversed.

Though different in subject, there is striking convergence with the analyses of Barry Commoner, Paul Ehrlich, Jay Forrester and other students of the near future (Commoner, 1972; Meadows, 1972; and see Maddox, 1972). These are all 'doomsday' analyses, with a millennialist character appropriate to the approach of the year A.D. 2000. Yet it would be foolish to ignore a message in which the diagnoses and prescriptions of so many professions, from the farthest and most 'infantile' Left to the equally extreme 'senile' Right and including a sober, philosophic and scientific centre, come together. And the message is that technology is now high enough, that the villain is not capitalism or human greed as such, not hierarchy or authoritarianism as such, but increase of specialisation, division of labour and task—'organisation' as such. The fear of organisation is the beginning of wisdom.

CHAPTER TWELVE

Theory and Practice in Public Administration

Should any practising administrator have chanced to pick up this volume, and persevered this far, he may have marvelled that so many pages could be written, all undeniably about administration in one or other of its senses, and none of them be about his own daily work—the reading and writing of correspondence, minutes, and memoranda, the use of the telephone, attendance at meetings, interviews, informal discussions with colleagues, the searching for needed information, the calculating and tabulating, and so on: the imagined ciné-record of an administrator's day. A practising politician, perhaps, has the same reaction to most books about politics: they describe the setting, the conditions, the issues—but seldom outside novels and autobiography does one get any description of the *practice*, the 'nitty-gritty' of what it is like to be a politician, the tricks of the trade—the sort of thing a politician's (and an administrator's) *talk* is full of. Again: for understanding what it is like to be a head of a college, there are almost no textbooks at all; the authorities are Snow, Cornford and Dundonald—the first writing novels, the other two in the tradition of *Fürstenspiegel* or 'advice to Princes', a genre that goes back well beyond Machiavelli.

The earliest 'text-books' were written-down talk: the *Dialogus de Scaccario*, which dates from 1179, is a procedure manual for the Court of the Exchequer, in the form of a conversation between Richard Fitzneal, Bishop of London and one of the Barons of the Exchequer, and one of his juniors (Johnson, 1950). Most descriptions of administration to this day are oral, between master and apprentice, and much of it is not written down, partly because it seems so specific to time and place and circumstances, partly

197

because it has that touch of the illicit or scandalous that inhibits a record—'you can't always say this out loud, but the facts are that more often than not . . .'

Yet there *are* books on memo-writing, on filing, on conduct of meetings and interviews, even on use of the telephone. They are usually written at a fairly elementary level, and the degree of time-and-place specificity that is feasible is strictly limited. It is the translation of the training function to the classroom that makes a market for written instruction in administrative practice; but the value of the one-to-one oral tradition, that enabled a flexible blend of specificity and generality, that taught as much by what was left unsaid as by what was said, that varied the syle to suit the persons concerned, has never been lost sight of, and few of such 'practical' books escape heavy criticism from practitioners. A useful classroom technique for replicating the occasion of oral advice is 'simulation', by use of purely documentary case-histories and problems, or more lifelike still, role-playing, games and other exercises. What can be more appropriately produced in the classroom, that used to take years of experience to produce in an inferior version, is understanding of the wider setting, the conditions of success and failure, the law and social mores, and so on; the high degree of specificity that accompanies the oral tradition may here be a handicap. Hence the greater number of books like that, a few actually of the 'written-down talk' kind, by practising administrators. Relatively, however, the number of civil servants who have written books on administration is very small (and of local government officers and public corporation executives, even smaller); such authors (e.g. Bridges, 1950; Munro, 1925; Sisson, 1959; Baker, 1972) have been, figuratively speaking, well thumbed.

Most books on administration, as on politics, painting and many other essentially practical professions, have been written not by practitioners for other practitioners or their apprentices, but by academics in colleges and universities, for their colleagues and students. Most of these books are not training manuals at all, though they may have a function in the training of those who do intend to follow these professions; rather are they designed to fulfil a general educational purpose, to provide information that it is felt should be available to educated people who are not themselves administrators or whatever and do not intend to become so; or they are reports of research or reflection, designed to advance one theory about administration or refute another. The general educational purpose needs but little emphasis on administrative method and practice; it stresses, rather, meaning and significance, the impact of what administration does, not how it is done; relations with other processes, rather than internal relations; background, rather than foreground.

But although that is not 'practice' as it is known by the practitioner, it is not 'theory' either. It could be called 'the study and teaching of administration', distinct both from 'training for administration' and 'theorising about administration', yet partaking of the nature of both. Ordinary nomenclature does not make any such distinctions: 'Administration' (or more frequently, in qualified form, 'Public Administration', 'Business Administration', 'Hospital Administration', and so on) can mean the collective noun for the substantive activities denoted, an extension of our earlier Tenth Meaning (see p. 16); or it can mean the title of a subject or course in a training programme, or in a general education programme; or it can mean the field and material of a research study, or a body of theorising upon such material. Since none of the fourteen meanings we isolated earlier accommodates such usages, perhaps we should recognise a Fifteenth Meaning:

(15) *title of a subject, field, discipline, course, or examination in a school, college, university or other institution of training or education*, whose content is provided by the study of administration in one or more of the foregoing Meanings;
an area of academic and theoretical research, the description and evaluation of the machinery or work associated with one or more of the foregoing Meanings.

Assumptions and observations

Although 'theory' and 'practice' are separated in the chapter title, and indeed there is a considerable difference between the characteristic modes of 'the practitioner' and 'the academic theorist', nevertheless it should not be pretended that 'practice' is wholly untheoretical and 'theory' quite divorced from practice.

Any practitioner of a practical art operates in a context of assumptions and suppositions about what follows what, and what is a condition of what, that (if there were need) could be expressed as a set of theories, susceptible of test and proof (or disproof). We all of us take for granted some understandings about the world we live in that are *not* proven truth—in fact, may have been proven quite inadequate as explanations of given phenomena: but these understandings are yet 'good enough' for us, they enable us to make sense out of what we see and hear. The most obvious example is that most of us to all intents and purposes live in a universe that is governed by the laws of Newtonian physics, although these laws are inadequate for most modern theoretical physicists—indeed, so are the laws of Einsteinian relativity for some of them: whereas some of us are just beginning to grasp *those* as an intellectual exercise of little application to daily life, the frontiersmen of sub-atomic physics live in a stochastic Heisenberg universe ordered by degrees of uncertainty and probability. The advanced thinking of one generation becomes the common property of educated men in the next, and the common sense of the one after that. The corollary is that what is 'common sense' to one man may be 'the obsolete theory of some defunct economist' to his educated critic, and 'philosophical nonsense' to another.

On the whole, the academic theorist is trained to be more self-conscious about 'common sense', to explore assumptions (or at least make them explicit), and to direct himself more towards coherence and consistency *between* theories, than the practitioner ever has need to be, or would have time to be. Newtonian physics is good enough for everyday purposes; and so, in our present field, is the politics/administration dichotomy, perhaps. Most practitioners, even at lower hierarchical levels, would agree that there is a need for *some* theory or another to justify the difference between the career official and the elected politician, and would find that the conventional dichotomy still made reasonably good sense in most circumstances. Some might accommodate the odd anomaly by doing something which to the academic theorist is quite unhelpful: switching from a description of the reason for the difference, to a *prescription* of the difference—'Well, we know it doesn't always work quite like that, but that is how it ought to be'. That is no good to the academic theorist, as a way of taking care of 'facts' that don't fit the theory: the only satisfactory way is to abandon that theory and look for a better one, that accommodates more of the 'facts' without anomalies. The same criticism has to be made of the frequent spurious contrast between theory and practice: 'Yes, we know that is the theory of it, but it just doesn't work like that in practice.' If that is so, then that merely shows how bad the theory in use is, and that it is high time a new theory was suggested.

But new theories may already have been suggested, of which the practitioner is unaware. There is inevitably a gap, between the first presentation of a new theory and its reception by the practitioner, which is not only a gap in time (ideas take time to diffuse), but also in comprehension (academics tend to speak to one another in special languages, testing consistency, before someone puts them into language that is accessible to the non-specialist). It may be that some of the assumptions about the world that a practitioner more-or-less unconsciously holds (perhaps, about human perception, about what 'authority' is, about the relationship of price and supply, etc.) are assumptions that have been replaced in advanced thinking, which if it were known to the practitioner might significantly alter his own understanding of his decision situation and the choices open to him.

The practitioner may, then, be (through no fault of his own) out-of-date in his perception of what are the going theories on his work and its conditions. On the other hand, the academic, who may be more advanced in his theorising, runs the danger of explaining 'facts' that are no longer the case, of using out-of-date data; or alternatively, of basing himself on generalised or stylised accounts of phenomena which ignore variations of time and place and setting, whereas any practitioner knows that the particularities of time and place and setting are much the more significant factors in those phenomena. The practitioner may have a highly sophisticated practical understanding of 'what is what' in his own corner of the world, even if he is not skilled in expressing this as an articulated special theory. So academics go on using material that is sometimes an object of practitioners' scorn, because of this other inevitable gap—again, a gap which is not only in time (new practices take time to diffuse, to become widespread enough to 'alter the general picture' perceptibly), but also in comprehension (practitioners tend to speak to one another in special languages, understanding much that is not said, sharing a common experience that is the real basis of communication); it needs a person with a foot in both camps to make what is happening accessible to outsiders.

It is questionable who is the more ludicrous: the academic theorising on obsolete observations, or the practitioner blindly proceeding on mistaken assumptions. There is undoubtedly a gap between practitioner and theorist; but it is not expressible by a 'theory/practice dichotomy', it is a mere communications gap.

Ivory towers and packaged teaching

The distinction between 'training' and 'education' can be similarly mis-stated. There is a difference, and it can perhaps be illustrated by presenting stereotypes of the extremes, contrasting 'the staff college' and 'the university'; I draw on an earlier paper (Dunsire, 1969) presented to a conference of civil servants and teachers of Public Administration.

The 'staff college' is a type of training establishment where in principle the trainees are all employees of one employer; and where the principle governing the inclusion or exclusion of any subject in or form the curriculum, or the choice of training method, or any other teaching decision, is whether an alternative is seen as likely to produce a more useful employee. There is nothing wrong in this. By contrast, 'the university' is a type of educational establishment where the students are nationwide or international in provenance, and where ultimately the governing principle for all teaching decisions is the advancement and transmission of knowledge for its own sake, superseding even a view of the social or national interest. There is nothing wrong in this either. But the two types of institution are clearly not interchangeable.

The first corollary of the contrast is this. A trainee's time at 'the staff college' is time taken from productive employment; even if it is reasonably seen as an investment, prudence indicates that the training result desired should be clearly specified and the training programme designed to produce this result as economically (in terms of time as well as money) as is consistent with effectiveness. There is thus a premium on systematic teaching, with selected bodies of knowledge prepared in easily-assimilated form, at the expense of a certain amount of accuracy in final detail; on simulation techniques, which condense periods of skill-developing, at a certain cost in depth of appreciation; and on rapid socialising processes, which reduce variety.

'The university', on the other hand, has a given period of time with the student, during which to take him as far along an endless path as he can manage to go; and the aim is not primarily the communication of a certain body of knowledge, but the learning of what it is 'to know', the understanding of the contingency of knowledge, the discovery and exploration of knowledge. Good teaching in 'the university' consists not of the exposition of 'facts' but of conscious exposition of rival theories of what the facts are.

As already suggested, a theory is a supposition which makes sense out of some set of observations; all theories are founded on assumptions, but better theories need fewer assumptions, and academic research is concerned with improving theories. Bad 'university' teachers are not those who cannot lecture well, but those who base their teaching on obsolete or discredited theories. A good student is not he who knows more than his fellows, but he who understands the subject better—he will know how to increase his own knowledge, and that of others.

So 'the university' sees the 'staff college' as teaching what is not truth, sacrificing accuracy and completeness and individuality for the sake of the neatness of the package in which the selected information is delivered. 'The staff college' sees 'the university' as self-indulgent, remote from actuality, stultified in action by their purity of theory.

A second corollary may be noted. Teaching in 'the staff college' (and also selection of trainees, examining and reporting) is imbued with hierarchic authority. Not only is the system taught to all relevant trainees the same single system, it is also seen as the approved system. The standardised capacities produced by authoritative uniform training can be expected to raise the level of average operational performance by a calculated amount, taking into account that some 'truth' is sacrificed; the marginal cost of raising the accuracy, etc., of the package to the level of the academic ideal would not be matched by any gain in performance, and might well result in a drop through the absence of the authoritative singleness of purpose.

Teaching in 'the university', by contrast, is imbued with sapiential authority only, an authority depending upon respect for knowledge, or confidence in superior technique. To some degree always, and increasingly at higher levels of scholarship, the 'university' teacher to teach must convince. A student who, using the teacher's own methods, can show the teaching to be in error, is highly valued indeed; for this is how knowledge advances. The most important thing taught in 'the university' is how to question what is taught; and this involves scepticism about the accepted bases of the subject, of society, of knowledge, and of reasoning itself. This faculty is the most inhibiting, the most immobilising of all; an employer could not be blamed who determined to keep his staff out of such institutions at all costs.

Of course, real and actual universities fall far short of the stereotype of 'the university', principally because the society expects them to be more useful institutions than that. A great deal of university teaching is preparatory to employment in particular professions, and even where it is not, is concerned to communicate generally-accepted knowledge more than to question it. University teaching as well as staff college teaching is governed by economic considerations.

Most actual staff colleges, too, see it as part of their function to 'broaden the horizons' of their trainees, to include a considerable amount of 'general education' in their curricula, to liberate employees from too narrow a specialist outlook, to deepen understanding of fellow-men, of society, of the environment.

Nor do universities and staff colleges exhaust the spectrum of educational and training establishments. Between them come a whole range of types: polytechnics, technical colleges and colleges of further education in the public sector, and a range of business and management schools and colleges in the private sector, not attached to particular employers. Curricula and approaches vary within each type of institution, and between subjects within a single institution, so that types of institution cannot be neatly arranged along the spectrum we began with, from ivory towers to packaged teaching. In none, however, is there such an emphasis upon 'exploratory learning' as there is in 'the university' (and also in some universities); in none, the exclusive concern with purely operational performance found in 'the staff college'. There is a good deal of vocational training, and of what a recent writer called 'good, solid, conscientious technical college teaching' (Constantine, 1972). This applies to the field of administration as to other subjects.

Public Administration teaching

There is no academic 'profession' or sizeable group of teachers and scholars in this country recognising 'Administration' as their subject (there is only one Chair in Administration, at Strathclyde, and a Department, at the University of Aston in Birmingham); but there are such groups for Public Administration, and Social Administration, and there are societies, courses, and qualifications in Hospital Administration and Nursing Administration, Health Service and Public Health Administration, Municipal and Local Government Administration, Industrial and Business Administration, Archive Administration, Traffic Administration, Weights and Measures

Administration, and no doubt many more. The question whether the common presence of the word Administration in these titles means that they are all branches of the same basic subject, which therefore could be extracted and taught as 'generic Administration' (the specialist aspects being added as appropriate), is a matter of high controversy, found in its acute form as between Public Administration and Business Administration. There is so much that appears to be common to the two spheres (particularly, it is usually thought, in respect of administrative techniques, decision theory, human relations, and other sectors of organisation theory) that the setting up of an all-branches school, to share teachers, equipment, premises and so on, seems only sensible; and indeed, it has occasionally been done. If the results have never been so clearly satisfactory as to encourage universal emulation, it may be because the teaching is at fault although the principle is a sound one, or it may be that it is the principle that is wrong-headed. The consensus of opinion in Britain appears to be that the fundamental ethos of business administration and of public administration are so different that each requires to be infused through all the teaching of the whole curriculum, not just 'optional' aspects. The atmosphere is of different composition, it seems; the public servant breathes social accountability, the businessman the keen airs of commercial competitiveness. Similar arguments can be led for special schools of hospital and health administration, and so on. Whether or not such arguments are wholly and finally convincing does not matter, for in practice the really weighty arguments are those of convenience and control, over finance, selection of members, staffing policy, and the like. Providing each such school is separately viable, there may be no great benefit in having combined 'all branch' training in Administration; and at middle and lower levels of the managerial hierarchy, there may be an advantage in the specialised school, in that cases and illustrations can all be drawn from a familiar field. At the higher levels, probably, the advantage swings to the multilateral conference or seminar, where there is less straight teaching, and where members from differing milieux can greatly inform and stimulate one another. This is the main *raison d'être* of the Administrative Staff College at Henley, which in spite of its name is not a 'staff college' as defined earlier, but an independent institution drawing its course members from all fields and sectors (Rapoport, 1971).

Amongst university teachers of Public Administration, this discussion has merged with another kind of heart-searching (Simon,

1967; Charlesworth, 1968; Henderson, 1969; Schaffer, 1971; Ridley, 1972; etc.). The question broadly is this: is there a true university subject, discipline, or 'profession' called Public Administration, which would (if adequately developed) take its place amongst the Arts and Social Sciences, and hold its own as a degree subject (perhaps in combination with Political Science) against Economics, Sociology, and others, attracting students by displaying the same properties as do English and History, for example—inherent interest of content, intellectual rigour, theoretical depth, and so on: or is Public Administration basically a vocational curriculum, like Medicine, Architecture, Law, and indeed Social Administration in most universities, preparing students for specific career openings in the public service, and to do so drawing on several university subjects including Economics, Sociology, Statistics, Law, and of course Political Science or Government?

At present, the answer is affirmative both ways; the same title, Public Administration, stands for both concepts. There are several degree and diploma qualifications offered in Public Administration (B.A. in Public Administration, or Diploma in Public Administration), with curricula including courses in Economics, Sociology, History, and so on, one of the component courses being Public Administration. This is surely unusual: one does not find, among the courses which form the curriculum for a degree in Law, or Medicine, or Architecture (or Economics, History, etc.), a component course called simply 'Law', 'Medicine', etc.

As the subject title, 'Public Administration' usually includes discussion of machinery of government, public service staffing, local and regional government and administration, and public corporations, as the core material (Gunn, 1969; 1971). Either under the same subject title, or under different titles, there may be elements of comparative administration ('ideographic' or 'nomothetic', sometimes both), administrative theory (or organisation theory), public finance, decision theory, administrative law, and relations with the public. Inside the subject title, the teaching may be coloured by a distinctive approach, e.g. heavily 'quantitative', heavily 'policy-oriented', or 'sociological', depending upon the predilections of the teacher; but there is little evidence as yet of the radical commitment among young teachers which produced the 'Minnowbrook Perspective' in the United States (Marini, 1971; Waldo, 1971). In universities and polytechnics, material covering Parliament, parties and elections, pressure groups, and political philosophy (or thought, or theory), is not usually found under the subject heading of Public Administration (though this material is found, under Political Science, Politics, or Government, in degree or diploma *curricula* called Public Administration). However, in the Civil Service College, there are five Directors of Studies, in Economics, Statistics, Social Policy and Administration, Public Administration, and Personnel Management (Grebenik, 1972); this political science and political philosophy material comes under the Director of Studies in Public Administration—so that the title there is neither 'subject' nor 'curriculum', but somewhere between—which, even though a special Civil Service usage, does nothing to clarify the confusion.

In the sister field of Social Administration, much the same double usage is found: 'Social Administration' can be the name of a degree or diploma qualification which forms the educational basis for a later professional training, which then qualifies for a career as a social worker; and within the degree or diploma curriculum, there will often be a course entitled 'Social Administration', describing the organisation of the social services and the problems of their administration. But in some quarters there is an attempt to keep a distinction, to reserve 'Social Administration' for the study of the organisation and working of the social services, and not apply it to studies preparatory to a field-work career. It might be helpful if 'Public Administration' meant always the subject, the study of the organisation and working of the public services, and if degree and diploma qualifications were called something else, say 'Public Service Administration'.

There is, however, another point of view. Such situations are confusing only when one attempts to see them whole, and so notices the ambiguities and anomalies. Given the number of senses in which, even today, the root term 'administration' is employed (often two or three senses in one sentence) with quite astonishing clarity of meaning from the context, the different senses of 'Public Administration' can be tolerated in the same way. It is seldom really not clear what is meant.

The important problem does not lie in the naming in any case. Let me illustrate from another of the specialised fields, 'Development Administration', which has its nominal ambiguity also, already mentioned—but has suffered from a confusion of *purpose* which is more fundamental. Schaffer has brilliantly illuminated the gap between the academic interests and pursuits of most of the members of the Comparative Administration Group of the American Society for Public Administration, containing scores of the leading scholars of 'Development Administration', and the practical needs of the developing countries themselves:

> But in practice, the members of the Group saw well enough that something or other consistently prevented them from being sufficiently 'action oriented'. To put it another and harsher way, they had their conferences and wrote their papers, but the practitioners did not seem to take much notice and changes in developing countries did not seem to be directly affected (*Schaffer, 1971, 330*).

This could, of course, be a result of the 'communication gap' between academics and practitioners that we have already noticed; and, in respect of the transferring of Western administrative science to developing country practitioners, the gap is a truly formidable one, not yet satisfactorily bridged after two whole decades of genuine hard work and sympathetic exploration of the 'engineering' involved (Weidner, 1964; Stone, 1969; Schaffer, in Leys, 1969; Jones, 1970; Gavaghan, 1972). But there is another difficulty, and it applies also in domestic Public Administration. A large number of academic scholars who find the study of administrative problems interesting, ripe for empirical investigation or philosophical exploitation, full of as yet unresearched puzzles and suffering under appallingly unsophisticated theory, have little interest in training public servants (especially at the lower levels), or even in administrative improvement. Given the high plane of their intellectual activity (it is what they are selected and trained for), it is also probable that not many of them, even if interested, would be good at it. It is an accident of the subject that, as Schaffer puts it,

> students of administration, unlike 'other' students of politics, may occasionally be supposed to be, asked to be, or claim to be 'useful', like some economists... [yet] at the very same time, a prescriptive position for them is peculiarly difficult (*Schaffer, 1971, 333*).

They see only too well how much more information and experience and understanding they would need before they would dare to teach or to recommend.

It may be the case that, among the comparatively small number of British scholars of Public Administration, a majority nevertheless is more interested in 'good solid, conscientious teaching' and improvement, than in the realm of high theory. The expansion of the 'profession' at the present time, certainly, is in the polytechnics and not in the universities, which may or may not be evidence for this view; and there is some real educational innovation in the subject taking place. If this is the case, it might account for Ridley's finding an 'astonishing shortage of academically-oriented studies of the administrative system' in this country, compared with America:

> It is not only the quality that differs but the range of subject matters and, in many cases the originality of the approach. Americans may place too high a premium on originality, theorize too easily, and produce too many dead-end original theories; and that in turn makes wholesale dismissal too easy. That we have no Herbert Simon, no Fred Riggs in Britain may be a factor of size: compare the number of political scientists in the two countries, or, indeed, the size of university departments... But it is chastening to think that we have nothing yet to compare with that theoretically-based and empirically-supported study of the French administrative system, *The Bureaucratic Phenomenon*. Where, one asks despondently, is the Crozier of Britain? France, after all, has even fewer political scientists and sociologists than we (*Ridley, 1972, 70*).

The answer to that last question might well be that Crozier is essentially a sociologist, and that the 'British Crozier' (if we need to call them that) is the pair of Scottish sociologists who three years before *The Bureaucratic Phenomenon* published *The Management of Innovation*. The names of Burns and Stalker are as renowned internationally as is that of the Frenchman, and it is perhaps mere accident that their investigations were not in the public sector whereas Crozier's were. That does not, of course, demolish Ridley's main point. *Some* British theory about public administration is being produced, and I should like now to give some examples of it; but it is fair to acknowledge that, of the six persons whose work is quoted from in the next sections, two are lecturers in Social Administration, one is a Professor of Law, and of the remaining three, one is now head of a training unit in a polytechnic but until recently was a civil servant, and the other two still are civil servants.

Public Administration theory: typologies

Nearly all theorising of the type we are concerned with (mainly *descriptive* theory, though it helps to confirm that one has a good description if one can essay a little mild prediction on the strength of it) begins from a 'typology', a multidimensional classification; which is as it were a squaring-off of the ground, a divination of the order or pattern that either really does underlie the appearances of the world (if one is a positivist) or which seems to group them in a useful way for the purposes one has in mind. Typologies, that is to say, are sometimes 'discovered'—suddenly things 'fall into place' when one happens to look at them in a particular way; or they can be developed, by imposing on the puzzling raw data a set of categories derived from some other source altogether—grouping things according to size and age, for instance, just to see what one gets.

In either case, a typology is a construction of the mind of the author first; and it is a sound maxim that no typology is unique—that is, that any set of observations is capable of being classified in a number of different ways, and no one of them is any more 'true' than any of the others. But a well-known property of the human mind applies to classifications as to other projections on the world; the shift from description to prescription. The division of the branches of English government into Legislative, Executive, and Judicial began as a new typology, to enable the British Constitution to be seen as it really was, as distinct from what the legal terminology of monarchy would imply. By a century or so later, that description was acquiring normative force—a picture of what the Constitution ought to be; and Bagehot developed a new typology, to show what the British Constitution was really like, that we did not really have 'separation of powers' at all. A typology which seems to 'fit the facts' very well will become 'common sense', and then will come to stand for the 'right' pattern of things, the principles which must be defended against change.

It needs a fresh and bold mind, therefore, to produce a new typology in an existing field of knowledge, and this breaking of an old mould in its turn can release further energy. A new typology can 'show up' or suggest relationships not previously obvious, which can then be the basis of hypotheses to be tested by empirical study. Like an economist's model, a typology starts as a supposition but is strengthened every time a prediction made from it is found to be supported. It is, in this context, difficult to find meaning in the question whether a particular typology is 'true' or not. It may be useful, promising, or satisfying; the test, as Ridley suggested, is whether or not it is a 'dead-end'.

This, to my mind, is the stage at which theorising in Public Administration is at the moment. It is not perhaps really important to define closely at what stage one has 'theories', as distinct from a hunch, or a model, or a set of unrefuted hypotheses, or mere conviction that one has made sense out of what was a puzzle. What is probably more important is self-conscious awareness of what one is doing, being explicit about one's assumptions, and clear-headed about classification and cross-classification. Sub-classifying and further sub-classifying is all too easy; but the more classes one produces, the less one is able to grasp, and so use, the typology that one has created: it is a dead-end.

The best way of illustrating these points is to give examples. I will mention some recent pieces of work in the field of British public administration; the first at what one may call 'micro-level', in the study of decisions; the second in the middle range, concerned with analysing the internal structure and functioning of an organisation; the third at 'macro-level', describing the differences between organisations. Beyond this level still, there is 'grand theory', of which the last British example may be the work of Jeremy Bentham; but Almond and Coleman (1960) and Riggs (1957) provide recent American examples.

Micro-theory

The 'micro' illustration is from an article by P. H. Levin entitled 'On Decisions and Decision Making' (Levin, 1972), which builds on earlier work by March and Simon (1958), Jaques (1966), Etzioni (1968) and Donnison and Chapman (1965) to produce a new model of public decision making. Three case histories are used for illustration, the most important of which is that of the Roskill Commission on the Third London Airport (1971); but I will omit the illustrative material from this account.

Trivial usage apart, the situations described are manifestations of a resolve upon action, a deliberate act of resolution (sometimes individual, sometimes collective). This is what Levin calls a *decision*. The action that is resolved upon may be more or less *specific*; that is it might be a decision to move in a certain direction only, or it might be a detailed blueprint which left very few options open at all. Between an original act of resolution and the fulfilment of what was resolved upon, there will be intermediate events: an immediate manifestation of a decision, for instance, might be its announcement; a somewhat later effect the procurement of materials, and so on; at these stages, further decisions of increasing specificity will be made.

A second variable is the degree of *commitment*, which can be high even for a decision of low specificity, or low even for a closely-specified action, so that one does not necessarily expect high specificity and high commitment to go together. Commitment is a measure of the penalty that is perceived as associated with substituting another action (or no action) for the one intended; commitment is the incentive (high or low) for a decision-maker to persist in his intention. Of course, a highly-committed actor may still abandon a course of action, if paying that penalty enables him to avoid paying a greater.

Decisions, then, can be described by these two dimensions 'specificity' and 'commitment to intention', together with the relationship that the decision maker sees between the action that he resolves on and the outcomes he expects. Every decision maker acts according to what Levin calls a *schema*: a set of perceptions of what is desirable for him in his situation, what it is possible for him to do in his situation, and what the relationship between those two is. Even for an individual actor who can resolve and implement his intentions independently of any other person's schema, there will be several separate schemata involved in the 'decision chain', for immediate, intermediate and ultimate implementations will require different consideration. If the intentions and schemata of other actors are involved in a decision process, it become an *interactive* one. Particularly in an organisational or governmental context, there will be sequences of decisions that are purely internal, designed mainly to alter the schemata of other actors in the same organisation rather than have any actual physical effects on the real world; so Levin divides decision chains into those concerned with the *institutional* changes that are intermediate between original resolve and fulfilment of intention, and *interventions*, changes in the real world.

These are the elements of the model. Decisions are of a certain specificity, they display a certain commitment, they manifest a certain relationship between actions and outcomes, immediate, intermediate, or ultimate, and they are concerned either with internal changes in men's perceptions or with actual changes in the physical world. The kinds of decision we are interested in are such as to require the interaction of several men or groups with differing schemata.

These elements are put together into three distinct processes through which schemata may develop; processes made up of

(i) decisions and actions leading to the independent develop- of an intervention schema only;

(ii) decisions and actions leading to the independent development of an institutional schema only; and

(iii) decisions and actions leading to the interactive development of schemata of both types (*Levin, 1972, 31*).

At this point, there is a 'discovery'; these three kinds of process are named (i) technical, (ii) administrative, and (iii) political. Levin says he has 'identified' these three: the implication is that 'interactive' developments of intervention schemata and institutional schemata, and 'independent' developments of both together, do not occur. Thus Levin has arrived at what can be called 'operational' definitions of technical, administrative, and political decision processes: the first, concerned only with actions in the real physical world, enabling an 'intervention' to be specified; the second, concerned only with actions inside an institution, enabling (by ensuring compliance with logical necessity and prescribed procedural rules) an intervention actually to be made; the third, 'mobilising support for it' (or against it).

The article then returns to the case-histories and re-analyses them through this new framework. There are many questions that one might ask about these definitions and their application to the material; but let us move to the last section, where Levin speculates on what his model might suggest about 'ideal' decision making processes from the three points of view, administrative, technical, and political:

> In a process that was perfect from the administrative point of view, there would never be any going back, no re-opening of decisions or annulment of actions once they were taken. A critical path programme which is designed to maximise the 'efficiency' of an administrative procedure also has the effect of maximising the disincentive to the retracing of steps. It was in the interests of efficiency that the Roskill Commission took the administrative step of refusing to permit any re-opening of the short list once it had decided on it. The implication is that in an administratively perfect process there would be 100 per cent commitment to each action as it was taken, notably to those actions that marked an increase in specificity of the envisaged proposal . . .
> A decision-making process that was perfect from the technical point of view would look very different. No commitment would be generated in the course of the searching and learning part of the technical process. Only when all possible interventions and their implications had been explored would preferences be formed and commitment thereby generated . . . Ideally a single preferred proposal would emerge and, to the commitment generated by the forming of the preference and the staking of judgement on it, would be added commitment

generated by the administrative and political processes as the project moved towards implementation. This commitment would be to a single course of action of maximum specificity. . . .

A process that is perfect from the political point of view, we have suggested, must begin with some commitment to a proposal of at least some specificity, but the commitment will not be so high as to inhibit political activity—bargaining, say, or meditation. As the area of conflict is progressively reduced— as agreement on certain 'sub-issues' is reached, for example— commitment and specificity will increase hand in hand. . . . (*Levin, 1972, 41–2*).

These, then, are three different modes in which commitment and specificity can develop. In an actual decision process, progress will be by different modes at different times, and it would be possible to formulate hypotheses about the conditions in which each mode could be expected to be dominant:

> Thus, where power lies with a single group the administrative mode might be expected to predominate. Where the problems are highly complex and their solution depends on finding solutions to nth order problems, the technical mode might be predominant. Where the co-operation of several groups is essential for the implementation of the ultimate action, the political mode might be most in evidence (*Levin, 1972, 42*).

There are some genuine new insights derivable from this model of the decision process, which adds to previous models (most of which are concerned with the 'rationality' of the process, what choices ought to be made for what goals) the notion of *commitment* and so provides a somewhat sharper and more discriminating tool with which to appreciate decision making in the public arena. One might wish to challenge some of the assumptions implicit in it, to reformulate or correct it in some way; that is but proof that it is not 'dead-end'.

Theory at middle level

The second example is from a book by Desmond Keeling, entitled *Management in Government* (1972), which is about the use of resources in public administration; with chapters on criteria for decisions, assessment of performance, PPB and PAR, and the like. But in one part of the book Keeling develops a typology which is of quite general interest, about the way in which the tasks of civil servants in a Department can be described.

This begins from some definitions, which are not merely conventional but are derived from the theory itself (as were Levin's meanings for 'technical', 'administrative', 'political'). *Management* always means

> The search for the best use of resources in pursuit of objectives subject to change.

Administration always means

> The review, in an area of public life, of law, its enforcement and revision; and decision-making on cases in that area submitted to the public service.

Keeling looked for a similar definition of 'policy' that he would be able to use consistently throughout the book, but having read other people's attempts, abandoned his own; though he uses 'strategy' in the sense of the relationship between an objective and a plan—'a series of related actions or proposed actions over time' (Keeling, 1972, 36).

Keeling sees the whole of the public service as a number of 'systems'—for instance, and as in common parlance, 'the judicial system'. The group of systems that is nearest in temper to private industry, including the nationalised industries, he proposes to call 'management systems', since their basic *raison d'etre* is describable in terms of *management* as previously defined—it is their 'primary task' (a concept borrowed from Rice, 1963). It is clear enough that, however 'judicial' might be defined, it would fall at the other end of some spectrum from 'the search for the best use of resources'; and Keeling suggests that *administration* also falls somewhere along the spectrum quite distant from *management*. But there are in the public service, systems where administration and management criteria have equal weight in the 'primary task'—for example, the siting of an airport, or planning in local government.

The spectrum is not exhausted by administration systems, management systems, and their hybrids. An important system in central government he names a 'diplomatic system'—not merely the Diplomatic Service, but such bodies as the Cabinet Office and the Private Offices of the various Departments, would be such systems. Some of them have no specific objectives; their primary task seems to be to keep the government machine going as it is. Other 'diplomatic systems' may have been set up to have oversight of a broad issue, like pollution, or to act as a co-ordinator of relations between Government and a particular industry. They neither administer any body of regulations nor deploy any resources other than their own staff time and accommodation, but they gather and circulate information, they may forecast and plan, and they try to foster good relations.

Other kinds of system might be identified: the education system, for instance, is a complex of central decision making and local execution; the central government aspects can be said to be an 'integrative-allocative management system'. There are similar systems in health and in defence. Keeling identifies other kinds of system, such as the 'police system', various welfare systems such as probation and child care, other 'professional' systems, 'research' systems, and others still undesignated. If I might for a moment move from exposition to criticism, I would say that, in consequence, the complexity of the typology is thus enormously increased, so that it admittedly becomes 'more like life', but almost as difficult to handle. Perhaps, if Keeling had stuck to seeing his 'systems' not as sets of posts, or actually-constituted sections and branches of Departments, but rather as 'tasks', or even 'sets of values' that would display a particular mix in any job, he would have ended with fewer categories and grouped the material differently.

For the most useful insights come when he does just this. Distinguishing between the 'primary' tasks of an agency and its 'secondary' and 'tertiary' tasks, he provides a matrix for the finer description of an agency than is given by its title: there are some agencies that have primary tasks that are *management*, secondary tasks that are *administrative*, and tertiary tasks that are *diplomatic* or *professional*, etc.; other agencies have different mix, and agencies with similar patterns of primary, secondary and tertiary task can be grouped together, and might be expected to behave similarly in certain situations. Keeling does not do this except by suggestion, but it is a fruitful idea.

Then, with a switch of metatheory away from the systems framework to a Weberian ideal-type analysis, Keeling begins to consider what an 'administrative' attitude of mind would be; and we have some very fine intuitive writing which would bear quotation at greater length than there is space for here. He says that 'it is from the criteria and attitudes of mind appropriate to a judicial system that public service administrative systems have derived many of their characteristic features', as can be seen in European countries where legal and administrative processes are not clearly distinguished (Keeling, 1972, 92); both are basically 'mistake-avoiding', have a clear concept of mistake or error, often procedural, and a similar attitude to time; both will tend to defensive strength, with the consequences found in équivalent military organisation:

... since action originates outside the system the resources are deployed on the basis of forecasts and assumptions of where the weight of activity is likely to fall. Parts of the line will be held very lightly—with no more than an occasional patrol involved in reconnaissance, and some frontiers may not be defended at all. If a major action develops at such points the whole defensive administration system may be by-passed. With the benefit of hindsight we can now see that pollution of the environment has broken through in this way and now needs to be counterattacked. And whereas in attack the military dictum 'always reinforce success' applies (the equivalent in management to Drucker's saying 'resources, to produce results, must be allocated to opportunities rather than to problems'), in defence and in administration it is the points of failure to which the reinforcements are rushed (*Keeling, 1972, 94*).

Operating successfully in an administration system therefore requires men of a certain attitude of mind:

> Means must be seen to be as important and at times more important than ends. There is a 'right' or 'correct' decision to be found if time is taken and the correct process of analysis applied to the case. Risks are by definition to be avoided ... (*Keeling, 1972, 95*).

He notes one difference from the judicial system: whereas judges are used to being appealed against, and even having a summing-up found unsatisfactory at a higher level, without the judicial system as a whole being imperilled, in administration systems where the only appeal is to the Minister in the House of Commons, 'the whole system tends to be, or to feel, "committed" to the original decision however low the level at which it was decided' (96).

In administration systems, conformity and consistency are regarded as criteria of efficiency; and compatibility of decision between systems is expected—a requirement that sounds simple, but is in fact extraordinarily difficult and expensive to approach. The objectives of administration systems tend 'to be as general, as infrequently reviewed and as little used in day-to-day decision making as the mottoes which form part of the crests of the oldest British families'.

> In some administration systems there may even be no explicit objectives to be discovered and the existence of implicit objectives has to be argued from the proposition that every activity must be intended to contribute to some purpose, or must at any rate have been started at some earlier period with some end in view (*98*).

In such situations it is not surprising if it is difficult to tell whether or not objectives are being achieved.

Keeling then proceeds to a similar analysis of the *management* attitudes of mind, and later the diplomatic, in the same style—incisive, witty, productive of that deeply satisfying flash of understanding in the reader, as things previously known, but disparately, click into place in a single pattern.

> The diplomatic system was ... difficult to name. It is as difficult to describe ... If a man working in an administration system arrives at the office intending to deal with cases correctly, the manager hoping to use resources more efficiently, the diplomat's ambition for the day is perhaps to see an advance in the affairs in which he is involved. . . . the 'advance' may amount to little more than to keeping abreast of developments, to end the day with no more business awaiting decision; with no more, and hopefully a few less decisions 'bogged down', than at the beginning of the day ...
>
> In many matters to which the management and administration systems reveal different attitudes, the diplomatic system will be found to have an approach distinct from either of them. On time, the administration system is insensitive within wide limits and inclined to patience: the management system strongly committed to that time-scale which seems likely to produce the best return on the resource use, and often impatient. The diplomatic system is both less committed to a prevailing attitude and more sensitively attuned to the opportunities of fine adjustment. It will choose to operate at times with more speed than any management system; at others more slowly than any administration system even of the most judicial variety. On the use of the written word, the statements emanating from the diplomatic system will convey meaning more readily than those from administration, in a style to which more attention has been devoted than in those from management. There will be no apparent ambiguity. If subsequently some is found, it will not have occurred inadvertently ...
>
> The diplomat will find statistical data and quantitative argument of less relevance to a decision than the manager, but will be more inclined to become involved with such data than the administrator—learning enough about, say, discounted cash flow to use such calculations when favourable to his case and to point out their limitations when the reverse situation arises. In personal relations, at which those successful in administration systems may be inadequate and those in management systems effective but possibly abrasive, the diplomatic system is likely to display the qualities needed to succeed in negotiations—and sooner or later every system finds that it needs to succeed in negotiation ... (*Keeling, 1972, 107–8*).

Keeling notes that where more than one such system exists in a single Department, there may develop, on an evolutionary time-scale, a 'pecking order' which sooner or later will be challenged.

Keeling's biggest contribution, perhaps, is his breakaway from the Civil Service tradition of naming as 'administration' what he calls the 'diplomatic' system. Perhaps 'diplomatic' is not *quite* right for a label; yet that is not the difficulty it might appear, because even if we think the cage is wrongly labelled, we all recognise the animal it contains, and recognise also that it really is a separate species from 'administration'. This is a mark of a useful typology, that however many questions it may arouse in those who inspect it, however many philosophical and methodological challenges it may attract (and Keeling's theoretical underpinnings are certainly very shaky), yet it is suggestive, it stimulates people to try to improve it, to stand on the author's shoulders and see if they can get a better perspective on their own terrain. There is a decade of development in this typology of management, administration, diplomatic, welfare, research, and other 'systems' (or perhaps only outlooks, mental sets, attitudes, criteria?) in an organisation.

Macro-theory in British Public Administration

The third theoretical level overlaps with Keeling's, as Keeling's overlapped with Levin's. We are considering, basically, a typology for central government as a whole. A now quite conventional typology divides all British government into central government, local government, and the public corporations, with discussion then possible about central-local relations, relations between central government and public corporations, and (though rarely) between local authorities and corporations. There are, nevertheless, a number of parts of government that do not fit neatly into this: Scottish and Welsh 'devolution', 'twilight' institutions like the Arts Council and Trinity House, the universities, the self-regulating statutory professions like medicine and the legal profession, and so on. Thus a typology can both reflect and engender expectations that, if not fulfilled, raise questions for examination.

In 'central government', a recent typology (suggested by the Head of the Home Civil Service, no less) pictures the Departments as occupying either the surface of a disc or the sections of a column that penetrates the disc vertically. The disc has five segments: 1. overseas and defence; 2. financial, economic, industrial; 3. physical:

4. social; 5. law and order; and the individual Departments are grouped apropriately (Scotland and Wales are acommodated by rim marks). The vertical column has sections marked 'Policy', 'Statistics', 'General Economic Policy', 'Expenditure Control', 'Conditions of Service, Manpower Control, etc.', and others, down to 'Printing and Publishing', 'Building and Some Transport', with the Departments furnishing such central and common services indicated. Again, such a diagram both reflects and engenders expectations of relationships, and sophisticated as it is, it does not cater for everything that its author wanted to convey, and it may, in some respects, convey more than its author intended. Typologies are like that. (Armstrong, 1970, 65; reproduced in Chapman and Dunsire, 1971, 320.)

An avowedly tentative treatment that falls somewhat short of a rigorous typology is that on which R. J. S. Baker bases Part II, 'The Nature of Public Administration in Britain', of his book *Administrative Theory and Public Administration* (1972). Baker first groups the 'functions' of government into eight: Basic functions, which include Defence, Law and Order, Taxation, and Intelligence; Modern functions, which are Regulatory, Conciliatory, or Service-providing; and Symbolic functions, the maintenance of national identity. On a second dimension are the 'tasks' of government: (i) control; (ii) decision-making; (iii) co-ordination; (iv) personnel management; (v) general planning. The third dimension is that of 'processes', of which there are perhaps four (this is not clear, since there are no diagrams or tables): (a) the secretarial process; (b) the delegation process; (c) legislation, directives, and other written communication; (d) internal discussion. If this were to be regarded as a typology, it would produce a three-dimensional matrix of 160 cells one of which, for instance, would be inhabited by 'the secretarial process of the control task in the Defence function' (Baker does not speak of such a matrix, the suggestion is entirely my own). However, the succeeding chapter in the book is on 'Forms and Structures of Government Departments', and the first sentences are:

> In contrast with some literature, this book has considered first the environment of public bodies and what they do and how they do it, and only after that their forms and structures. The forms and structures of organisations derive from environment, functions, tasks and processes, rather than the reverse...
> (*Baker, 1972, 141*).

This seems to argue that Baker does have a theory of how form and structure in a particular Department might be predicted from its functions, its tasks and its processes—the 'space' it can be shown to occupy in a putative typology. Nothing of the kind follows in the present book, but it remains the case that Baker shows the way: a somewhat simpler typology, with fewer terms and preferably 'exhaustive' on each dimension, might yet yield viable theories about form and structure.

In a rather more restricted field, that of central-local relations, J. A. G. Griffith noted (1966, 515–528) that there were differences between Departments in their 'philosophy about local government'. He distinguished three separate attitudes: *laissez-faire*, regulatory, and promotional; noted that different parts of a Department some-times had different attitudes in dealing with different kinds of ser-vice, although one attitude that was 'traditional' in a Department might colour the rest; that a particular attitude seemed to go along with a particular style of communication, or of contact, between Department and local authority; and finally, that a particular attitude seemed to be associated with the political importance of the service concerned. Griffith has no diagrams either, but if this piece of acute observation had been presented as a typology with four variables, predictive hypotheses could have been generated: given the kind of service and its degree of political importance (independent variables), one could expect a certain attitude in the Department and a certain style of contact (dependent variables). Such terminology is usually associated with highly quantitive analysis, with correlations and regressions; but it need not be so.

The last illustration is from an article by Adrian Webb (1971) which does have diagrams, and is entitled 'Social Service Admini-stration: A Typology for Research'. It is again concerned with attitudes in Government Departments, this time towards individual clients.

Webb begins from the Blau and Scott classification of organisa-tions according to their relationships with clients (Blau and Scott, 1962, 42); statutory social services can be regarded as 'Service' organisations operating within the context of a 'Commonweal' organisation—the parliamentary-governmental system. 'Common-weal' goals and 'Service' goals interact and may conflict; most social services can be used as a means of social control, and this sometimes raises deep ethical dilemmas for the professions involved. Social services can therefore be distinguished according to how far their 'Service' orientation is influenced by social control orienta-tions: broadly, into 'regulatory service', 'adaptive services' (where a dominant objective is to effect in the client an adjustment to his social environment), and 'non-regulatory' (or 'pure service') services.

The social services can also be classified by the nature of the contacts between organisation and client: a high degree of face-to-face relationship at one end, to impersonal contact, or even no contact at all, at the other. The highest degree of interaction is found in 'total institutions'—service organisations in which the clients live, such as prisons and hospitals; the least, in the purely 'paper-work' cash benefit services.

Putting both classifications together in a single matrix provides the basis of Webb's typology. Individual social services may have activities in more than one box: the pattern that a particular organisation takes up in the matrix can give an 'indication of the kind and range of issues facing its administrators'. But a particular organisation will probably, nevertheless, acquire dominant characteristics that will enable comparison with other organisations. And the view that the official or field-worker has of the service's characteristics may, of course, differ from that of the client. The typology is illustrated in the table.

Client organisation contact		Goal orientation		
		Regulatory	Adaptive	Service
Total institutions		Prisons	Psychiatric hospitals	General hospitals
Quasi-total institutions		Attendance centres	Hostels for the mentally disordered	Boarding schools
Non-total institutional services	Expressive contact		Probation Some child care functions	Day schools General Practitioner services
	Instrumental contact		'Workshy' and other unemployed applicants for supplementary benefits	Pensioner claimants of supplementary benefits
	No contact	Clean Air and other environmental controls	National Insurance supplementary benefits	National Insurance pensions (*Webb, 1972, 326*)

Webb then considers three problem areas which may be illuminated by the use of the typology. The first is that of safeguarding clients' interests: organisations in the 'adaptive' cells, for example, must rely for this on staff training and 'professionalization', so 'fraught with ambiguous value choices' is the decision making that faces field staff. In purely regulatory services, judicial and quasi-judicial appeal procedures may suffice.

The second problem area is that of 'clients as an organisational variable': the fairly-well-researched phenomenon of 'institutionalisation', inmate subcultures, and nowadays, 'client organisation' (of the Claimants' Union type). Differing forms of response can be seen to correspond to different cells of the typology; some forms of 'client support' (kin and neighbourhood support) are almost beyond the influence of the service providers, and yet can be the channels of misinformation and inaccurate role expectations.

The third problem area is that of organisational structure and management style. Here Webb makes several suggestions:

> Services in which difficult choices between commonweal and service objectives have to be made by staff low in the hierarchy (especially services in the 'adaptive' cells in [the table]) may need to provide more support and job satisfaction to these staff than is possible in a firmly hierarchical organisation.... Services with dominant commonweal regulatory functions will be most likely to adopt authoritative styles of management... Total institutions and services where the cost of mistakes and failures is especially high (surgical wards) may also rely on authoritative management to meet their needs.... Services in the bottom row ... seem *a priori* to be suited to traditional bureaucratic organisation ... (*Webb, 1972, 335*).

If the table is used to classify activities in a single organisation, some questions for further research are suggested:

> How do administrators unify an organisation which occupies considerable 'space' in such a typology, and with what consequences? What combinations of objectives, and client-service relationships prove difficult to reconcile—regulatory and service objectives, or predominantly instrumental, with a minority of expressive relationships? Where basically irreconcilable objectives or methods are incorporated in one service, can they be reconciled by being structurally isolated, or does one become dominant to the detriment of the others? (*Webb, 1972, 337–8*).

Research evidence is presented of the results of separating different types of social welfare into distinct administrative units, and to distinct 'styles of management'; but a diversity of activities within one service may also be beneficial—staff in a discretionary income maintenance service may obtain job satisfaction from helping 'deserving' retirement pensioners, which compensates them for having to deal with 'difficult', 'deviant', or 'less deserving' clients, even if there is a case to be made for specialising in the latter.

Once again, the utility of such a piece of work may lie only partly in what it immediately states, and partly in its heuristic value—what it suggests for further thought by others. What, one asks oneself, are the relationships between objectives and modes of communication in other government services, besides the central-local and social service Departments? If a client-oriented approach is enlightening for the appreciation of administrative problems in the social services, what fresh perspective might be appropriate in the taxation and national economy field, or in foreign and commonwealth relations?

There is a great deal of typology-making and -mongering to be done in British Public Administration, before we are ready to talk of 'general theories'.

Conclusion

I am sure no reader will expect, at the end of this book, a carefully written definition of what 'administration' really means, or even what seems to be the common element in all the Meanings that have been described. The spirit of the treatment has been that each different sense is legitimate, and the same would go for all the nuances of usage that have not been described—every reader probably has his own example.

Yet I trust that this does not leave readers *confused* about 'administration'. A field would properly be called confusing if all agreed that there was in it only one legitimate meaning for a term, and then there was found a multiplicity of incompatible usages. A reader would be understandably confused if an author promised to clarify a term, and then, having produced a great many different clarifications, left him without a key to what was true and what was false clarity. But a field is not confusing just because there are in it, for example, many different growing things all called 'weeds'; we appreciate that, if necessary, the various plants could be uniquely distinguished and named. So in 'administration': it may be tiresome, but it is not inevitably confusing, that there are a large number of senses in which the word is used. Like 'weed', 'administration' is a term which gets its content from its context; very often, it gains its precise meaning from contrast and exclusion more than from positive identification—it is being said to be *not* something else. Just as there is no point in synthesising the essence of 'weed' from the characteristics of all the plants that from time to time are called 'weeds', so one would run into difficulty in trying to distil the nature of 'administration' from consideration of its usage in various contexts.

Let us not, then, even start up that blind alley. But let us not, either, deny ourselves the use of the term altogether. Let us, rather, just get on with the job of 'administering', whatever it is, and let the context take care of the meaning. But, if this book has done its job, we will never again fall into the mire of arguing backward, from the use of the term to the context.

The same general outlook can be brought to bear on the 'science' as on the word. To speak of an 'administrative science' has been too often, in this century at least, to engender expectations that one is able to 'reduce administration to a science', to encourage contrasts between 'art' and science, somehow to be manifestly promising a great deal more than one can deliver. Some of the disparity may be due to lay misconceptions of what 'science' is, to confusion perhaps between science and technology—though that is another of those easy contrasts that is at the root tautologous: the words are mere labels, and the contrast is not that intended, between two methods, or fields, or institutions of education, but between two purposes: the one academic, pursuing knowledge for its own sake, or out of pure curiosity; the other practical, using knowledge as an instrument, as a means to some other end. Simon pointed out that propositions in a science can be expressed as practical imperatives, commands can be written as descriptive propositions (Simon, 1947, 248). Any scientist, if asked, could probably think of practical applications for a discovery he has made or hopes to make; but those were not his reasons for making the search, and the discovery is for him its own reward, while among his academic peers the fact that he has 'advanced the state of learning' in his field is justification enough for his work, and their own. The name 'technologist' may be given to someone who avowedly does not attempt to advance knowledge, but only to apply existing knowledge to practical ends. Yet there is continual feedback between the two, and only at the extremes is the contrast a marked one—clear demonstration of a useless dichotomy. Perhaps many people who say 'administrative science' have 'administrative technology' in mind, the direct improvement of administrative practice through the application of academic knowledge; but that presupposes the existence of an administrative science and thus begs the question.

Another part of the disparity between the promise and the fulfilment may be due to ambiguity in the meaning of 'administration' being employed. An Administrative Class civil servant (or 'diplomatic', in Keeling's terms), may reasonably be highly sceptical about the possibility of an administrative science, given what he understands by 'administration'. An industrialist, already installing on-line computer facilities, centralised records and accounts, and other hardware, may think 'administrative science' merely a fancy name for modern clerical technology, as 'management science' means decision techniques to aid his entrepreneurial function. An academic student of Administration may think in terms of making Administration more susceptible to the hypothetico-deductive manner of thinking, more like Economics (while some economists are realising that working with models is just that—it is not 'studying the economy' (Worswick, 1972)).

There is, to my mind, no way to answer the question 'Is an administrative science possible?' because the answer already lies in the questioner's reason for asking the question. The same is true of another question, 'Can the study of administration be made scientific?', even though it is so much narrower a question, for the answer depends on what is meant by 'scientific'. I would want to by-pass the 'scientific' argument, and deal with questions which may in any case carry the same import; they have already been touched on in the last chapter. 'Is administrative theory possible?' 'Can the study of administration be made theoretical?' I would answer both questions affirmatively; add that 'theory' can be sought for and discovered for all levels and senses of administration; that, moreover, if it can be, it ought to be; but that the search for theory does not entail but one method, the so-called 'scientific method' of the falsifiable hypothesis—that is only one of the routes to theoretical understanding, appropriate for some areas (and where appropriate, indispensable), but not the only shot in the locker—as any scientist from one of the 'exact sciences' would readily agree.

If pressed, then, the search for theory is what I would call 'administrative science'—a usage compatible with both eighteenth century senses and usages in 'other' twentieth century scientific fields. It is certainly a pity to deny ourselves the use of such an elegant term.

APPENDIX

The Meanings of 'Administration'

11. *the duties of the Administrative Class*, 1920; work concerned with the formation of policy, with the co-ordination of and improvement of Government machinery, and with the general [administration and] control of the Departments of the public service   26

12. *work of analysing, balancing, and presenting for decision complex policy considerations;* assigning due weights to each factor (technical, financial, political, etc.), balancing short-term considerations against long-term considerations; to be contrasted with the work of giving specialist advice on any one factor;
   work of persons trained in and experienced in this task, as distinct from the work of persons trained in a specific professional capacity or technical expertise before entry and employed in such capacity   36

13. *ancillary housekeeping and 'office' or 'desk' work in an organisation,* or part of the work of an individual, contrasted with but inseparable from the work of producing the goods or services whose production defines the public role of the organisation or individual; work of logistic support, structuring and programming, procedural record and control, contrasted with direction of production, and with making of corporate policy, as well as with productive operations;
   collective noun for persons engaged in such work in an organisation.   50

14. *work of book-keeping, registration, accounting, and other internal communication* of record; 'clerical' work, as contrasted with the use of such records in control or in policy-making;
   collective noun for persons engaged in such work   51

15. *title of a subject, field, discipline, course, or examination in a school, college, university or other institution of training or education,* whose content is provided by the study of administration in one or more of the foregoing Meanings;
   an area of academic and theoretical research, the description and evaluation of the machinery or work associated with one or more of the foregoing Meanings.   199

Books and Articles Referred to in the Text

ADDISON, Christopher (Viscount) (1924), *Politics from Within 1911–1918*, 2 vols., London: Herbert Jenkins, 1924.

ALBROW, M. (1970), *Bureaucracy*, London: Pall Mall Press 1970; Macmillan Papermac, 1970; New York: Praeger 1971.

ALMOND, Gabriel, and COLEMAN, James eds. (1960), *The Politics of Developing Areas*, Princeton: Princeton University Press, 1960.

ALMOND, Gabriel, and VERBA, Sidney (1963), *The Civic Culture: Political Attitudes and Democracy in Five Nations*, Princeton: Princeton University Press, 1963.

ALDERSON, M. (1970), *Government in France: An Introduction to the Executive Power*, Oxford: Pergamon Press, 1970.

APPLEBY, Paul H. (1949), *Policy and Administration*, Alabama: University of Alabama Press, 1949.

ARGENTI, J. (1969), *Management Techniques*, London: George Allen and Unwin, 1969.

ARGYRIS, Chris (1957), 'The Individual and Organization: Some Problems of mutual Adjustment', *Administrative Science Quarterly* 2(1): 1–22, 1957.

ARGYRIS, Chris (1960), *Understanding Organizational Behavior*, Homewood, Ill: Dorsey Press, 1960; London: Tavistock Publications, 1960.

ARMSTRONG, Sir William (1970), 'The Civil Service Department and Its Tasks', *O & M Bulletin* 25(2): 63–79, May 1970. Reprinted in CHAPMAN and DUNSIRE, 1971.

ARROW, Kenneth J., and SCITOVSKY, Tibor eds. (1969), *Readings in Welfare Economics*, London: George Allen and Unwin, 1969.

BAGEHOT, Walter (1867), *The English Constitution*, London: 1867; ed. R. H. S. Crossman, London: C. A. Watts, New Thinkers Library, 1964.

BAILEY, Stephen K. et al., (1955), *Research Frontiers in Politics and Government*, Washington, D.C.: The Brookings Institution, 1955.

BAKER, R. J. S. (1972), *Administrative Theory and Public Administration*, London: Hutchinson University Library, 1972.

BAKKE, E. Wight (1959), 'Concept of the Social Organization', *in* HAIRE, 1959: 16–75.

BANE, W. T. (1968), *Operational research, models, and government*, CAS Occasional Papers No. 8, London: HMSO, 1968.

BANKS, A. S., and TEXTOR, R. B. (1963), *A Cross-Polity Survey*, Cambridge, Mass.: M.I.T. Press, 1963.

BARKER, Ernest (1944), *The Development of Public Service in Western Europe 1660–1930*, London: Oxford University Press, 1944.

BARNARD, Chester I. (1938), *The Functions of the Executive*, Cambridge, Mass.: Harvard University Press, 1938.

BARNETT, Malcolm Joel (1969), *The Politics of Legislation: the Rent Act 1957*, London: Weidenfeld and Nicolson, 1969.

BEARD, Charles A. (1926), *Government Research, Past, Present and Future*, New York: Municipal Administration Service, 1926.

BEER, Stafford (1966), *Decision and Control*, London: John Wiley, 1966.

BEER, Stafford (1967), *Management Science, The Business Use of Operations Research*, London: Aldus Books, 1967.

BELL, Daniel (1960), *The End of Ideology, On the Exhaustion of Political Ideas in the Fifties*, New York: The Free Press; London: Collier-Macmillan, 1960. Revised *edn.*, 1962.

BENDIX, Reinhard (1960), *Max Weber—An Intellectual Portrait*, London: Heinemann, 1960.

BENNIS, Warren G. (1966), *Changing Organizations*, London: McGraw-Hill, 1966.

BENTHAM, Jeremy (1782), *Of Laws in General*, ed. H. L. A. Hart, *Gen. ed.* J. H. Burns, London: The Athlone Press, 1970.

BENTHAM, Jeremy (1791), *Panopticon, or The Inspection-House*, in BOWRING, 1843, vol. IV: 37–172.

BENTHAM, Jeremy (1806a), *The Rationale of Evidence*, in BOWRING, 1843, vol. VI.

BENTHAM, Jeremy (1806b), *Reform of Scotch Justice*, in BOWRING, 1843, vol. V.

BENTHAM, Jeremy (1816), *Chrestomathia*, in BOWRING, 1843, vol. VIII.

BENTHAM, Jeremy (1819), *The Radical Reform Bill*, in BOWRING, 1843, vol. III.

BENTHAM, Jeremy (1820–30), *Constitutional Code*, in BOWRING, 1843, vol. IX.

BENTLEY, Arthur F. (1908), *The Process of Government*, Chicago: University of Chicago Press, 1908; Bloomington, Ind.: Principia Press, 1949.

BERGER, Morroe (1957), 'Bureaucracy East and West', *Administrative Science Quarterly* 1(4): 518–529, 1957.

BERLE, A. A. (1954), *The 20th Century Capitalist Revolution*, New York: Harcourt, Brace, 1954.

BERLINER, Joseph S. (1956), 'A Problem in Soviet Business Administration', *Administrative Science Quarterly* 1(1): 86–101, 1956.

BLAU, P. M., and SCOTT, W. Richard (1962), *Formal Organizations*, San Fancisco: Chandler Publishing Co., 1962. London: Routledge and Kegan Paul, 1963.

BLAUNER, Robert (1964), *Alienation and Freedom: The Factory Worker and his Industry*, Chicago: University of Chicago Press, 1964.

BOULDING, Kenneth E. (1964), review of BRAYBROOK and LINDBLOM (1963) in *American Sociological Review*, 29: 931, 1964.

BOURN, J. B. (1968), 'The Main Reports on the British Civil Service since the Northcote-Trevelyan Report', Memorandum No. 10 submitted to the Committee on the Civil Service, *Report* of the Committee, 3(2): 423–465, London: HMSO, 1968.

BOWRING, John *ed.* (1843), *The Works of Jeremy Bentham*, 10 vols., Edinburgh: William Tait, 1843.

BRAIBANTI, Ralph, *ed.* (1969), *Political and Administrative Development*, Durham, N.C.: Duke University Press, 1969.

BRAYBROOK, D., and LINDBLOM, C. E. (1963), *A Strategy of Decision*, New York: The Free Press, 1963.

BRECH, E. F. L., *ed.* (1953), *The Principles and Practice of Management*, London: Longmans, Green and Co, 1953; 2nd *edn.*, 1963.

BRIDGES, Sir Edward (Lord Bridges) (1950), *Portrait of a Profession*, The Rede Lecture, London: Cambridge University Press, 1950.

BRODIE, M. B. (1962), 'Henri Fayol: "Administration industrielle et générale"—a reinterpretation', *Public Administration* 40: 311–7, 1962.

BROWN, J. A. C. (1954), *The Social Psychology of Industry*, Harmondsworth, Middlesex: Penguin Books, 1954.

BROWN, R. G. S. (1970), *The Administrative Process in Britain*, London: Methuen, 1970.

BUCHANAN, J. M., and TULLOCK, Gordon (1962), *The Calculus of Consent*, Ann Arbor, Michigan: University of Michigan Press, 1962.

BUNBURY, Sir Henry (1930), 'Rationalising the Processes of Administration', *Public Administration* 8: 275–282, 1930.

BURNHAM, James (1941), *The Managerial Revolution*, New York: John Day, 1941; Harmondsworth, Middlesex: Penguin Books, 1945.

BURNS, Tom and STALKER, G. M. (1961), *The Management of Innovation*, London: Tavistock Publications, 1961.

CAPLOW, Theodore (1957), 'Organizational Size', *Administrative Science Quarterly* 1(4): 484–505, 1957.

CHADWICK, Edwin (1885), *On the Evils of Disunity in Central and Local Administration, especially with relation to the Metropolis: and also on the new centralisation for the people, together with improvements in codification and in legislative procedure*, London: Longmans and Co., 1885.

CHAMBERLAIN, Rt. Hon. Sir Austen (1936), *Politics from Inside*, London: Cassell and Company, 1936.

CHAPMAN, Brian (1959), *The Profession of Government, The Public Service in Europe, London:* George Allen and Unwin, 1959.

CHAPMAN, Brian (1963), *British Government Observed, Some European Reflections*, London: George Allen and Unwin, 1963.

CHAPMAN, Richard A. (1969), *Decision Making, A Case Study in the Decision to raise the Bank Rate in September 1957*, London: Routledge and Kegan Paul, 1969.

CHAPMAN, Richard A. (1970), *The Higher Civil Service in Britain*, London: Constable, 1970.

CHAPMAN, Richard A., and DUNSIRE, A. *eds.* (1971), *Style in Administration: Readings in British Public Administration*, London: George Allen and Unwin, 1971.

CHARLESWORTH, James C., *ed.* (1962), *The Limits of Behaviouralism in Political Science*, Monograph 1, Philadelphia: The American Academy of Political and Social Science, 1962.

CHARLESWORTH, James C., *ed.* (1968), *Theory and Practice of Public Administration: Scope, Objectives, and Methods*, Monograph 8, Philadelphia: The American Academy of Political and Social Science, 1968.

CHESTER, D. N. *ed.*, and WILLSON, F. M. G. (1957), *The Organization of British Central Government 1914–1956*, London: George Allen and Unwin, 1957. 2nd *edn.*, 1968.

COHEN, Emmeline W. (1941), *The Growth of the British Civil Service 1780–1939*, London: George Allen and Unwin, 1941; Frank Cass, 1965.

COHN-BENDIT, Gabriel, and COHN-BENDIT, Daniel (1968), *Obsolete Communism, The Left-Wing Alternative*, London: André Deutsch, 1968; Harmondworth, Middlesex: Penguin Books, 1969.

COLE, G. D. H. (1948), *A History of the Labour Party from 1914*, London: Routledge and Kegan Paul, 1948.

COMMONER, Barry (1972), *The Closing Circle*, London: Jonathan Cape, 1972.

CONSTANTINE, T. (1972), 'Universities must face up to the fact that a large number of engineering students are not fit for a traditional university education, but need good, solid, conscientious technical college teaching', Manchester: *The Guardian*, 28 July, 1972.

CRICK, Bernard (1959), *The American Science of Politics*, London: Routledge and Kegan Paul, 1959.

CRICK, Bernard (1962), *In Defence of Politics*, London: Weidenfeld and Nicolson, 1962; Harmondsworth, Middlesex: Penguin Books, 1964.

CROZIER, Michel (1964), *The Bureaucratic Phenomenon*, Paris: Editions du Seuil, 1963; London: Tavistock Publications, 1964; Chicago: University of Chicago Press, 1964.

CTCC (1963), *Handbook on Transport Users Consultative Committees*, London: The Central Transport Consultative Committee, 2nd *edn.*, 1963.

CAUDILL, William (1956), 'Perspectives on Administration in Psychiatric Hospitals', *Administrative Science Quarterly* 1(2): 155–70, 1956.

DAHL, Robert A. (1947), 'The Science of Public Administration: Three Problems', *Public Administration Review* 7: 1–11, 1947.

DAHL, Robert A. (1961), 'The Behavioural Approach in Political Science: Epitaph for a Monument to a Successful Protest', *American Political Science Review* 55: 763–72, 1961.

DAHL, Robert A., and LINDBLOM, C. E. (1953), *Politics, Economics, and Welfare*, New York: Harper and Bros., 1953.

DALE, Ernest (1956), 'Contributions to Administration by Alfred P. Sloan Jr., and GM', *Administrative Science Quarterly* 1(1): 30–62, 1956.

DALE, H. E. (1941), *The Higher Civil Service of Great Britain*, London: Oxford University Press, 1941.

DEMERATH, Nicholas F., and THIBAUT, John W. (1956), 'Small Groups and Administrative Organizations', *Administrative Science Quarterly* 1(2): 139–54, 1956.

DE SOLA POOL, Ithiel, *ed.* (1967), *Contemporary Political Science, Toward Empirical Theory*, New York: McGraw-Hill, 1967.

DIAMANT, Alfred (1962), 'The Bureaucratic Model: Max Weber Rejected, Rediscovered, Reformed', *in* HEADY and STOKES, 1962: 59–96.

DIMOCK, Marshall E. (1937), *Modern Politics and Administration*, New York: American Book Company, 1937.

DONNISON, D. B., and CHAPMAN, V. (1965), *Social Policy and Administration*, London: George Allen and Unwin, 1965.

DORSEY, John T. Jr. (1958), 'A Communication Model for Administration', *Administrative Science Quarterly* 2(3): 307–24, 1958.

DOWNS, Anthony (1957), *An Economic Theory of Democracy*, New York: Harper and Bros., 1957.

DOWNS, Anthony (1967), *Inside Bureaucracy*, Boston: Little, Brown and Co., 1967.

DROR, Yehezkel (1967), 'Policy Analysts: A New Professional Role in Government Service', *Public Administration Review* 27(3): 197–203, 1967.

DROR, Yehezkel (1968), *Public Policymaking Re-examined*, San Francisco: Chandler Publishing Co., 1968.

DROR, Yehezkel (1971), *Design for Policy Sciences*, Amsterdam: Elsevier Publishing Company, 1971.

DUBIN, Robert (1957), 'Power and Union-Management Relations', *Administrative Science Quarterly* 2(1): 60–81, 1957.

DUNSIRE, A. *ed.* (1956), *The Making of An Administrator*, Manchester: Manchester University Press, 1956.

DUNSIRE, A. (1969), 'Why university courses at all? Which universities?', *PAC Bulletin* No. 6: 44–52, May 1969.

DURKHEIM, Emile (1893), *De la division du Travail Social: études sur l'organisation des sociétés supérieures*, Paris: 1893. *The Division of Labour in Society*, transl. by George Simpson, New York: Macmillan, 1933; Glencoe, Ill.: The Free Press, 1947.

EASTON, David (1953), *The Political System: An Enquiry into the State of Political Science*, New York: Alfred A. Knopf, 1953.

EASTON, David (1957), 'Traditional and Behavioral Research in American Political Science', *Administrative Science Quarterly* 2(1): 110–15, 1957.

EASTON, David (1965), *A Systems Analysis of Political Life*, New York: John Wiley and Sons, 1965.

EATON, Dorman B. (1880), *Civil Service in Great Britain: A History of Abuses and Reforms and Their Bearing upon American Politics*, New York: Harper, 1880.

ELBOURNE, E. T. (1914), *Factory Administration and Accounts*, London: Longmans and Co, 1914. New *edns.*, 1919, 1921, 1934.

EMERY, F. E. *ed.* (1969), *Systems Thinking*, Harmondsworth, Middlesex: Penguin Books, 1969.

ENGELS, Friedrich (1878), *Herr Engen Dühring's Revolution in Science* (The Anti-Dühring), Berlin: 1878. Some chapters publ. as *Socialism; Utopian and Scientific*, Paris: 1880; *transl.* Aveling, London: 1892. Reprinted in Karl Marx and Frederick Engels, *Selected Works*, 2:151, Moscow: Foreign Languages Publishing House, 1958; and in *Marx and Engels, Basic Writings on Politics and Philosophy*, ed. Feuer, New York: Anchor Books; London: Fontana Library, 1969, 147.

ETZIONI, Amitai (1961), *A Comparative Analysis of Complex Organizations*, Glencoe, Ill.: The Free Press, 1961.

ETZIONI, Amitai (1967), 'Mixed-Scanning: A "Third" Approach to Decision-Making', *Public Administration Review* 27(5): 385–92, 1967.

ETZIONI, Amitai (1968), *The Active Society, A Theory of Societal and Political Processes*, New York: The Free Press, 1968.

EULAU, Heinz (1963), *The Behavioral Persuasion in Politics*, New York: Random House, 1963.

FAYOL, Henri (1916), 'Administration Industrielle et Générale', *Bulletin de la Société de l'Industrie Minérale*, No. 3, 1916; Paris: Dunod, 1925, new edn. 1962; *transl.* Coubrough, *Industrial and General Administration*, Geneva: International Management Institute, 1929; *transl.* Storrs, *General and Industrial Management*, London: Pitman, 1949.

FELDSTEIN, Martin S. (1964), 'Cost-Benefit Analysis and Investment in the Public Sector', *Public Administration* 42: 351–72, 1964.

FINER, Herman (1932), *The Theory and Practice of Modern Government*, London: Methuen and Co., 1932; 2nd *edn.*, 2 vols., 1946; 3rd *edn.*, 1954; 4th *edn.*, 1961.

FISCHEL, Edouard (1862), *Die Verfassung Englands*, Berlin: Schneider, 1862; *transl.* Shee, *The English Constitution*, London: 1867.

FLETCHER, Ronald (1971), *The Making of Sociology, A Study of Sociological*

Theory, vol I, Beginnings and Foundations; vol. II, Developments, London: Michael Joseph, 1971.

FLOUD, Sir Francis (1923), 'The Sphere of the Specialist in Public Administradition', *Public Administration* 1: 117–26, 1923.

FOLLETT, Mary Parker (1925), 'The Giving of Orders', and 'Business as an Integrative Unity', first presented in Jan. 1925; *in* METCALF and URWICK, 1941: 50–70, 71–94.

FRIEDRICH, Carl J. (1937), *Constitutional Government and Politics*, New York: Harper and Bros., 1937.

FRIEDRICH, Carl J. (1940), 'Public Policy and the Nature of Administrative Responsibility', *in* FRIEDRICH and MASON, 1940.

FRIEDRICH, Carl J., and MASON, Edward S., *eds.* (1940), *Public Policy*, Yearbook of the Graduate School of Public Administration, Cambridge, Mass.: Harvard University Press, 1940.

FROMM, Erich (1942), *The Fear of Freedom*, London: Routledge and Kegan Paul, 1942.

FRY, Geoffrey K. (1969), *Statesmen in Disguise, The Changing Role of the Administrative Class of the British Home Civil Service 1853–1966*, London: Macmillan, 1969.

GALBRAITH, J. K. (1967), *The New Industrial State*, London: Hamish Hamilton, 1967.

GAUS, John M. (1936), 'American Society and Public Administration', *in* GAUS, WHITE, and DIMOCK, 1936.

GAUS, John M. (1947), *Reflections on Public Adminstration*, University, Ala.: University of Alabama Press, 1947.

GAUS, J. M., WHITE, L. D. and DIMOCK, M. E. (1936), *The Frontiers of Public Administration*, Chicago: University of Chicago Press, 1936.

GAVAGHAN, Terence J. (1972), 'Public Administration Abroad: Between Theory and Practice', *PAC Bulletin* No. 12: 16–22, June 1972.

GELLNER, Ernest (1970), 'Concepts and Society', *in* WILSON, 1970: 18–49.

GEORGE, Claude S. Jr. (1968), *The History of Management Thought*, Englewood Cliffs, N.J.: Prentice-Hall, 1968.

GERTH, H. H. and MILLS, C. Wright *eds.* and *transl.* (1946), *From Max Weber: Essays in Sociology*, New York: Oxford University Press, 1946; London: Routledge and Kegan Paul, 1948; 4th impression, 1961.

GILBRETH, Lillian M. (1914), *The Psychology of Management*, New York: Sturgis and Walton Co., 1914; London: Pitman, n.d.

GNEIST, H. Rudolph von (1857), *Das heutige englische Verfassungs- und Verwaltungsrecht*, 3 parts, Berlin: 1857–63; vol. 2, 'Self-government, Communalverfassung und Verwaltungsgericht in England.'

GOFFMAN, Erving (1957), 'On the Characteristics of Total Institutions', *Symposium on Preventive and Social Psychiatry*, Washington D.C.: Walter Reed Army Institute of Research, 1957: 43–84; enlarged, *in* Donald R. Cressey *ed.*, *The Prison*, New York: Holt Rinehart and Winston, 1961; reprinted in Goffman, *Asylums*, New York: Doubleday, 1961; Harmondsworth, Middlesex: Penguin Books, 1968.

GOLDTHORPE, John H., LOCKWOOD, David, BECHHOFER, Frank and PLATT, Jennifer (1968), *The Affluent Worker, Industrial Attitudes and Behaviour*, London: Cambridge University Press, 1968.

GOLEMBIEWSKY, Robert T. (1964), 'Toward the Administrative Sciences: Methodological Directions for Public Administration', *International Review of Administrative Sciences* 30 (2): 113–23, 1964.

GOODNOW, Frank J. (1900), *Politics and Administration*, New York: The Macmillan Company, 1900.

GOULDNER, Alvin W. (1958), 'Cosmopolitans and Locals: Toward an Analysis of Latent Social Roles', *Administrative Science Quarterly* 2(3): 281–306 and 2(4): 444–80, 1958.

GRAY, Alexander, *The Socialist Tradition, Moses to Lenin*, London: Longmans, Green, 1946; new *edn.*, 1947.

GREBENIK, Eugene (1972), 'The Civil Service College: The First Year', *Public Administration* 50(2): 127–38, 1972.

GRIFFITH, John A. G. (1966), *Central Departments and Local Authorities*, London: George Allen and Unwin, 1966.

GROSS, Bertram (1967), *Action Under Planning, The Guidance of Economic Development*, New York: McGraw-Hill, 1967.

GULICK, Luther (1933), 'Politics, Administration, and the "New Deal"', *Annals of the American Academy of Political and Social Science* 169: 55–66, 1933.

GULICK, Luther (1937), 'Notes on the Theory of Organization, with special reference to Government in the United States', A Memorandum prepared as a member of the President's Committee on Administrative Management, December 1936; revised June 1937; Paper I in GULICK and URWICK, 1937: 1–45.

GULICK, Luther, and URWICK, Lyndall F. *eds.* (1937), *Papers on the Science of Administration*, New York: Institute of Public Administration, 1937.

GUNN, Lewis A. (1969), 'Public Administration Teaching in British Universities', *PAC Bulletin* No. 6: 29–43, 1969.

GUNN, Lewis A. (1971), 'Public Administration as Management', *PAC Bulletin* No. 11: 76–93, 1971.

GUNNELL, John G. (1969), 'The Idea of the Conceptual Framework: A Philosophical Critique', *Journal of Comparative Administration* 1: 140–176, 1969.

HAIRE, Mason, *ed.* (1969), *Modern Organization Theory*, New York, John Wiley, 1959; London: Chapman and Hall, 1959.

HANHAM, H. J. *ed.* (1969), *The Nineteenth-Century Constitution, 1815–1914, Documents and Commentary*, London: Cambridge University Press, 1969.

HANSON, A. H. (1959), *Public Enterprise and Economic Development*, London: Routledge and Kegan Paul, 1959.

HARRIS, Nigel (1968), *Beliefs in Society, The Problem of Ideology*, London: C. A. Watts, The New Thinkers Library, 1968; Harmondsworth, Middlesex: Penguin Books, 1971.

HART, H. L. A. *ed.* (1970), *Jeremy Bentham: Of Laws in General, a continuation of An Introduction to the Principles of Morals and Legislation*, substantially completed in 1782, unpublished until discovered in 1939 (*The Collected Work of Jeremy Bentham, Gen. Ed.* J. H. Burns); London: The Athlone Press, 1970.

HEADY, Ferrel (1966), *Public Administration: A Comparative Perspective*, Englewood Cliffs, N.J.: Prentice-Hall Inc., 1966.

HEADY, Ferrel, and STOKES, S. L. *eds.* (1962), *Papers in Comparative Public Administration*, Ann Arbor, Mich.: University of Michigan Press, 1962.

HECLO, H. Hugh (1972), 'Review Article: Policy Analysis', *British Journal of Political Science* 2(1): 83–108, 1972.

HEILBRONNER, André (1965), *Prevention of Cattle Diseases, with special reference to Foot-and-Mouth Disease*, Brussels: International Institute of Administrative Sciences, 1965.

HEINZEN, Karl (1845), *Die Preussische Büreaukratie*, Darmstadt: Leske, 1845.

HENDERSON, A. M. and PARSONS, Talcott, *transl.* and *eds.* (1947), Max Weber, *The Theory of Social and Economic Organization*, Glencoe, Ill.: The Free Press, 1947.

HENDERSON, Keith M. (1966), *Emerging Synthesis in American Public Administration*, London: Asia Publishing House, 1966.

HENDERSON, Keith M. (1969), 'Comparative Public Administration: The Identity Crisis', *Journal of Comparative Administration* 1(1): 65–84, 1969.

HERRING, E. Pendleton (1936), *Public Administration and the Public Interest*, New York: McGraw-Hill, 1936.

HERTZ, Frederick (1944), *Nationality in History and Politics*, London: Routledge and Kegan Paul, 1944; new *edn.*, 1957.

HEWART, Rt. Hon. Lord (1929), *The New Despotism*, London: Benn, 1929.

HIRSCHMANN, A. O., and LINDBLOM, C. E. (1962), 'Economic development, research and development, policy making: some converging views,' *Behavioral Science* 7: 211–222, 1962; reproduced in EMERY, 1969: 351–371.

HOMANS, George C. (1950), *The Human Group*, New York: Harcourt, Brace, 1950; London: Routledge and Kegan Paul, 1951.

HUME, David (1740), *A Treatise of Human Nature*, ed. L. A. Selby-Bigge, Oxford: Clarendon Press, 1896.

HURWITZ, Nils (1958), 'Publicity of Official Documents in Sweden', *Public Law* 1958: 50–69, 1958.

HUXLEY, Aldous L. (1932), *Brave New World*, London: Chatto and Windus, 1932; Harmondsworth, Middlesex: Penguin Books, 1955.

JAQUES, Elliott (1966), 'The Nature of Decision Making', paper presented at a meeting of the Operational Research Society, London: 15 February 1966 (cited in LEVIN, 1972, 27).

JENKINS, Peter (1971), 'Thinks ᵤ . .', Manchester: *The Guardian*, September 13, 1971.

JOHNSON, Charles, *transl.* and *ed.* (1950), Richard Fitz Neale, Bishop of London, *De necessariis observantiis Scaccarii dialogus qui vulgo dicitur Dialogus de Scaccario (The Course of the Exchequer)*, Latin and Engl., London: Thomas Nelson and Sons, 1950. Earlier *edn.*, Arthur Hughes, G. C. Crump, and C. Johnson, Oxford: Clarendon Press, 1902.

JONES, Garth N. (1970), 'Failure of Technical Assistance in Public Administration Abroad', *Journal of Comparative Administration* 2(1). 3–51, 1970.

KAST, Fremont (1968), 'Systems Concepts and Organization Theory', *in* LE BRETON, 1968: 147–54.

KATZ, D., and KAHN, R. (1966), *The Social Psychology of Organizations*, New York: John Wiley, 1966.

KEELING, Desmond (1972), *Management in Government*, London: George Allen and Unwin, 1972.

KEIR, Sir David Lindsay (1938), *The Constitutional History of Modern Britain 1485–1937*. London: Adam and Charles Black, 1938; 5th *edn.* (*1485–1951*), 1953.

KEITH LUCAS, Bryan ed. (1958), *The History of Local Government in England, being a reissue of Book I of Local Government in England by Joseph Redlich and Francis W. Hirst*, London: Macmillan, 1958; 2nd edn., 1970.

KLEIN, Josephine (1956), *The Study of Groups*, London: Routledge and Kegan Paul, 1956.

KOESTLER, Arthur (1964), *The Act of Creation*, London: Hutchinson, 1964.

LANDSBERGER, H. (1958), *Hawthorne Revisited*, Ithaca, N.Y.: Cornell University Press, 1958.

LA PALOMBARA, Joseph ed. (1963), *Bureaucracy and Political Development*, Princeton N.J.: Princeton University Press, 1963.

LASKI, Harold J. (1933), *Democracy in Crisis*, London: George Allen and Unwin, 1933.

LAWRENCE, J. R. ed. (1966), *Operational Research and the Social Sciences*, London: Tavistock Publications, 1966.

LE BRETON, Preston P. ed. (1968), *Comparative Administrative Theory*, London: University of Washington Press, 1968.

LENTZ, Edith M. (1957), 'Hospital Administration—One of a Species', *Administrative Science Quarterly* 1(4): 444–63, 1957.

LEPAWSKY, Albert ed. (1949), *Administration: The Art and Science of Organization and Management*, New York: Alfred A. Knopf, 1949.

LE PLAY, F. (1864), *La Réforme Sociale en France*, Paris: Plon, 1864.

LEVIN, P. H. (1972), 'On Decisions and Decision Making', *Public Administration* 50: 19–44, 1972.

LEWIS, J. Slater (1896), *The Commercial Organisation of Factories*, London: E. and F. N. Spon, 1896.

LEYS, Colin, ed. (1969), *Politics and Change in Developing Countries*, London: Cambridge University Press, 1969.

LINDBLOM, Charles E. (1959), 'The Science of "Muddling Through" ', *Public Administration Review* 19: 79–85, 1959.

LINDBLOM, Charles E. (1965), *The Intelligence of Democracy, Decision Making Through Mutual Adjustment*, New York: The Free Press, 1965.

LINDBLOM, Charles E. (1968), *The Policy-Making Process*, Englewood Cliffs, N.J.: Prentice-Hall Inc., 1968.

LIPSON, Leslie (1939), *The American Governor: From Figurehead to Leader*, Chicago: University of Chicago Press, 1939.

LITCHFIELD, Edward H. (1956), 'Notes on a General Theory of Administration', *Administrative Science Quarterly* 1(1): 3–29, 1956.

LITTERER, Joseph A. ed. (1969), *Organizations: Systems, Control and Adaptation*, New York: John Wiley, 1969. (Vol. 2 of a two-volume work, which is the 2nd *edn.* of a one-volume work first published in 1963).

LITWIN, Josef (1965), *Control of River Pollution by Industry*, Brussels: International Institute of Administrative Sciences, 1965.

LOCKYER, K. G. (1964). *An Introduction to Critical Path Analysis*, London: Pitman, 1964.

LOWENSTEN, Karl (1944), *Report* of the Research Panel on Comparative Government of the Research Committee of the American Political Science Association, *American Political Science Review*, 38: 540–8, 1944.

LYDEN, Fremont J. (1968), 'Synthesis—Cross-Cultural Comparative Study in Public Administration', *in* LE BRETON, 1968: 139–43.

LYDEN, Fremont J., SHIPMAN, George A., and WILKINSON, R. W. Jr. (1968), 'Decision-Flow Analysis: A Methodology for Studying the Public Policy-Making Process', *in* LE BRETON, 1968: 155–68.

McBain, Howard Lee (1927), *The Living Constitution*, New York: The Macmillan Company, 1927.

McEwen, William J. (1956), 'Position Conflict and Professional Orientation in a Research Organization', *Administrative Science Quarterly* 1(2): 208–224, 1956.

McGregor, Douglas (1960), *The Human Side of Enterprise*, New York: McGraw-Hill, 1960.

Mack, Mary P. (1962), *Jeremy Bentham, An Odyssey of Ideas 1748–1792*, London: Heinemann, 1962.

Mackenzie, W. J. M. (1967), *Politics and Social Science*, Harmondsworth, Middlesex: Penguin Books, 1967.

Mackenzie, W. J. M. (1970), *The Study of Political Science Today*, Paris: Mouton/UNESCO, 1970; London: Macmillan, 1971.

Maddox, John (1972), *The Doomsday Syndrome: an assault on pessimism*, London: Macmillan, 1972.

Mannheim, Karl (1935), *Mensch und Gesellschaft im Zeitalter des Umbaus*, Leiden: 1935; *Man and Society in an Age of Reconstruction*, London: Routledge and Kegan Paul, 1940; New York: Harcourt, Brace, 1940.

March, James G., and Simon, Herbert A. (with the collaboration of Harold Guetzkow) (1958), *Organizations*, New York: John Wiley, 1958; London: Chapman and Hall, 1958.

Marchant, J. R. V. and Charles, J. F. eds. (1941), *Cassell's Latin Dictionary*, 22nd *edn.*, London: Cassell and Co., 1941. (First *edn.* 1887.)

Marcuse, Herbert (1964), *One Dimensional Man: Studies in the Ideology of Advanced Industrial Society*, London: Routledge and Kegan Paul, 1964; Boston: Beacon Press, 1964.

Marini, Frank, ed. (1971), *Toward a New Public Administration: The Minnowbrook Perspective*, Scranton, Penn.: Chandler Publishing Co., 1971.

Marx, F. Morstein (1969), 'A new look at administrative science in Europe', *International Review of Administrative Sciences* 35(4): 291–301, 1969.

Marx, Karl, and Engels, Friedrich (1846), *The German Ideology*, in Lewis S. Feuer *ed.*, *Marx and Engels, Basic Writings on Politics and Philosophy*, New York: Anchor Books, Doubleday, 1959; London: Fontana Library, Collins, 1969.

Maslow, A. H. (1954), *Motivation and Personality*, New York: Harper Bros., 1954.

Mayo, Elton (1933), *The Human Problems of an Industrial Civilisation*, New York: Macmillan, 1933.

Meadows, Dennis, et al. (1972), *The Limits to Growth*, A Report by the Massachusetts Institute of Technology for the Club of Rome project The Predicament of Mankind, Boston: M.I.T. and Potomac Associates, 1972; London: Earth Island, 1972.

Megill, Kenneth A. (1970), *The New Democratic Theory*, New York: The Free Press; London: Collier-Macmillan Ltd., 1970.

Merson, F. (1923), 'Public Administration: A Science', *Public Administration* 1(1): 220–7, 1923.

Merton, Robert K. (1949), *Social Theory and Social Structure*, Glencoe, Ill.: The Free Press, 1949.

Merton, Robert K., Gray, Ailsa P., Hockey, Barbara, and Selvin, Hanan C., eds. (1952), *Reader in Bureaucracy*, New York: The Free Press, 1952; London: Collier-Macmillan Ltd., 3rd printing, 1968.

Metcalf, Henry C., and Urwick, Lyndall F. eds. (1941), *Dynamic Admin-*

istration, The Collected Papers of Mary Parker Follett, London: Pitman, 1941.

MILIBAND, Ralph (1961), *Parliamentary Socialism,* London: George Allen and Unwin, 1961.

MILL, John Stuart (1848), *Principles of Political Economy, with some of their applications to Social Philosophy,* 2 vols., London: 1848; *ed.* Ashley, London: Longmans, 1909.

MILL, John Stuart (1859), *On Liberty,* London: 1859; People's Edition, London: Longmans Green, 1867.

MILL, John Stuart (1861), *Considerations on Representative Government,* London: 1861; *in* A. D. Lindsay *ed.,* John Stuart Mill, *Utilitarianism, Liberty, and Representative Government,* London: J. M. Dent, 1910.

MILLER, George A., GALANTER, Eugene, and PRIBRAM, Karl H. (1960), *Plans and the Structure of Behavior,* New York: Henry Holt and Co., 1960.

MILLETT, John D. (1956), 'A Critical Appraisal of the Study of Administration', *Administrative Science Quarterly* 1(2): 171–88, 1956.

MILLS, C. Wright (1956), *The Power Elite,* New York: Oxford University Press, 1956; Galaxy Books, 1959.

MISHAN, E. J. (1971), *Cost-Benefit Analysis,* London: George Allen and Unwin, 1971.

MOHL, Robert von (1846), *Aktenstücke betreffend den Dienst-Austritt des Professors R. von Mohl in Tübingen,* Freiburg in Breisgau: 1846; *in Staatsrecht, Völkerrecht und Politik,* Monographieen, 3 vols., Tübingen: Laupp, 1862.

MOLITOR, André (1959), *The University Teaching of the Social Sciences: Public Administration,* Paris: UNESCO, 1959.

MONTGOMERY, John D., and SIFFIN, William J. *eds.* (1966), *Approaches to Development: Politics, Administration, and Change,* New York: McGraw-Hill, 1966.

MOONEY, James D., and REILEY, A. C. (1931), *Onward Industry,* New York: Harper Bros., 1931; 2nd *edn.* as *The Principles of Organization,* New York: Harper Bros., 1939; revised *edn.* by Mooney, 1947.

MUIR, Ramsay (1910), *Peers and Bureaucrats,* London: Constable, 1910.

MUMFORD, Lewis (1964), *The Myth of the Machine vol. II, The Pentagon of Power,* New York: 1970; London: Secker and Warburg, 1971.

MUNRO, C. K. (1952), *The Fountains in Trafalgar Square,* London: Heinemann, 1952.

MURRAY, D. J. (1965), *The West Indies and the development of colonial government 1801–1834,* London: Oxford University Press, 1965.

NEWELL, A., SHAW, J. C., and SIMON, H. A. (1958a), 'The elements of a theory of human problem solving', *Psychology Review* 65: 151–66, 1958.

NEWELL, A., SHAW, J. C., and SIMON, H. A. (1958b), 'Chess-playing programs and the problem of complexity', *IBM Journal of Research and Development,* 2: 320–35, 1958.

NEWMAN, Sir George (1939), *The Building of a Nation's Health,* London: Macmillan and Co., 1939.

NICHOLSON, Max (1967), *The System, The Misgovernment of Modern Britain,* London: Hodder and Stoughton, 1967.

OGLESBY, Carl, ed. (1969), *The New Left Reader,* New York: Grove Press Inc., 1969.

ORWELL, George (1949), *Nineteen Eighty-Four,* London: Secker and Warburg, 1949; Harmondsworth, Middlesex: Penguin Books, 1954.

PARKER, R. S. and SUBRAMANIAM, V. (1964), 'Public and Private Administration', *International Review of Administrative Sciences* 30: 1964.

PARRIS, Henry (1969), *Constitutional Bureaucracy, The Development of British Central Administration Since the Eighteenth Century*, London: George Allen and Unwin, 1969.

PARSONS, Talcott (1956), 'Suggestions for a Sociological Approach to the Theory of Organizations', *Administrative Science Quarterly* 1(1): 63–85 and 1(2): 225–39, 1956.

PARSONS, Talcott (1964), *Structure and Process in Modern Societies*, Glencoe, Ill.: The Free Press, 1964.

PARSONS, Talcott, and SHILS, E. A. eds. (1961), *Toward a General Theory of Action*, Cambridge, Mass.: Harvard University Press, 1951.

PATEMAN, Carole (1970), *Participation and Democratic Theory*, London: Cambridge University Press, 1970.

PELLEGRIN, Roland J., and COATES, H. (1957), 'Executives and Supervisors: Contrasting Definitions of Career Success', *Administrative Science Quarterly* 1(4): 506–17, 1957.

PELLING, Henry (1961), *A Short History of the Labour Party*, London: Macmillan, 1961.

PFIFFNER, J. M. (1935), *Public Administration*, New York: The Ronald Press, 1935.

POLLARD, Sidney (1965), *The Genesis of Modern Management, A Study of the Industrial Revolution in Great Britain*, London: Edward Arnold, 1965; Harmondsworth, Middlesex: Penguin Books, 1968.

PORTER, George (1965), *The laws of disorder: an introduction to chemical change and thermodynamics*, London: British Broadcasting Corporation, 1965.

PULZER, Peter G. J. (1967), *Political Representation and Elections in Britain*, London: George Allen and Unwin, 1967.

RANNEY, Austin ed. (1962), *Essays on the Behavioural Study of Politics*, Urbana, Ill.: Illinois University Press, 1962.

RANNEY, Austin ed. (1968), *Political Science and Public Policy*, Chicago: Markham Publishing Co., 1968.

RAPOPORT, Robert N. (1971), *Mid-Career Development*, London: Tavistock Publications, 1971.

RAPOPORT, Anatol, and HORVATH, W. J. (1960), 'Thoughts on Organization Theory and a Review of Two Conferences', *General Systems Yearbook* 4(2); 1960.

REDLICH, Josef, ed. HIRST, Francis W. (1903), *Local Government in England*, 2 vols., London: Macmillan, 1903. (German edn., 1901).

RHODES, Gerald (1967), 'The Committee System', paper commissioned by the Committee on Management in Local Government (The Maud Committee), printed as Appendix B in Volume 5, 'Local Government Administration in England and Wales' by Margaret Harrison and Alan Norton, of the *Report* of the Committee, London. HMSO, 1967: 613–20.

RICHARDSON, Stephen A. (1956), 'Organizational Contrasts on British and American Ships', *Administrative Science Quarterly* 1(2): 189–207, 1956, reprinted in THOMPSON, 1969: 39–54.

RICHARDSON, J. J. (1969), *The Policy-Making Process*, London: Routledge and Kegan Paul, 1969.

RIDGWAY, Valentine F. (1957), 'Dysfunctional Consequences of Performance Measurements', *and* 'Administration of Manufacturer–Dealer Systems',

Administrative Science Quarterly 1(2): 240–7, 1956, *and* 1(4): 464–83, 1957.

RIDLEY, Clarence E., and SIMON, Herbert A. (1938), *Measuring Municipal Activities*, Chicago: International City Managers Association, 1938; 2nd *edn.*, 1943.

RIDLEY, F. F. (1966), 'French Technocracy and Comparative Government', *Political Studies* 14: 34–52, 1966.

RIDLEY, F. F. *ed.* (1968), *Specialists and Generalists: A Comparative Study of the Professional Civil Servant At Home and Abroad*, London: George Allen and Unwin, 1968.

RIDLEY, F. F. (1972), 'Public Administration: Cause for Discontent', *Public Administration* 50: 65–78, 1972.

RIDLEY, F. F., and BLONDEL, J. (1964), *Public Administration in France*, London: Routledge and Kegan Paul, 1964; 2nd *edn.*, 1969.

RIGGS, Fred. F. (1956), 'Public Administration: A Neglected Factor in Economic Development', *Annals of the American Academy of Political and Social Science* 305: 70–80, 1956.

RIGGS, Fred. W. (1957), 'Agraria and Industria: Toward a Typology of Comparative Administration', *in* SIFFIN, 1957: 23–110.

RIGGS, Fred. W. (1961), *The Ecology of Public Administration*, Bombay, London and New York: Asia Publishing House, 1961.

RIGGS, Fred W. (1962), 'Trends in the Comparative Study of Public Administration', *International Review of Administrative Sciences* 28(1): 9–15, 1962.

RIGGS, Fred W. (1964), *Administration in Developing Countries, The Theory of Prismatic Society*, Boston: Houghton Mifflin Company, 1964.

RIGGS, Fred W. (1965), 'Relearning An Old Lesson: The Political Context of Development Administration', *Public Administration Review* 25: 70–9, 1965.

RIGGS, Fred W., *ed.* (1971), *Frontiers of Development Administration*, Durham N.C.: Duke University Press, 1971.

ROBERTS, D. (1960), *Victorian Origins of the British Welfare State*, New Haven: Yale University Press, 1960.

ROETHLISBERGER, Fritz J. and DICKSON, William J. (1939), *Management and The Worker*, Cambridge, Mass.: Harvard University Press, 1939.

ROSE, Richard *ed.* (1969), *Policy-Making in Britain, A Reader in Government*, London: Macmillan, 1969.

ROSENBERG, Hans (1958), *Bureaucracy, Aristocracy, and Autocracy, The Prussian Experience 1660–1815*, Cambridge, Mass.: Harvard University Press, 1958.

ROSSI, Peter H. (1957), 'Community Decision Making', *Administrative Science Quarterly* 1(4): 415–43, 1957.

ROSSITER, Clinton *ed.* (1961), *The Federalist Papers: Alexander Hamilton, James Madison, John Jay*, New York: Mentor Books, The New American Library, 1961; London: The New English Library, 1961.

ROSZAK, Theodore (1968), *The Making of a Counter Culture, Reflections on the Technocratic Society and Its Youthful Oppositon*, New York: 1968; London: Faber and Faber, 1970.

ROTH, Günter (1968), 'Lorenz von Stein (1815–1890),' *in International Encyclopaedia of the Social Sciences* 15: 257–9, New York: The Free Press, 1968.

ROWAT, D. C. (1965), *The Ombudsman*, London: George Allen and Unwin, 1965; 2nd *edn.*, 1968.

ROWNTREE, B. Seebohm (1921), *The Human Factor in Business; Experiments in Industrial Democracy*, London: Longmans, Green and Co., 1921; 2nd edn., 1925; 3rd edn., 1938.

RUBENSTEIN, Albert H., and HABERSTROH, Chadwick J. eds. (1960), *Some Theories of Organization*, Homewood, Ill.: The Dorsey Press, 1960.

RUSSELL, Bertrand (1932), *Education and the Social Order*, London: George Allen and Unwin, 1932; new impression, 1951.

RUSSETT, Bruce M., ALKER, Hayward R., DEUTSCH, Karl W., and LASSWELL, Harold (1964), *World Handbook of Political and Social Indicators*, New Haven, Conn.: Yale University Press, 1964.

SALTER, Lord (1961), *Memoirs of a Public Servant*, London: Faber and Faber, 1961;

SAYLES, Leonard R. (1958), *Behavior of Industrial Work Groups*, New York: John Wiley, 1958.

SAYRE, Wallace S. (1958), 'Trends in the Study and Teaching of Public Administration', *in* SWEENEY, 1958: 37–43;

SCHAFFER, Bernard B. (1957), 'The Idea of the Ministerial Department: Bentham, Mill and Bagehot', *Australian Journal of Politics and History* 3: 60–78, 1957.

SCHAFFER, Bernard B. (1969), 'The Deadlock in Development Administration', *in* LEYS, 1969: 177–211.

SCHAFFER, Bernard B. (1971), 'Comparisons, Administration and Development', *Political Studies* 19(3): 327–37, 1971.

SELF, Peter (1971a), 'Tests of Efficiency: Public and Business Administration', *PAC Bulletin* No. 11: 28–41, 1971;

SELF, Peter (1971b), 'Elected Representatives and Management in Local Government: An Alternative Analysis', *Public Administration* 49: 269–78, 1971.

SELF, Peter (1972), *Administrative Theories and Politics*, London: George Allen and Unwin, 1972.

SELZNICK, Philip (1948), 'Foundations of the Theory of Organization', *American Sociological Review* 13: 25–35, 1948; reprinted in EMERY, 1969: 261–80.

SHARKANSKY, Ira (1970a), *Public Administration: Policy-making in Government Agencies*, Chicago: Markham Publishing Co., 1970.

SHARKANSKY, Ira ed. (1970b), *Policy Analysis in Political Science*, Chicago: Markham Publishing Co., 1970.

SHELDON, Oliver (1924), *Philosophy of Management*, London: Pitman, 1924;

SHONFIELD, Andrew (1965), *Modern Capitalism, The Changing Balance of Public and Private Power*, London: Oxford University Press, 1965.

SHORE, Peter (1966), *Entitled to Know*, London: MacGibbon and Kee, 1966.

SIFFIN, William J. ed. (1957), *Toward The Comparative Study of Public Administration*, Bloomington, Ind.: Indiana University Press, 1957.

SILVERMAN, David (1970), *The Theory of Organizations, A Sociological Framework*, London: Heinemann, 1970.

SIMON, Herbert A. (1937), 'Comparative Statistics and the Measurement of Efficiency', *National Municipal Review* 26: 524–7, 1937.

SIMON, Herbert A. (1944), 'Decision-Making and Administrative Organization', *Public Administration Review* 4: 20–1, 1944.

SIMON, Herbert A. (1946), 'The Proverbs of Administration', *Public Administration Review* 6: 53–67, 1946.

SIMON, Herbert A. (1947), *Administrative Behavior, A Study of Decision-Making Processes in Administrative Organization*, New York: The Macmillan Company, 1947; 2nd edn., 1957.

SIMON, Herbert A. (1950), 'Modern organization theories', *Advanced Management* 15: 2–4, 1950.
SIMON, Herbert A. (1952), 'Comments on the Theory of Organizations', *American Political Science Review* 46(4): 1130–9, 1952.
SIMON, Herbert A. (1953), 'Birth of an Organization: The Economic Co-operation Administration', *Public Administration Review* 13: 227–36, 1953.
SIMON, Herbert A. (1955), 'Recent Advances in Organization Theory', *in* BAILEY, 1955: 23–44.
SIMON, Herbert A. (1957), *Models of Man, Social and Rational*, New York: John Wiley, 1957.
SIMON, Herbert A. (1967), 'The Changing Theory and Changing Practice of Public Administration', *in* DE SOLA POOL, 1967: 86–120.
SIMON, Herbert A., and RIDLEY, Clarence E. (1938), *Measuring Municipal Activities*, Chicago: The International City Managers Association, 1938; 2nd *edn*. 1943.
SIMON, Herbert A., SMITHBURG, Donald W., and THOMPSON, Victor A. (1950), *Public Administration*, New York: Alfred A. Knopf, 1950.
SISSON, C. H. (1959), *The Spirit of British Administration, and some European Comparisons*, London: Faber and Faber, 1959.
SJOBERG, Gideon (1971), 'Ideology and Social Organization in Rapidly Developing Societies', *in* RIGGS, 1971: 274–301.
SMALL, Albion W. (1909), *The Cameralists*, Chicago: University of Chicago Press, 1909.
SMELLIE, K. B. (1937), *A Hundred Years of English Government*, London: Duckworth, 1937; 2nd *edn. rev.*, 1950.
SMELLIE, K. B. (1946), *A History of Local Government*, London: George Allen and Unwin, 1946; 4th *edn.*, 1968.
SMITH, Adam (1776), *An Inquiry into the Nature and Causes of the Wealth of Nations*, 2 vols., London: 1776; 3 vols., Edinburgh and London: 1812; a careful reprint of the 1812 3 vols. *edn.*, with Notes by J. R. McCulloch, 1 vol., London: Ward, Lock and Co., World Library of Standard Books, 1875; and see Andrew Skinner *ed.*, Harmondsworth, Middlesex: Penguin Books, 1970.
SMITH, J. Toulmin (1851), *Local Self-Government and Centralization: The Characteristics of each, and its practical tendencies . . .*, London: 1851.
SPENCER, Herbert (1876), *The Principles of Sociology*, Parts I, II and III (vol. I), 1876; Part IV, 1879, and Part V, 1882 (vol. II); London: Williams and Norgate, 3rd *edn.*, 3 vols, 1893.
SPENCER, Herbert (1882), *The Principles of Sociology, Part V, Political Institutions*, London: 1882; New York: D. Appleton and Co., 1883.
SPIELMEYER, Gunter (1965), *Ascertaining Entitlement to Compensation for an Industrial Injury*, Brussels: International Institute of Administrative Sciences, 1965.
STANYER, Jeffrey (1971), 'Elected Representatives and Management in Local Government: A case of applied sociology and applied economics', *Public Administration* 49: 73–97, 1971.
STEIN, Lorenz von (1865), *Die Verwaltungslehre*, 3 vols., Stuttgart: Cotta, 1865, 1868, 1869.
STEWART, John D. (1969), *New Approaches to Management in Local Government*, London: Local Government Chronicle, 1969.
STONE, Donald C. *ed.* (1969), *Organizing Schools and Institutes of Administration*, Washington, D.C.: Agency for International Development, 1969.

STORING, Herbert J. ed. (1961), *Essays on the Scientific Study of Politics*, New York: Holt, Rinehart, 1961.

SWEENEY, Stephen B. ed. (1958), *Education for Administrative Careers in Government Service*, Philadelphia: University of Pennsylvania Press; London: Oxford University Press, 1958.

SWERDLOW, Irving ed. (1963), *Development Administration: Concepts and Problems*, Syracuse: Syracuse University Press, 1963.

TAINE, Hippolyte (1890), *The Modern Regime*, New York: Henry Holt and Co., 1890.

TAYLOR, Frederick Winslow (1903), 'Shop Management', paper to the American Society of Mechanical Engineers; *Shop Management*, New York: Harper Bros., 1910.

TAYLOR, Frederick Winslow (1911), *Principles and Methods of Scientific Management*, New York: Harper Bros., 1911.

TAYLOR, Sir Henry (1836), *The Statesman*, London: 1836; reprinted in *Collected Works* 1878, and with introduction by H. J. Laski, Cambridge: Heffer, 1927; with introduction by L. Silberman, Cambridge: Heffer, 1957; with introduction by C. N. Parkinson, New York: Mentor Books, The New American Library, 1958.

TEODORI, Massimo ed. (1969), *The New Left, a Documentary History*, New York: 1969; London: Cape, 1970.

THOMPSON, James D. (1956), 'On Building an Administrative Science', *Administrative Science Quarterly* 1(1): 102–11, 1956.

THOMPSON, James, and BATES, Frederick L. (1958), 'Technology, Organization and Administration', *Administrative Science Quarterly* 2(3): 325–43, 1958.

THOMPSON, James D., HAMMOND, Peter B., HAWKES, Robert W., JUNKER, Buford H., and TUDEN, Arthur, eds. (1959), *Comparative Studies in Administration*, Pittsburgh: University of Pittsburgh Press, 1959.

TODD, Alpheus (1869), *On Parliamentary Government in England: its Origin, Development and Practical Operation*, 2 vols., London: 1867–9; 2nd edn. 1887–9.

TÖNNIES, Ferdinand (1887), *Gemeinschaft und Gesellschaft, Abhandlung des Communismus und des Socialismus als empirischen Culturformen*, Leipzig: 1887; transl. C. S. Loomis, *Community and Association*, New York: American Book Co., 1940; London: Routledge and Kegan Paul, 1955.

TRIST, E. L., and BAMFORTH, K. W. (1951), 'Some social and psychological consequences of the longwall method of coal-getting', *Human Relations* 4: 3–38, 1951.

TRIST, E. L., HIGGIN, J. W., MURRAY, H. and POLLOCK, A. B. (1963), *Organizational Choice*, London: Tavistock Publications, 1963.

TULLOCK, Gordon (1965), *The Politics of Bureaucracy*, Washington, D.C.: Public Affairs Press, 1965.

UDY, Stanley H. Jr. (1959), *Organization of Work: A Comparative Analysis of Production among Non-Industrial Peoples*, New Haven, Conn.: Human Relations Area Files Press, 1959.

UNITED NATIONS, (1961), Technical Assistance Program, *A Handbook of Public Administration*, New York: United Nations, 1961.

URWICK, Lyndall F. (1929), *The Meaning of Rationalisation*, London: Nisbet and Co., 1929.

URWICK, Lyndall F. (1943), *The Elements of Administration*, London: Pitman, 1943; 2nd *edn.*, 1947.

URWICK, Lyndall F. (1969), 'Are the Classics Really Out of Date—a Plea for Semantic Sanity', *Advanced Management Journal*, July 1969.

URWICK, L. and BRECH, E. F. L. (1945–8), *The Making of Scientific Management*, London: Management Publications Trust; vol. 1, Thirteen Pioneers, 1945; vol. 2, Management in British Industry, 1946; vol. 3, The Hawthorne Investigations, 1948.

VICKERS, Sir Geoffrey (1965), *The Art of Judgement: A Study of Policy Making*, London: Chapman and Hall, 1965; New York: Basic Books, 1965.

VILE, M. J. C. (1967), *Constitutionalism and the Separation of Powers*, Oxford: Clarendon Press, 1967.

WALDO, Dwight (1948), *The Administrative State, A Study of the Political Theory of American Public Administration*, New York: The Ronald Press, 1948.

WALDO, Dwight (1961), 'Organisation Theory: An Elephantine Problem', *Public Administration Review* 21: 210–25, 1961.

WALDO, Dwight (1964), *Comparative Public Administration: Prologue, Problems, and Promise*, Chicago: Comparative Administration Group, The American Society for Public Administration, 1964.

WALDO, Dwight ed. (1970), *Temporal Dimensions of Development Administration*, Durham, N.C.: Duke University Press, 1970.

WALDO, Dwight ed. (1971), *Public Administration in a Time of Turbulence*, Scranton, Penn.: Chandler Publishing Co., 1971.

WALKER, Charles J., and GUEST, Robert H. (1952), *The Man on the Assembly Line*, Cambridge, Mass.: Harvard University Press, 1952.

WALLAS, Graham (1908), *Human Nature in Politics*, London: Constable and Co., 1908.

WALLAS, Graham (1928), 'The British Civil Service', *Public Administration* 6: 3–15, 1928.

WALSH, H. G., and WILLIAMS, Alan (1969), *Current issues in cost-benefit analysis*, CAS Occasional Paper No. 11, London: HMSO, 1969.

WARREN, J. H. (1952), *The Local Government Service*, London: George Allen and Unwin, 1952.

WEBB, Sidney, and WEBB, Beatrice (1908), *The Manor and The Borough 1689–1834*, vols. 2 and 3 of *English Local Government from the Revolution to the Municipal Corporations Act*, London: Longmans, 1908; Frank Cass, 1963.

WEBB, Sidney, and WEBB, Beatrice (1922), *Statutory Authorities for Special Purposes 1689–1834, with a Summary of the Development of Local Government Structure*, vol. 4 of *English Local Government from the Revolution to the Municipal Corporations Act*, London: Longmans, 1922; Frank Cass, 1963.

WEBB, Beatrice (1948), *Our Partnership*, ed. Barbara Drake and Margaret I. Cole, London: Longmans, Green and Co., 1948.

WEBB, Adrian (1971), 'Social Service Administration: A Typology for Research', *Public Administration* 49: 321–39, 1971.

WEBER, Max (1947), *The Theory of Social and Economic Organization*, transl. A. M. Henderson and Talcott Parsons, Glencoe, Ill.: The Free Press, 1947.

WEIDNER, Edward W. (1964), *Technical Assistance in Public Administration Overseas: The Case for Development Administration*, Chicago: Public Administration Service, 1964.

WEIDNER, Edward W. ed. (1970), *Development Administration in Asia*, Durham, N.C.: Duke University Press, 1970.

WELSCH, Lawrence A., and CYERT, Richard M., eds. (1970), *Management Decision Making, Selected Readings*, Harmondsworth, Middlesex: Penguin Books, 1970.

WHITE, Leonard D. (1926), *Introduction to the Study of Public Administration*, New York: Macmillan, 1926; 2nd *edn.*, 1939; 3rd *edn.*, 1948; 4th *edn.*, 1955.

WHITE, Leonard D. (1927), *The City Manager*, Chicago: University of Chicago Press, 1927.

WILDAVSKY, Aaron (1966), 'The Political Economy of Efficiency: Cost-Benefit Analysis, Systems Analysis and Program Budgeting', *Public Administration Review* 26(4): 292–310, 1966.

WILLOUGHBY, W. F. (1919), *The Government of Modern States*, New York: D. Appleton-Century Co., 1919; 2nd *edn.*, 1936.

WILLOUGHBY, W. F. (1927), *Principles of Public Administration*, Washington D.C.: The Brookings Institution, 1927.

WILLSON, F. M. G. (1955), 'Ministries and Boards: some aspects of Administrative Development since 1832', *Public Administration* 33: 43–59, 1955.

WILSON, Bryan R. ed. (1970), *Rationality*, Oxford: Key Concepts in the Social Sciences, Basil Blackwell, 1970.

WILSON, Woodrow (1887), 'The Study of Administration', *Political Science Quarterly*, 2: 197–222, 1887; reprinted *American Political Science Quarterly* 56: 481–506, 1941.

WOODWARD, Joan (1958), *Management and Technology*, London: Department of Scientific and Industrial Research, Problems and Progress in Industry 3, HMSO, 1958.

WOODWARD, Joan (1965), *Industrial Organization: Theory and Practice*, London: Oxford University Press, 1965.

WORSWICK, G. D. N. (1972), *Uses of Economics*, Oxford: Basil Blackwell, 1972.

YOUNG, D. Murray (1961), *The Colonial Office in the Early Nineteenth Century*, London: Longmans, 1961.

British Official Papers
Referred to in the Text

Report on the Organisation of the Permanent Civil Service (The Northcote-Trevelyan Report), C.1713, London: HMSO, 1854; reproduced in Appendix B of the Report of the Committee on The Civil Service (The Fulton Committee), Cmnd. 3638, London: HMSO, 1968, vol. 1: 108–18.

Reports of the Commission to Enquire into the Civil Service (The Playfair Commission), C.1113 and C.1226, London: HMSO, 1875.

Reports of the Royal Commission on Civil Establishments (The Ridley Commission), C.5226, C.5545, C.5748, C.6172, London: HMSO, 1887, 1888, 1889 and 1890.

Report of the Committee on the Reorganisation of the War Office (The Esher Committee), Cd.1932, London: HMSO, 1904.

Reports of the Royal Commission on the Civil Service (The MacDonnell Commission), Cd.6209, Cd.6534, Cd.6739, Cd.7338, Cd.7832, London: HMSO, 1912–15.

Final Report of the Health of Munition Workers Committee, Cd. 9065, Ministry of Munitions, London: HMSO, 1918.

Report of the Machinery of Government Committee (The Haldane Committee), Ministry of Reconstruction, Cd.9230, London: HMSO, 1918.

Interim Report of the Joint Committee on the Organisation of the Civil Service (The Reorganisation Committee), London: Civil Service National Whitley Council, 1920.

Report of the Royal Commission on the Civil Service (The Tomlin Commission), Cmd.3909, London: HMSO, 1931.

Report of the Committee of Inquiry on the Post Office (The Bridgeman Committee), Cmd.4149, London: HMSO, 1932.

Report of the Committee on the Staffing of Local Government (The Mallaby Committee), Ministry of Housing and Local Government, London: HMSO, 1967.

Report of the Committee on the Management of Local Government (The Maud Committee), Ministry of Housing and Local Government, London: HMSO, 1967.

Report of the Committee on the Civil Service (The Fulton Committee), Cmnd.3638, London: HMSO, 1968.

Report of the Commission on the Third London Airport (The Roskill Commission), London: HMSO, 1971.

Report of the Committee on Local Government Management (The Bains Report), *The New Local Authorities: Management and Structure*, London: HMSO, 1972.

Index of Names

(Persons named once in a book-reference are not included in this index.)

Index of Subjects

253